Beyond the Casino Economy

Beyond the Casino Economy

Planning for the 1990s

NICHOLAS COSTELLO, JONATHAN MICHIE &
SEUMAS MILNE

VERSO
London · New York

First published by Verso 1989

Verso
UK: 6 Meard Street, London W1V 3HR
US: 29 West 35th Street, New York, NY 10001–2291

Verso is the imprint of New Left Books

British Library Cataloguing in Publication Data
Costello, Nicholas
Beyond the casino economy : planning for the 1990s.
1. Economics
I. Title II. Michie, Jonathan III. Milne, Seumas
330

ISBN 0–86091–252–3
ISBN 0–86091–967–6 pbk

Library of Congress Cataloging-in-Publication Data
Costello, Nicholas.
Beyond the casino economy : planning for the 1990s / Nicholas Costello, Jonathan Michie & Seumas Milne.
p. cm.
Bibliography : p.
ISBN 0–86091–252–3. — ISBN 0–86091–967–6 (pbk.)
1. Great Britain—Economic policy—1945- 2. Great Britain—Economic conditions—1945- 3. United States—Economic conditions—1981- 4. Economic forecasting. 5. Economic policy.
I. Michie, Jonathan. II. Milne, Seumas. III. Title.
HC256.6.C665 1989
338.941'009'049—dc20

Typeset in 11pt Dutch by ThumbPrint
Printed in Great Britain by Bookcraft (Bath) Ltd

Contents

The Authors

Nicholas Costello works as a consultant on telecommunications policy for the European Commission in Brussels. He has an MSc in economics from the London School of Economics. He has worked as an economist for British Telecom, and at the National Institute of Economic and Social Research and the City University Business School. He translated *Profit and Crises* by Arghiri Emmanuel in 1981, is co-author of the 1986 Campaign for Labour Party Democracy publication *The Case for Public Ownership*, and of *Telecommunications in Europe*, 1988. He has been assistant secretary of the Campaign for Labour Party Democracy and of Tottenham Labour Party.

Jonathan Michie is a Research Fellow and economics lecturer at Brunel University, an external expert for the European Commission and a tutor in economics for the Open University. He has an MSc in economics from Queen Mary College, London, and a DPhil in economics from Oxford University. He taught economics at Oxfcrd University and Polytechnic before working in the economics department of the TUC from 1983 to 1988. He is the author of *Wages in the Business Cycle*, 1987.

Seumas Milne has been a staff journalist on the *Guardian* since 1984. He studied philosophy, politics and economics at Balliol College, Oxford and economics at Birkbeck College, London University. He worked for three years on *The Economist*, covering local government, education and the motor industry. He is author of *Economic Perspectives* published by the Economics Association and co-author of *The Case for Public Ownership*. He is a member of the National Executive Council of the National Union of Journalists and Chair of Hammersmith Constituency Labour Party.

Preface and Acknowledgements

This book grew out of a conference on the prospects for the British economy and a new economic strategy for the left, organized in February 1988 by the Campaign for Labour Party Democracy (CLPD). A broad group of economists, trade union and Labour Party activists and Labour MPs took part. Discussion focussed on the implications of economic globalization, the 1980s swing to the market, new technology and changes in the labour force for capitalism and socialism in the coming years. There was wide agreement on the need for detailed work on a radical economic programme for a Labour government in the 1990s – and in particular, for research on strategies for particular industries based on public ownership and planning.

CLPD itself was founded in 1973 after Harold Wilson announced that he would ignore the Labour Conference's support for the proposal to nationalize at least twenty-five major companies; the organization went on to lead the successful campaign for democratic reform inside the Labour Party at the beginning of the 1980s. Without CLPD this book would not have been commissioned or written and thanks are particularly due to Vladimir Derer and Victor Schonfield for their support.

The book's other main sponsors have been the National Communications Union (NCU) and the National Union of Mineworkers (NUM), who jointly launched the project at the 1988 TUC Congress in Bournemouth and have given vital political and financial backing. Advice and comments from Bill Fry and Dave Ward of the NCU, and from Peter Heathfield, Dave Feikert, and Roger Windsor of the

NUM were extremely useful. Policy and financial support was also generously given by the Association of Cinematograph, Television and Allied Technicians (ACTT), the Associated Society of Locomotive Engineers and Firemen (ASLEF), the Broadcasting and Entertainment Trades Alliance (BETA), the Bakers, Food and Allied Workers' Union (BFAWU), the Furniture, Timber and Allied Trades Union (FTAT), and the Transport and General Workers' Union (T&GWU) Regions 1 and 6.

Special thanks are due to Bob Tennant, secretary of CLPD's public ownership working party, who played a central role in initiating and supporting the project – as well as in discussing and improving the contents through its various drafts, and in consulting a broad range of trade unionists.

Substantial pieces of research for the book were undertaken and written up by Marj Mayo, tutor at Ruskin College, Oxford, in particular on local economic strategies; Ben Fine, Reader at Birkbeck College, London, on the energy sector and changes in the labour market; Tony Cutler, lecturer at Middlesex Polytechnic, on the motor industry; and Bruce Allan and Martin Moriarty of the Public Transport Information Unit, on public transport. Detailed suggestions and comments were added on urban and regional policy, and the role of local government by Carolyn Downs, Policy Analyst for the London Borough of Haringey; on public transport by Laurie Harris, Head of Research at the National Union of Railwaymen, and Ken Fuller, Transport and General Workers Union Divisional Officer; on telecommunications by John Starmer, NCU Political Officer; and on the City of London by Professor Laurence Harris, head of the Open University's Economics Department. Comments on specific industrial sectors were contributed by Jack Adams, T&GWU National Officer for the motor industry, and on local economic strategies by Michael Ward, director of the Centre for Local Economic Strategies and former chair of the employment committee of the Greater London Council (GLC). Marj Mayo, Ben Fine and Carolyn Downs also commented at length on various drafts.

Especially useful contributions to the 1988 conference came from Ken Livingstone MP and member of Labour's NEC, Les Huckfield MEP, Mick Costello, Peter Haggar of the T&GWU Executive Committee and Tom Hart, T&GWU Region 6 Education Officer.

Valuable suggestions and criticisms of different drafts of the book were also received from Hussein Agha; Barry Camfield, T&GWU

Regional Organizer; Trevor Carter of the Inner London Education Authority's Equal Opportunities Unit; Diane Coyle of the *Investors Chronicle*; Vera Derer of CLPD; Gregory Elliott; Ken Fuller, T&GWU Regional Officer; Andrew Glyn, Fellow and Economics Tutor at Corpus Christi College, Oxford; Charles Grant of *The Economist*; Douglas Hayward; Les Huckfield MEP; Ken Livingstone MP; Kevin Magill; Cathy Mandi; Kirsty Milne; Cristina Montanari; Kevin Morgan of Sussex University's Science Policy Research Unit; Jim Mortimer, former General Secretary of the Labour Party; Andrew Murray, T&GWU media officer; Sándor Nagy, Deputy Director of the Budapest Centre for Social Sciences; Louisa Saunders; Anne Tennant of CLPD; Marc Vlessing, associate director of a UK merchant bank; Lord Wedderburn, Professor of Company Law at the LSE; and Tess Woodcraft. We are grateful to them all. Thanks are also due to Simon Braunholtz at MORI; Melanie McFadyean of the *Guardian*; and Roger Simon at the Labour Research Department for their help. Colin Robinson of Verso deserves a special mention for his encouragement and creative suggestions through successive drafts; as do Verso's Anna del Nevo and Lucy Morton, without whose help and support the drafts would never have become a book. The final text is, of course, the responsibility of the three authors alone.

Tony Benn MP not only wrote the Foreword but also made comments on the text and spent considerable time discussing the economic and industrial record of previous Labour governments. This was invaluable, given that – as a former Minister of Technology, Energy Secretary and Industry Secretary – he has more cabinet experience than the entire current Shadow Cabinet put together.

A draft of the book was submitted in full to the Labour Party's Policy Review in April 1989 by CLPD. *Beyond the Casino Economy* aims to present an outline of a programme for the labour movement in the 1990s, but it is not intended to be the last word: an enormous amount of work needs to be done. Nevertheless, one thing at least can be said of current Labour Party policy: there is an alternative.

Foreword

Ten years after the Conservative government was elected, the full and horrific implications of their policies are becoming apparent to many who have so far accepted them, with rising inflation, higher interest and mortgage rates, low levels of manufacturing investment and a massive balance of payments deficit. All this has been combined with a widening gap between rich and poor, growing homelessness and poverty, the neglect of our public services and infrastructure, continuing mass unemployment and mounting attacks on local government and the trade unions.

Unfortunately the response of some on the left to these developments has been weak and superficial – either harking back to the policies adopted by earlier Labour governments, which did not themselves succeed, or concentrating on personal attacks on the ministers responsible and implying that the situation could be remedied by better management of the status quo. Another school of thought has emerged, associated with *Marxism Today* and some leading figures in the Labour Party, who seem to have accepted key elements in the Thatcherite analysis and, in the name of 'New Realism', argue that changes in the world economy and British society must be accepted as the basis of future policy-making.

The importance of *Beyond the Casino Economy* lies in the detailed examination it gives to the implications of those changes: the globalization of capital, the increasing power of multinational companies, and the damaging effect of financial gambling on the strength of Britain's industrial base, which is likely to accelerate from 1992 as the EEC's Single Market comes into force. It also looks at the changing structure of industry, the increase in women's employment, usually in low-paid work, and the ecological factors which are rightly dominating so much of the contemporary public debate. This is a highly political book which goes beyond the narrow arguments about management and looks to the future of working people in a country still in decline. The hectic and frothy growth of recent years has been fed by a consumer credit boom, and relied on oil and privatization revenues. But all these special factors are now being exhausted.

The main conclusion which the authors reach is that we shall, once again, have to see the relevance of common ownership of the key sectors of the economy if we are to be able to build up the industrial and service base which we shall need in the 1990s and the next century. The arguments for this are well documented, with meticulous attention to detail, and as they proceed it is possible to see why the social democratic attachment to Keynesianism failed, and why we have to go beyond the Alternative Economic Strategy adopted by the left in the 1970s. Indeed it is essential, if we are to prepare for the future, that we should realize that it was during that decade that many of the ideas now associated with Mrs Thatcher were first accepted and applied. And it was the adoption of them that paved the way for Labour's defeat in 1979.

The Thatcher era is now coming to an end, and the British establishment itself is getting increasingly concerned at the damage that has been done, and at the possibility that public disenchantment might lead to the election of a Labour government by default. It is for these very reasons that socialists should be intensifying their work on policies that would both deal with the immediate crisis and start the long process of rebuilding our economic base and reconstructing our society. For unless that work is done well in advance, the change of government that may well lie ahead could amount to little more than one big cabinet re-shuffle, where the incoming ministers were left to struggle with a situation that cannot be improved without major structural changes.

Preparatory work on the scale that is required depends on our having the confidence that those tasks can be performed, and that there really is an alternative to the present injustice and decay. The publication of *Beyond the Casino Economy*, at this moment, will go a long way towards building that confidence. 'Popular capitalism' has obviously failed Britain. Our best hope for the future lies in a socialism that is democratic, accountable and internationalist in its outlook, and is one we construct for ourselves.

Tony Benn
May 1989

Introduction

> *Constant revolutionizing of production, uninterrupted disturbance of all social conditions, everlasting uncertainty and agitation distinguish the bourgeois epoch from all earlier ones.*
>
> Karl Marx and Friedrich Engels, 1847[1]

The 1970s and 1980s were years of crisis and turbulent economic change throughout the world, which repeatedly shook and overturned established political ideas. The breakdown of the post-war capitalist boom in the late 1960s at first gave way to an inflationary slump in the 1970s, and later spawned a period of frenetic economic restructuring which has still far from played itself out. This economic pattern was matched by a rapidly evolving political scene. Economic turmoil and the failure of social democratic policies were met during the 1970s by an upsurge of working class militancy in countries like Britain, France and Italy. Fascism was overthrown in Portugal, Spain and Greece; and American global power was successfully challenged by anti-imperialist movements in Southeast Asia, Africa, Latin America and the Middle East.

By the 1980s the freedom of manoeuvre of international capital had been drastically narrowed by the exhaustion of the special post-war conditions for growth. A new strategy had to be imposed. Politicians in the advanced capitalist states abandoned their attempts to find a way out of the crisis with the Keynesian formulas of the post-war years. Most, including the socialist and social-democratic leaders of Western Europe and Australasia, succumbed to a latter-day economic liberalism which gave free rein to the transnational giants to re-fashion the Western world to their own design. Armed with the micro-chip, multinationals and their political partners assumed a new confidence and aggression.

Hot money now swirls around the globe in what has become a virtual free-fire zone in the search for increased profitability. Production centres are opened and closed without regard for social costs. Whole industries – like shipbuilding and consumer electronics – are transferred from one continent to another, while millions of workers are being shaken out of traditional industries to become a pool of low-cost service labour. Mass unemployment has become a permanent feature of the developed capitalist countries, where over thirty million people were on the dole in the mid 1980s.[2] Inequality and crime have advanced hand in hand with ecological destruction and credit-card consumerism. The restructuring of the major capitalist economies and their relations with the rest of the world is not simply a technical adjustment, but is being carried out at the expense of the working class – which is itself undergoing profound change and recomposition – as well as other important sections of society. The untrammelled power of the largest capitalist monopolies that has been the hallmark of the 1980s has forced up the productivity of labour and the level of company profits, but at the same time brought widespread social insecurity and poverty in its wake.

Between the advanced and the developing regions of the capitalist world, a new economic relationship is emerging which combines a re-division of international labour with a new parasitism based on the harness of colossal debts. The International Monetary Fund (IMF) and the World Bank have succeeded in prising open more and more Third World economies for Western business. During the 1980s it became commonplace for desperately poor countries to find themselves paying the bulk of their export earnings in interest payments to American, British, Japanese and West German banks. Net capital outflows from the Third World in the form of debt repayments between 1983 and 1988 totalled US$143 billion, while indebtedness continued to rise. The result was a fall in living standards of between a tenth and a quarter in Latin America and Africa during the decade and growing impoverishment for 900 million people.[3]

Britain has a special place in this process of economic change because of its chronic relative decline. The peculiar dominance of financial capital in Britain and the overseas orientation of the British economy meant record profits for British-owned transnational corporations during the international capitalist boom of the 1980s at the same time that British manufacturing industry slipped into the red on the trade account for the first time since the industrial revolution of the eighteenth century.[4] Despite the claims of the Thatcher government to have turned the economic corner, those profits have not been translated into the scale and breadth of investment throughout the country which could bring a sustainable and rising quality of life for the mass of the people. Thatcherite policies have failed either to tackle the inherited weaknesses of the British economy or to prepare it for the opening up of the Single European Market and the international conditions of the 1990s. The government has frittered away oil revenues to the value of £100 billion paying for mass unemployment and an unprecedented scale of capital export. Britain now faces the prospect of a drift towards de-skilled, low-wage employment for large sections of the labour force unless there is a sustained modernization and investment drive which could equip the British economy to face the rigours of the international economic environment of the 1990s. If the domination of the City of London, the drain of high military spending and years of under-investment have been debilitating for Britain in the past, that burden now risks becoming critical.

The aim of this book is to contribute to laying the policy foundations for a complete change of direction for the British economy which could start to meet basic goals of the labour movement – first-class collective services, full employment for all sections of society and better living standards in all areas of the country – and at the same time carry out that long-overdue economic modernization without which only the wealthy few can be confident of their future. Neither the right nor centre of British politics has shown itself capable of bringing about the necessary changes in the structure and performance of British business. Conservative government ministers and their supporters in the media are forever hailing the arrival of the long-awaited economic miracle which will break the familiar cycle of failure. But £150 billion-worth of British capital exported overseas under the Thatcher governments and a return to profitability for what remains of home-based manufacturing are no basis for sustainable growth. The credit-fuelled Tory consumer boom was bound to come to grief without a dramatic investment-led increase in productivity to match internationally competitive levels. Yet despite significant increases in the late 1980s, British industrial investment remains at strikingly low levels compared with other advanced capitalist countries. Even by 1988, British manufacturing investment was still below its 1979 level.[5] By the end of the 1980s, as the vital cushion of North Sea oil was gradually being deflated, the underlying industrial weakness of the British economy was once again making itself felt in a swollen trade deficit, rising inflation and the highest interest rates of any major capitalist economy.

It is hardly surprising that if big business is given a free hand, as it has been during the Thatcher years, it will vigorously pursue its own interests. The last ten years have shown that those interests do not coincide with the needs and interests of the majority of the British people. Nothing more clearly illustrates the fact that capitalist criteria of success are not the best guide to real economic health than the coincidence of runaway profits and soaring unemployment in Britain in the early 1980s. But the Keynesian remedies that were tried and ultimately failed in the 1950s and 1960s stand even less chance of tackling such deep-seated problems in today's much harsher economic conditions than they did the first time around. Carrot-and-stick tax incentives and regulations are not up to the job of convincing scores of large and determined multinationally-orientated British companies radically to change their ways.

Towards a Cure

It would be absurd in such a situation for the left and the labour movement simply to regurgitate formulas and strategies inherited from the past. But it would be equally wrong to throw up one's hands at the problems created by the new environment and discard policies based on years of experience and discussion because they are politically unfashionable. A realistic analysis of current trends in both the British and international capitalist economies shows that the basic goals of the labour movement would require far greater changes in the structures of social and economic power in the 1990s than in the mid 1970s when the last Labour government split over whether to bow to the dictates of the IMF. The only way to restructure the British economy on the scale necessary to meet the challenge of the changes in the world economy – to re-orientate Britain's huge resources of capital and skilled labour towards building up a core of hi-tech industries to meet people's needs and aspirations – is through large-scale public ownership and intervention.

While the package of reflationary economic policies and import controls which the left of the Cabinet championed in the 1970s could have been accommodated by the City and large monopolies without a major threat to the balance of class power, that could not be said of any credible economic strategy aimed at changing direction in the conditions of today. Against such a background, it is perhaps not surprising that there has been a drift away from support for radical economic policies among different sections of the labour movement during the 1980s. But arguments which justify rejecting or watering down such a programme on the grounds that it would no longer work in the brave new world of globalized markets and inter-penetrated capitalist economies are seriously flawed. These trends call, on the contrary, for more far-reaching change.

The evolution of technology also increasingly favours the socialization of the key sectors of the economy. The role played by the market and small private companies in the early stages of the microchip revolution has now exhausted itself. As will be argued in detail later, information technology demands the integration and compatibility of systems and networks, and that can only be ensured by public ownership and intervention. Private enterprise is becoming a brake on the development of modern production techniques, which are dissolving the boundaries of the traditional firm. Private ownership and the patent system are blocking the free spread of industrial knowledge at a time when the information economy is supposed to be on the rise, and the cost of necessary research and development has escalated beyond the reach of even some of the largest private companies. These underlying trends – which are common to all industrial economies – are pushing in the direction of more direct social ownership and control in economic life and exactly the kind of interventionist policies that are essential if Britain's special economic problems are to be overcome.[6]

If it is correct that only a radical, sustained government-led policy of intervention and restructuring can build a modern industrial and technological base in Britain, then the demands of modernization and the political interests of working people potentially coincide far more clearly than they do in other capitalist countries – or than they have done in Britain in the past. This conclusion is in striking contrast to the common assumption which has come to associate the labour movement with an outdated smokestack ideology. Far wider strata of the population beyond the working class and traditional Labour supporters could be attracted towards a programme which put the re-industrialization and modernization of Britain at the head of its priorities in a broad framework of social justice. Already, polls show that 52 per cent of the population believe profits should go into investment and improved pay and conditions, but only 38 per cent believe that that is where they will go. Moreover, 55 per cent think higher profits are more likely to end up in the pockets of shareholders and managers as increased dividends and bonuses, while only 3 per cent believe that this is the right use of them.[7]

Scientists who are denied the backing and status they see given to their colleagues in other countries; technologists who find their skills spurned by domestic industry; teachers and academics who are frustrated by lack of funds from a government determined to tie them to the dubious priorities of private industry; women who are hampered from developing their lives by the government's refusal to provide a collective child-care system; black people who lose out in the jobs and housing market because of racism and inadequate training; professional people living outside the south east who find their opportunities cramped by the colossally wasteful neglect of large parts of the rest of the country – all these social groups could be won to a labour movement programme aimed at changing the direction of British society. Add to these the people who are disgusted by the ballooning inequalities of late-twentieth-century Britain and you have a potentially powerful alliance of social groups around the organized working class.

There are already signs that disaffected industrialists and professionals who could be won to an interventionist and modernizing platform are finding champions-in-the-making in Tory politicians like the former cabinet minister Michael Heseltine and the Welsh Secretary Peter Walker. Having staked his claim as the champion of a European strategy for British hi-tech during the Westland affair in the mid 1980s, Heseltine moved on to advance an active, corporatist approach to the modernization of the British economy which clearly strikes a chord with sections of domestically-based industry. The palpable irrationality of unplanned and regionally-skewed economic development, the failure of the market to manage the problems of industrial change and urban blight, the danger to the countryside and the environment from unbridled profiteering – Heseltine articulates all these problems in a way which avoids challenging the existing system of social relations.[8]

But the experience of both Tory and Labour governments shows that the causes of British capitalism's relative decline over the last century, which the interventionist Tories recognize as serious problems – the dominance of financial interests, the overseas orientation of British capital, its resistance to government guidance, the culture of short-term profiteering – cannot be overcome by exhortation and incentive. Big business has been peculiarly resistant in Britain to even the most generous curbs on its independence or attempts to point it in a more productive direction. The 1960s and 1970s were littered with the failures of such projects – from George Brown's National Plan of the mid 1960s to Edward Heath's U-turn Industry Act of 1972. British capital has very strong structural interests in carrying on as it has in the past, which is one reason why the more successful capitalist economic regimes operated in countries like Japan, Sweden or West Germany cannot just be transplanted by a well-meaning British government.

Even under a radically different leadership, the Tory party, with all its historic links with the City of London and overseas interests, could never deliver the sort of state-led restructuring and regional regeneration programme that Heseltine is increasingly drawn towards, even on the most favourable terms to capital. There is not the slightest sign that the most powerful groups in the Tory party would stand for it. The only political party capable of mobilizing a broad enough social constituency behind the kind of sweeping institutional and political change necessary to turn round the British economy is Labour. Only the working-class movement has the overriding interest in the necessary scale of change of direction, the potential collective strength to deliver it and hence the possibility of attracting and uniting other social groups for progressive advance.

The Chasm of Credibility

But between this potential and the current reality is a chasm of credibility and political will. Much of the analysis offered by the Labour front bench accurately pinpoints weaknesses in the British economy and dangers posed for the future. But there is an eerie echo of early 1960s rhetoric. One of the principal lessons of the first Wilson administration was that modernizing rhetoric by itself butters no parsnips – and certainly doesn't buy new plant and machinery. The National Plan was sacrificed on the altar of the exchange rate in 1966, and Tony Benn's more radical planning agreements of the mid 1970s were blocked at the Cabinet table by Harold Wilson and his allies. The weaknesses of British industry that Wilson's 'white heat' modernization programme was supposed to tackle are far more serious today than twenty-five years ago. Yet the methods advocated by the current Labour leadership are less radical than the tried and failed remedies of the 1960s.

Today's Labour leaders are less interventionist, more cautious, less prepared to step on the toes of the captains of industry and far more prepared to cede decision-making in industry to the market – in other words to the banks and transnationals – than even Wilson or George Brown. If the tools at hand proved utterly inadequate for the job in the 1960s, it is hardly rational to believe that more modest equipment will suffice for the 1990s. Relying on tax carrots to meet common goals – such as adequate training, regional balance and a boost to investment – begs the credibility question: where would the money come from? It reflects the hope of achieving desirable goals without making any of the difficult choices which lie along any realistic road to their attainment. Of course tax incentives have a place in any coherent strategy, but a radical Labour government cannot afford – literally – to bribe capital to act in the interest of society; and claims that Labour will do so lead to cynicism among voters. Now more than ever, major social and economic changes demand far-reaching measures, often involving legislative compulsion. Any programme which does not openly recognize this will not be believed. Labour's 1989 Policy Review is a case in point.[9]

Facing up to the Future?

The origins of the programme for re-industrialization and social justice outlined in this book can be traced to the package of policies known as the Alternative Economic Strategy (AES), which was developed in the early 1970s in response to the failure of the Wilson governments, and which heavily influenced Labour's 1973 and 1982 programmes. There were always a variety of versions of the strategy – some more radical than others – and the basic package evolved over time. But common to all its variants was an expansionary public spending programme, backed up by import controls to prevent the recurrent balance of payments crises that plagued Labour and Tory governments in the 1950s and 1960s. On the supply side of the economy, the AES envisaged an extension of public ownership and a system of compulsory planning agreements with major private sector firms as the basis for managing an expansion of output and investment. Many of those on the left who were once most enthusiastic for the strategy – such as the Labour Co-ordinating Committee – now regard such a potentially radical challenge to capitalist power as utopian or sloganistic. Sometimes former supporters argue that such a programme is no longer relevant because it is too radical to win mass support in the wake of ten years of Thatcherite rule. Others believe that it should be rejected because the growing internationalization of the world economy makes it outdated.

It is perfectly true that what may have been an appropriate strategy for the conditions of the 1970s and even the early 1980s cannot mechanically be wheeled out in the changed circumstances of the 1990s. In addition, there were always both technical and political problems with the old AES which were not fully addressed by many of its supporters. It was presented by some as a clever way of sticking with Keynesian demand reflation techniques while avoiding the persistent headache of balance of payments crises by means of import controls. In reality, this was always something of a sleight of hand which would have simply shifted the problems – which arise because of the chronic weakness of British industry – to some other part of the economy. But at least in the early 1980s, when the combined effects of an emerging world capitalist recession and the Tory-engineered slump had cut manufacturing output by almost a fifth, more than doubling unemployment, a reflation-centred programme made sense.

After the wave of capital-scrapping that took place in the wake of the 1979–81 slump, that is no longer the case. By the late 1980s, Britain's economy was running at the highest levels of capacity utilization ever recorded, domestic output of the most basic construction materials was being stretched to breaking point and credit-fuelled inflationary pressures had built up throughout the economy.[10] Unemployment was falling – though not to the manipulated official figure of 1.8 million recorded for mid 1989, at which time it really stood around 2.5 million. Even with recessionary conditions returning, a reflation-centred programme would be able to do little to stimulate domestic industries which no longer exist or set factories humming which have long since disappeared.

The focus needs to shift away from how to buoy up demand towards how to rebuild the supply side of the economy: how to provide the goods and services people need. Labour's experience in the 1960s and 1970s shows that while it is essential to maintain consistent levels of demand, stimulating consumption will simply suck in imports and push up prices unless domestic factories and businesses are able and willing to meet the demand. The Labour leadership has recognized this and even appropriated the slogan of 'supply-side socialism'.[11] But unless a government is prepared to take far-reaching powers and intervene directly to create new industrial capacity, all the good will and tax-and-subsidy carrots in the world will not succeed in making the priorities of Britain's banks, industrial monopolies and foreign-owned transnationals match the priorities of a Labour government.

Another way in which the typical formulations of the Alternative Economic Strategy are no longer adequate is in their response to the problems posed by the growing integration of the advanced capitalist economies – in particular the continuing internationalization of capital and exchange markets. It would be hard to claim that there has been a qualitative change in the process of economic internationalization, which has been developing for hundreds of years. But the deregulatory policies followed by most advanced capitalist countries during the 1980s, increased trade within the European Economic Community (EEC), and the accelerating globalization of currency markets, have all highlighted the power of transnational capital, and the challenge it poses to any attempt to pursue progressive economic strategies against the grain of the rest of the advanced capitalist world.

The debacle of the first Mitterrand government in France – which in many ways echoed that of earlier Labour governments – and the endless promotion of the Single European Market of 1992 have rammed the lesson home to the point where some have abandoned any hope of a Labour government pursuing a genuinely independent economic strategy. It has become fashionable to believe that 'reflation in one country wouldn't work any more'. In reality, reflation in one country never did work in Britain's case, as every Labour government has found to its political cost. But the approach to international pressures and economic relations in most versions of the old Alternative Economic Strategy – which can be broadly summed up under the two headings of import controls and exchange controls – is neither politically nor technically a sufficient response to the scale of the problem. A far more sophisticated and wide-ranging package of policies is needed to overcome the international constraints on a radical programme of economic change, including an active strategy of planned trade expansion and new relationships of economic co-operation with a wider range of partners.

The Critical Core

At the heart of any viable economic programme must be the planned expansion and development of a group of core industries of the future that could provide Britain with a secure economic base for the 1990s and beyond. Some of those industries are basically infrastructural – such as transport and electricity generation – and are not generally traded internationally. Others depend for their success on the development of international markets, as the costs of design and research and development have ballooned. Any vision of go-it-alone autarchy is, and has long been, hopelessly unrealistic for an advanced industrial economy. That does not, however, mean that a Labour government has to allow transnational companies to allocate Britain whatever economic role they choose. Instead it points to the necessity of reconstructing the country's trade and currency policies in a way that would allow the building of a modern industrial base. That would involve a new relationship with the EEC, a regulated foreign exchange system, active joint venture policies and a new orientation towards economic co-operation with the Third World and socialist countries.

Once it is accepted that the major monopolies and transnationals which dominate the economy will not by themselves create a modern industrial base – simply because it is not profitable for them – and once the sorry history of regulations and incentives to convince them to do what they do not want to do is reviewed, the case for a major extension of democratic public ownership and direct statutory intervention becomes apparent. For a Labour government to have the leverage and information to plan effectively would require a publicly-owned stake in most major sectors of the economy. In some, especially hi-tech industries, it might only be necessary to nationalize one company for the viability of the reconstruction programme. In other sectors – for example, pharmaceuticals – it would make more sense to take a group of vertically-integrated businesses into public ownership. In others – such as retailing – it would probably be unnecessary to make any social inroads into the sector in the short term at all. The scale of nationalization envisaged is roughly comparable with the public ownership programme carried through by the Mitterrand government in 1982 – though the way those nationalized firms would be run would have to be quite different.[12]

Using this core of publicly-owned advanced industry, it would be possible to begin to re-orientate the vast resources of the private corporate sector towards the modernization of the economy using a mix of direct statutory controls, taxation policies, negotiated planning agreements, purchasing policies and social pressure. What would be essential – and this is where both Harold Wilson and François Mitterrand came unstuck in different periods and circumstances – is that the government should be in a position to guarantee a stable and steadily expansionary macroeconomic environment. At the very least that would demand the regulation of the British economy's highly exposed foreign currency markets and intervention to keep the expansion of imports in line with export growth.

Such a programme would undoubtedly collide head on with the interests of the City of London. For the relatively modest net foreign exchange earnings made by the banks and financial institutions, the price that is paid in terms of the distorting effects on the rest of the economy, on government policy and on the country's industrial base is enormous – not to mention the parasitic relationship that the City has with Third World countries. The City of London both epitomizes and reinforces the chronic sickness of the British economy and its business culture of speculative short-term gain. The first two economic measures the Thatcher government took when it came to power in 1979 were to cut the top rate of income tax from 83 per cent to 60 per cent and to abolish exchange controls. The feather-bedding of the City as the centre of the hot money industry has become a major potential block on the industrial and regional regeneration of the country. The City has a corrosive effect on British industry through its control of exchange and interest rates and its tradition of staying at arm's-length from its industrial borrowers; and it encourages investment in overseas and paper assets rather than in the long-term modernization of British industry. The mobilization of finance for a major programme of industrial re-equipment and investment would certainly require the nationalization of the major banks and financial institutions and a radical restructuring of their role.

Politics in Command

The kind of measures that could tackle the deep-seated weaknesses of the British economy would of necessity involve a challenge to the interests of the banks, transnationals and largest industrial monopolies that dominate this society. Such a programme could only succeed by mobilizing an extensive alliance of different social groups around a united working class able to confront the power of big business and its policies and priorities. It would not in itself be a programme for abolishing capitalism and introducing socialism. But its full implementation would undoubtedly involve a major class confrontation and could begin to raise in a practical way the question of the transition to a socialist society.

The economic foundation of a programme for radical change is only part of the story. It is self-evident that any Labour government elected on such a platform would also have to be committed to a wide range of democratic and socialist policies across the whole social and political field: policies to democratize the constitutional and political system, to attack the roots of racism in society, to open up cultural opportunities for the mass of the people, to bring about a British withdrawal from Ireland, policies for disarmament and new international relationships. Except in so far as they directly relate to an economic programme, such policies are beyond the scope of this book. That is not because these questions are any less important and it is certainly artificial to separate the strictly economic from the political. But it is in the field of economic policy where most confusion reigns on the left, and we have tried to stick to that brief.

The Thatcherite 'counter-revolution' has not only failed to turn round Britain's underlying economic performance, it has also widened inequalities between social groups and regions; pushed millions into poverty; divided the working class; vandalized our cities and financed the over-exploitation of the countryside; pandered to racism; successfully encouraged the exploitation of women and young people at work and in bogus training schemes; strait-jacketed the trade union movement; turned the mass media into its creature; eaten away at civil rights; set the police on striking workers and young blacks while crime has soared; strangled the public services; and undermined the movement for international disarmament at every turn. It is not just economically and industrially vital to take Britain in a radically different direction; it is an elementary democratic and social necessity.

Notes

1. *Manifesto of the Communist Party* (1848), Part 1, 'Bourgeois and Proletarians', London 1967, p. 83.

2. There were between thirty-one and thirty-two million unemployed in the Organization for Economic Co-operation and Development (OECD) countries at the end of 1984, representing more than eight per cent of the workforce. Although unemployment fell in the late 1980s in most OECD countries, France, Italy, Spain and Holland all had more than ten per cent official unemployment in the spring of 1989.

3. Figures from World Bank, *Debt Tables*, 1988, and Unicef, *Annual Report*, 1988.

4. The share of profits made by British industrial and commercial companies (excluding finance and oil) as a proportion of GDP rose from a low point of 6.1 per cent in 1981 to 13.4 per cent in 1988, the highest level since 1964. The net rate of return on capital was up from less than 3 per cent in 1981 (5.6 per cent in 1979) to 10.5 per cent in 1988. That was also the highest since the mid 1960s. Figures from *UK Economics Analyst*, Goldman Sachs, and Central Statistical Office, 1989.

5. In 1988, the volume of fixed investment in manufacturing industry rose by 9.4 per cent, but the total of around £11 billion at 1985 prices was still 1.5 per cent below the 1979 figure of £11.2 billion. See *Labour Research*, vol. 78 no. 4, April 1989.

6. Detailed discussion of how trends in new technology favour public ownership and planning can be found in chapters 3, 5 and 7 below.

7. Roger Jowell, Sharon Witherspoon and Lindsay Brook, *British Social Attitudes*, Aldershot 1988, p. 115.

8. See, for example, the interview with Michael Heseltine by John Lloyd in *Marxism Today*, March 1988.

9. *Meet the Challenge, Make the Change*, the final report of Labour's Policy Review for the 1990s, London 1989.

10. Manufacturing capacity utilization in January 1989 had reached 94.3 per cent in Britain. That was by far the highest rate of any EEC country and well above the peak levels of the last two cycles. In 1979, the figure was 87.6 per cent; in 1973, 90.6 per cent. These statistics, which are based on Confederation of British Industry (CBI) data, are taken from *European Economy*, Supplement B, European Commission, Brussels February 1989.

11. The phrase appeared both in the 'Productive and Competitive Economy' report adopted by the 1988 Labour Party conference and in the final Policy Review docu-

ment, p. 6. It was originally used in *The Case for Public Ownership*, published by CLPD in 1986, p. 27.

12. In 1981–2, the French government nationalized 12 industrial firms (7 of which were among France's 20 biggest companies), 36 banks and two finance companies. After the takeovers, 25 per cent of all manufacturing and 13 out of the country's 20 main industrial groupings were in the public sector. See Howard Machin and Vincent Wright, eds, *Economic Policy and Policy-Making under the Mitterrand Presidency 1981–84*, London 1985.

PART I

A Brave New World?

Technological, economic and political changes are transforming advanced capitalist societies. Employment and production patterns are being redrawn; capital is becoming ever more international in its operations; denationalization and new forms of government regulation have been enforced in different ways throughout the globe and a new international division of labour is emerging.

It has become a commonplace – even among some on the left – to regard all these developments as together somehow signalling the end of the road for socialism and any prospect for political advance by the working class in the capitalist world. There are three main strands to this attitude. Industrial change is reckoned to be leading to the disappearance of the working class; the nation-state is seen as increasingly powerless in the face of the international economy; and the market is thought certain to defeat any attempts at planning in a deregulated world. What is striking about such views is how little they are rooted in a thorough analysis of actual developments.

In this part, recent changes are examined and an attempt made to sift out the fundamental from the superficial. Chapter 1 focusses on the new forms of industrial organization which have been glorified under the term Post-Fordism and considers whether they herald the revival of small-scale competitive capitalism with a workforce to match. Chapter 2 examines the implications of the continuing globalization of capital and markets, and what it means for progressive economic strategies in Britain. Chapter 3 then looks behind the cult of markets and deregulation that took hold in the 1980s and its implications for the future of socialist economic planning.

1

The Strange Death of Fordism

The reports of my death are greatly exaggerated.

Mark Twain, 1897[1]

At the heart of the left's confusion in recent years has been a widespread fear that changes in technology and society are somehow leaving socialism and the labour movement behind. Stoked up by the triumphalist talk of conservative ideologists and political and industrial defeats, an impression has been created that many of the traditional concerns of socialists – collectivism, class politics, economic planning, public ownership and trade unionism – are becoming relics of a bygone age, swept away or marginalized by the emergence of a brave new world of individualism, free markets and private enterprise.

In Britain, the onrush of new technology and industrial restructuring common to the rest of the capitalist world has been given a special ideological twist by its association with the successive governments led by Margaret Thatcher, who has proclaimed her intention to eradicate socialism from the country for ever. On the left, some have come to believe that the labour movement must not only rapidly adjust to new social and economic conditions, but must also accept the dominant political interpretation of them. In economic policy, that would certainly mean the abandonment of any radical programme for the transformation of the British economy.

Fordism and Post-Fordism

Part of the basis for such attitudes can be found in a particular view of recent industrial and economic change. In the 1970s, it became fashionable to argue that Britain and other advanced capitalist countries were becoming 'post-industrial' societies, as manual and manufacturing work gave way to employment in services. A much broader theory of 'Post-Fordism' has since been developed to explain where modern economies are – or should be – going.[2] Post-Fordists argue that the old industrial world built on large-scale production and uniform mass consumption, pioneered by the American capitalist Henry Ford in the early years of the century, has had its day. In its place small-batch flexible production systems based on robotics and information technology, combined with increasingly specialized markets, are making way for a pluralistic and innovative new social order.

Ford's original production methods, developed before the First World War, are taken by the Post-Fordists as the model on which industrialization has been based since the 1920s. At the root of Ford's system was the mass production of a small range of standard products. It involved an extensive division of labour, the use of special-purpose (or 'dedicated') machinery, and a concentration of manufacturing processes and services within one firm. More broadly 'Fordism' is seen as the whole system of mass production and consumption based on semi-skilled labour and easy credit which underpinned the post-war boom and the welfare state. The economic breakdown of the 1970s is in turn interpreted as a crisis of Fordism.

Against this old Fordist model of industry and society the Post-Fordists hold up modern manufacturing systems based on the principle of 'flexible specialization' ('flec spec' to its friends) as the emerging way of the future. Under flec spec, a large number of customized products are manufactured in small units by skilled staff working on a variety of different tasks, using re-programmable manufacturing technology. Smaller companies employ a stable core of well-paid, secure workers, supplemented by a peripheral workforce of part-timers or temporary employees hired in line with order books. And firms subcontract to specialized suppliers of different services rather than depend on direct employment. The overall effect, as one academic study of flexible specialization describes it, is 'to rely far more on the market to bring different aspects of production together, rather than to rely on management in a much larger production unit organizing everything with its own work-force.'[3]

For some sections of the left and centre in British politics, this sort of analysis of industrial change and the diversification of consumption it implies has become the basis for a vision of a new world of fragmentation, weakening collective solidarity, work flexibility and choice through personal consumption, which the labour movement ignores at its peril. From David Marquand of the Social and Liberal Democrats to Labour's Bryan Gould to the *Marxism Today* group in the Communist Party, a whole swathe of opposition politicians and intellectuals in Britain appears to have decided that adjusting to a post-Fordist future is the key to success. In the debate over the labour movement's economic strategy, the argument has been developed most clearly by Robin Murray, who ran the GLC's Industry and Employment Branch. The sort of flexible market specialization and subcontracting practised by retailers like Benetton and Sainsbury's could not only be the salvation of London's declining clothing and furniture industries, he argues, but potentially opens the way for new forms of local municipal intervention and economic planning. At the same time, it makes traditional national policies for public ownership and intervention increasingly out-dated.[4]

If all this were true and modern capitalist industry was turning small scale and competitive, while workers were becoming flexible, atomized and consumerist, it would have enormous importance for the labour movement's policies, not only in Britain, but all over the world. But have the Post-Fordists in fact got it right about industrial and social trends in the most advanced capitalist countries? And if their picture is distorted, what kind of industrial conditions would a radical Labour government in the 1990s actually face?

The Evidence: Where's the Beef?

To understand where modern industry is going, and what is happening to the size of firms, it is necessary to distinguish between three different types of economic advantage to be had from large-scale production:

- 'Economies of scale' will be used here to refer to the savings to be made from the scale of plants, as opposed to the size of production runs for particular product variants;
- 'Economies of scope' are the advantages to be had from spreading overheads, particularly research and development costs, over a wide scope of product variants; and
- 'Economies of integration' represent the advantages of all stages of production being carried out within a single firm.

Economies of integration appear to have fallen in recent years – that at least is clearly the belief of some industrialists who have moved towards a Japanese model of industrial organization, in which large firms rely increasingly on a cluster of smaller components and servicing firms instead of doing everything in-house. In the 1980s large manufacturing companies tended to restructure their internal organization and contract out not only 'peripheral' work such as catering, cleaning and transport, but also production itself. By contracting out a significant proportion of their intermediate production and services, large firms are able to continue to dominate the overall production process – while not having to take the risks of developing specialized expertise in all areas, and letting others do the dirty work of cutting labour costs by driving down conditions of employment.

Contracting out

The figures show a marked rise in the proportion of 'peripheral' workers during the 1980s. Self-employment registered a significant increase, from 9.7 per cent of the total in 1981 to 13.3 per cent in 1988.[5] Between 1983 and 1987 the number of full-time employees fell by over one per cent at a time when the total number of people in full-time and part-time employment grew by 6 per cent.[6] But there was no real growth in temporary employment: once participants in government 'special employment measures' are excluded, it stuck at 5.7 per cent of total employment from 1984 through to 1988.[7]

Increased contracting-out of work, as well as the use of temporary employment contracts and outwork, was partly a response to the increased economic uncertainties facing firms in Britain in the 1980s. One of the problems in sorting out the evidence on flexible specialization is the difficulty of separating those changes which have happened because of underlying technological and economic development from those which have been pushed through because of political pressure or the opportunities created by years of recession. For example, the Thatcher governments have enforced contracting-out of services on local authorities. And the use of unemployed people on training schemes as casual labour is more a direct result of mass unemployment than of any novel employment strategy. In the labour market of the 1980s, flexibility mostly became a code word for union-bashing and increased intensity of work, especially among low-paid, part-time casualized women workers.[8] These different processes cannot be fully separated, since technological development is influenced by class conflict. But those aspects of restructuring which are a product of the temporary weakness of organized labour cannot be regarded as a permanent trend.

Nor do technology and work organization develop in the same way in different sectors. Technological advance is not a uniform process; and the organization of the modern factory is not much of a guide, say, for construction or agriculture.[9] While some pundits and academics have hailed the arrival of the 'flexible firm' with a Japanese-style two-tier workforce,[10] the evidence on flexibility shows that British management made relatively modest headway in the direction of these kind of personnel and industrial relations practices within firms in the 1980s.[11]

The power of industrial groupings

Parallel with these uneven changes in work organization, there was a trend during the 1980s to reduce what is sometimes called the 'depth' of manufacturing processes. In the post-war years, a Ford motor plant would take in iron ore at one end and pour out finished cars at the other. Today an increasing proportion of output is accounted for by intermediate components. Long-term and reliable relations with components suppliers and producer services firms have become key to the strategies of most major manufacturers. This tendency is being boosted at the moment by the development of advanced telecommunications services, notably electronic data interchange. As relationships with suppliers become closer, the need for reliable and rapid exchange of information between firms increases. The automation of this process makes co-operating firms more and more transparent to each other, and their increasingly detailed partnership locks them into each others' strategies, with the result that an increasing number of firms represents a decreasing number of industrial groupings.

The very same trends which allow separate firms to carry out functions which once had to be integrated within a single organization also tighten the bonds between those firms. This applies both to organizational innovations – such as the Japanese 'kanban' system for organizing the movement of components around a factory – and to technological developments. Organizationally, for example, outside suppliers who used to deliver to a central warehouse now often deliver directly to the production line. The necessity for co-ordination and close relations between the workers of the two firms is greatly increased: where previously they were part of two separate production processes, cushioned by transport and warehousing, they are now really part of a single process. Similarly, the communication technologies which make it possible for workers to be physically separate from each other, also allow them to co-operate in new ways: today's local area networks, and tomorrow's wide area networks, can be used as effectively by workers to plan industrial action as by management to issue orders. The technology is introduced to increase management's control of the production process; but once introduced, it can be wielded by workers.

The number of firms has risen in Britain over the 1980s, though much of this increase is due to the proliferation of small businesses typical of periods of mass unemployment, combined with particular encouragement from government.[12] The growth in the number of firms, however, has not been matched by a reduction in either the size or power of the monopolies. Nor does increased industrial contracting-out by itself increase the number of relatively smaller firms to which such contract work has traditionally gone. Take the case of the British motor industry, which has always relied heavily on a large and varied independent supplier network. In recent years, these component suppliers have increasingly been performing contracted-out 'sub-assembly' work, such as the assembly of complete seats and braking systems. But this growth in the proportion of work going to supplier firms has been accompanied by a trend towards fewer, larger contracts going to just one supplier to ensure the necessary economies of scale.[13] This is reinforced by the trend for primary, and even secondary, contractors to carry out more of their own research and development.

Batch production

An essential part of the Post-Fordist argument is that robotics and re-programmable production equipment have started a shift from standardized, mass-produced goods to the batch production of an increased number and variety of products. Critics have rightly pointed out that many commercial developments in 1980s Britain, such as the gobbling-up of the country's high streets by identical retail chains and supermarkets, reveal the opposite tendency at work: MacDonalds is the ultimate in standardized Fordism on a world scale,[14] and video cassette recorders are the products of large-scale Japanese assembly factories sold in mass markets across the globe.

The mistake of the Post-Fordists has been to jump from the fact that new technology allows smaller production runs for particular model variants to the conclusion that this will mean smaller, more competitive firms. Of course, the Post-Fordists are not the only ones to make that assumption – *The Economist* has, for example, been insisting on the point for years.[15] But the evidence points in the other direction. The paradoxical fact is that as new technology allows shorter economic production runs and at the same time smaller concentrations of production workers in factories, the very same trends demand larger and larger firms for the research and development required by these technologies in the first place, and often increased total production of the wider range of product variants taken together. Many of the leading-edge areas of the economy require increasingly huge scale. In 1989 it already cost a minimum of US$100 million to establish a semiconductor plant of moderate volume, while companies were thinking in terms of around US$300 million for the next generation of facilities.

Modern batch-production is not, then, simply being undertaken by new firms competing against the old-timers who are still mass-producing clapped-out standardized products. On the contrary, batch production of diversified products is being carried out by the giant Fordist firms themselves. Companies like Ford itself are able to make smaller batches of a wider range of model variants because the same production line can be used for a varied output by re-programming the capital equipment – though robots cannot simply be re-programmed for a new model range at the press of a few buttons, but have to be expensively re-commissioned.[16]

Scale and scope

One of the main reasons why the up-and-coming Post-Fordist economy is, and will continue to be, dominated by a similar or greater degree of monopoly as was the old Fordist one, is the advantage of having a large enough output, not only of one product, but of an entire product range to justify the development and full use of the new re-programmable capital equipment. Until recently, it was thought that the introduction of flexible manufacturing systems would reduce economies of scale as capital equipment could be re-programmed for different models instead of having to invest in special-purpose, dedicated machinery for each new product. But the smaller size of a single product's production run only reduces the importance of economies of scale by increasing the importance of economies of scope. The bigger the firm, the greater the scope of different related products it can produce and so the more it can spread overheads and use the same costly capital equipment for more than one of its product variants.

Research and development, which used to be tightly tied to the development of particular products, is increasingly non-specific, aimed at the creation within a firm of capability in a particular technology or product area. To recoup the costs of this, the capability must be used for a wide variety of products. In the telecommunications industry, minimum efficient scales of production – equivalent to national monopolies in some cases – favour the global corporation rather than the small 'hi-tech' firm. And it is the increased range of products and services produced by a single firm which – by allowing the spreading of overheads, especially the escalating costs of research and development, over more products – is giving an even more decisive advantage to the giant firms.[17]

There is evidence of increasing flexibility in Britain and other advanced industrial countries, but in terms of products rather than firm size. Applying information technology to production, companies are able to shorten design cycles; reduce levels of stocks at all stages of the production process by using Japanese 'just-in-time' manufacturing techniques; manage shorter, rapidly changing production runs; and respond more rapidly and precisely to demand. And this growing capacity to produce a wider variety of products often leads to pressure for increased firm size – as argued for example by Michiyo Nakamoto in a discussion of the Japanese audio consumer electronics industry.

> The growing diversification of consumer preferences is perhaps the most important market change for the industry. Young people look for products specifically tailored to their individual tastes. The life span of any one product has become much shorter: the typical audio set is used for anywhere from six months to one year. This means manufacturers must be able to put a wide range of products on the market and must keep producing new ones very quickly, to keep pace with changing demand and to create new demand. Success in the supply and demand market depends on heavy investment in research and development. Manufacturers need to have a production system flexible enough to allow them to change models quickly. With products changing at such a frantic pace, a wide and efficient distribution network also becomes crucial. In all these respects, the larger manufacturer has a definite advantage over small and specialized companies.[18]

The growth of monopoly

So the demand for flexibility and specialization does not mean a trend to smaller firms or the break-up of the giant monopolies. Costs of research and development and design have grown enormously in the last fifteen years or so. In the car industry the cost of designing and developing a new model has risen to over one billion dollars, a figure which is expected to rise to around ten billion dollars by the end of the century.[19] The result is that only the largest monopolies can make the grade, and small volume producers like Rover – for whom flexible manufacturing systems were supposed to be a godsend – are floundering. Industrial concentration – the degree of monopoly – in the advanced capitalist countries was stable or even fell during the 1970s.[20] However, the wave of mergers at the end of the decade held up concentration levels, including in the UK.[21] 'Merger mania' then accelerated with a vengeance throughout the 1980s despite the 1987 stock market crash, and expenditure in the takeover market rose from £2.3 billion in 1983 to £27.7 billion in 1987.[22]

The trend towards industrial globalization has intensified the international integration of firms through mergers, takeovers and joint ventures. Previously monopolized national markets have increasingly become 'oligopolistic' ones,[23] fought over by rival groups. But increased international competition of this type is in no way associated with a greater number of smaller firms. The firms fighting over globalized markets are often larger than the previous national monopolies. And the economic benefits which are supposed to flow from a post-1992 increase in competition within the European Community are not expected from a rise in the number of smaller firms competing against each other but, on the contrary, from a reduction in the number of firms, each becoming greater in size.[24] There is some scepticism among academic economists that the boost to concentration and mergers from the completion of the Single Market will in fact make EEC-based firms more competitive. Western Europe already has a high level of industrial concentration by US and Japanese standards, and Britain has a particularly disproportionate share of giant companies. The experience of the Labour government's promotion of mergers policy in the 1960s proved that size is not enough for success. But the effect of 1992 on the drive to greater monopoly in Europe is not in doubt.[25]

The overall picture in the most advanced capitalist countries is of increasingly globalized markets fought over by ever-larger industrial companies and groupings. The modern trend towards greater monopoly is the result both of the higher costs of technology, design, marketing, and research and development – but also of the long-established tendency under capitalism for larger capitals to drive out smaller ones, and for big business to use its greater financial and political resources to destroy its lesser rivals. As Marx commented more than a hundred years ago: 'one capitalist always kills many.'[26]

Political Implications

The editor of *Marxism Today*, Martin Jacques, summed up the Post-Fordist 'new times' he believes the advanced capitalist countries are now entering as follows:

> Our world is being remade. Mass production, the mass consumer, the big city, big-brother state, the sprawling housing estate, and the nation-state are in decline: flexibility, diversity, differentiation, mobility, communication, decentralization and internationalization are in the ascendant.[27]

Labour's trade and industry spokesperson and self-proclaimed modernizer, Bryan Gould, called this 'the map of the territory we have to capture'[28] – and it is an interpretation of the way society is moving which has gained wide currency among certain sections of the left.

The basic political message that the Post-Fordists draw from their analysis of industrial change is that there is a solid material basis for the growth of individualism in society, which therefore needs to be integrated into the labour movement's political strategy. They paint a picture of a past in which workers drank the same beer, wore the same clothes, went to Blackpool for their holidays, watched the same TV programmes and talked about them at work the next day in huge factories and mines. Today, by contrast, lifestyles are thought to be differentiated; workplaces are smaller and cleaner; in the evening people sit at home and watch videos or cable television, during the day they shop for an unprecedented variety of products. These social changes are supposed to have undermined the basis for class solidarity and socialist change.

But this picture-postcard of the 'old working class' lifestyle is no more true to life than those you find in Blackpool. The work-life and home-life of nineteenth-century workers was very sharply stratified and regionally differentiated.[29] Furthermore, the bourgeoisie has always embraced a host of differentiated lifestyles and yet manages to sustain a very strong sense of class consciousness whenever its basic interests are called into question. In the nineteenth century, which after all saw the original growth of proletarian consciousness – as well as Marx's classic analysis of capitalism – individual workforces were far smaller than they could ever become on the basis of today's trends. While the number of workers in some industrial plants is shrinking, their potential industrial muscle is actually growing, as the power workers have demonstrated. And concentrations of employees in service sector workplaces – like hospitals and supermarkets – are expanding rapidly. The rise and fall of Fordism all took place in the twentieth century. It was associated with some stability in the economy, politics and society, so its demise would, if anything, suggest increased economic and political instability into the twenty-first century.

The Post-Fordist analysis – and its cruder variants in the mass media – is curiously reminiscent of arguments common in the late 1950s and early 1960s, another period when Labour had lost three general elections in a row. An influential book of the time, *Must*

Labour Lose?, claimed for example that Labour's class appeal was being undermined because:

> the working class itself, even the lower categories within it, is emerging from its earlier unhappy plight; manual workers are gradually moving into the white-collar category, which does not identify itself with the unskilled or semi-skilled labourers; and many, particularly among the young, are now crossing the class frontiers into the middle class. The ethos of class solidarity is beginning to crumble in the face of the new fluidity of our society, the new opportunities for advancement through individual effort.[30]

Those words were written in 1960. As things turned out, Labour won four out of the following five general elections and within a few years the proportion of the workforce involved in strike action rose to its highest level for fifty years – a cautionary tale for the labour movement's perennial prophets of doom.

The Post-Fordists have, in their enthusiasm, plainly over-egged the pudding. They are right to emphasize the need to understand the direction of change, and to warn against ostrich-like behaviour on the left. But they have picked on some real trends and generalized them out of all recognition, with the result that their 'map' is of little use as a guide for the labour movement's economic strategy for the 1990s. Technology is certainly transforming the nature of work and the composition of the working class, while production, distribution and marketing techniques – as well as increased levels of trade – have made a far larger range of goods available than in the past. But consumption patterns have never been a guide to basic class consciousness, which remains high in Britain.[31] Sixty-six per cent of the population regarded themselves as working class in 1986 – though obviously working-class consciousness implies more than simply self-identification.[32] A close analysis of the theory of flexible specialization and the case for interpreting it as the basis for a new industrial and social system of fundamental significance suggests that it jumps from insufficient evidence to over-ambitious theoretical constructs.[33]

Where the Post-Fordists really go off the rails is in their insistence that changes in manufacturing technology represent the 'end of mass society', or a general reversal of the trend to concentration and centralization. The reality, as we have tried to show, is essentially the opposite. The Post-Fordist claim that modern capitalism is stimulating a revival of small and medium-sized companies is a direct echo of the 'Revisionist' case championed by Eduard Bernstein in Germany in the 1890s. In support of his view that the German Social Democrats should abandon Marxism in favour of reformist gradualism, Bernstein argued that capitalism was becoming highly flexible and production ever more varied, the middle class was growing and, contrary to Marx's theory of capital concentration, small-scale enterprise was thriving.[34] The Polish-born revolutionary, Rosa Luxemburg's reply to Bernstein could have been just as well directed at today's partisans of Post-Fordism. The progressive monopolization of industry did not imply the disappearance of small firms, she wrote:

> Small capitalists play in the general course of capitalist development the role of pioneers of technical change. ... The struggle of the average-sized enterprise against big capital cannot be considered a regularly proceeding battle in which the troops of the weaker party continue to melt away directly and quantitatively. It should rather be regarded as a periodic mowing down of the small enterprises, which rapidly grow up again, only to be mowed down once again by large industry.[35]

The subsequent history of German capitalism, through Hitler to the current Federal Republic – dominated as it is by monopolies which dwarf the giants of Bernstein's day – must judge Luxemburg the clear winner of the debate.

Today new technology, globalization tendencies and the drive to the Single European Market are all encouraging the growth and influence of even bigger firms in the key industries. The confusion of the Post-Fordists over company size trends has led them to focus on policies for the support and development of small firms – often based on the experience of communist local government in Italy.[36] But the economy of the Emilia Romagna region, where such strategies have been most successful, has a long and unique tradition of networks of small-scale producers. That does not apply to other advanced industrial economies, or even to decisive sectors of the Italian economy. While such policies may have lessons for local planning strategies in particular industries, such as textiles, they cannot be the basis for a labour movement strategy to change the whole direction of an economy dominated by monopolistic giants. For a Labour government to succeed in restructuring the British economy in the 1990s, large-scale intervention and public ownership would be essential. By ignoring actual corporate trends, the theory of Post-Fordism risks disarming the labour movement of the policies it needs.

Notes

1. Cable from Europe to the Associated Press, 2 June 1897.

2. The Italian Communist, Antonio Gramsci, first used the term 'Fordism', but the modern analysis of Fordism and its breakdown was pioneered by a group of French economists known as the Regulation School. See Michel Aglietta, *A Theory of Capitalist Regulation*, London 1979, and Alain Lipietz, *The Enchanted World*, London 1985. The most detailed exposition of the theory of Fordism and Post-Fordism is to be found in Michael Piore and Charles Sabel, *The Second Industrial Divide*, New York 1984.

3. John MacInnes, 'The Question of Flexibility', Department of Social and Economic Research, Glasgow University, 1987.

4. 'Benetton Britain – The New Economic Order', *Marxism Today*, November 1985; and as argued more recently at the *Marxism Today* 'New Times' Conference, 11 February 1989, Caxton House, London.

5. *Department of Employment Gazette*, London April 1989, Table 1.1.

6. Central Statistical Office, *Social Trends*, London 1989, p. 75.

7. *Department of Employment Gazette*, London, April 1989, p. 188.

8. Part of the success of 'flexibility' may, however, have been due to the potential benefits it could offer to workers. Tess Woodcraft drew to our attention the relative popularity she found as NALGO's Women's Officer of work flexibility among women workers who were often prepared to trade a degree of job security and even higher pay for the opportunity such flexibility offered them of combining all the conflicting demands on their time. Unfortunately, from being a progressive demand in the 1970s, work flexibility was often imposed by employers in the 1980s as a cost-cutting exercise. Flexible work needs to be reaffirmed as a right not an imposition, and a progressive employment strategy should provide for genuinely flexible working practices.

9. See Michael Ball, *Rebuilding Construction*, London 1988, pp. 31–2.

10. See John Atkinson, 'Manpower Strategies for Flexible Organizations', *Personnel Management*, August 1984; also John Atkinson and Nigel Meagre, *Changing Working Patterns*, London 1986.

11. See John MacInnes, 'The Question of Flexibility', Department of Social and Economic Research, University of Glasgow, 1987; and Tim Walsh, 'Segmentation and Flexibility: Part-time and Temporary Work in the Retail and Hotel Trades', paper presented to the *Restructuring Work and Employment* Conference, University of Warwick, 1988.

12. Dr Colin Mason, 'Explaining Recent Trends in UK New Firm Formation Rates', *Urban Policy Research Unit*, Southampton University, 1988.

13. Peter Turnbull, 'Employment Restructuring and Management Strategy', paper presented to the *Restructuring Work and Employment* Conference, University of Warwick, 1988.

14. As some enthusiasts for Post-Fordism are ready to admit: see Stuart Hall in *Marxism Today*, October 1988. See also the remarkable exposure of MacDonalds' industrial practices and vicious anti-unionism in *Working for Big Mac*, Transnationals Information Centre, London 1987.

15. Recent examples include 'The Rise of the Small American Firm', *The Economist*, 21 January 1989, or 'New Products, New Markets, New Competition, New Thinking', *The Economist*, 4 March 1989.

16. See Karel Williams, Tony Cutler, John Williams and Tony Haslam, 'The End of Mass Production', *Economy and Society*, vol. 16, no. 3, 1987.

17. See for example D.R. Charles, P.J. Monk and E. Sciberras, *Technology and Competition in the Telecommunications Industry*, London 1989.

18. *Financial Times*, 16 February 1989.

19. See 'The $1 Billion Motor Car', *Investors Chronicle*, 31 March 1989.

20. OECD, *Merger Policies and Recent Trends in Mergers*, Paris 1984.

21. See Andrew Glyn, Alan Hughes, Alan Lipietz and Ajit Singh, 'The Rise and Fall of the Golden Age', World Institute for Development Economics Research of the United Nations University, *Working Paper*, Cambridge 1988, p. 59; and 'Takeover Activity in the 1980s', *Bank of England Quarterly Bulletin*, no. 1, 1989 .

22. *Acquisitions Monthly*, various issues.

23. Oligopolistic markets are those with a few firms, rather than many (as in a competitive market) or just a single firm (monopoly).

24. This is the argument of the Cecchini Report, sponsored by the European Commission. Paolo Cecchini, *The European Challenge. 1992 – the Benefits of a Single Market*, Aldershot 1988.

25. See *1992: Myths and Realities*, published by the London Business School's Centre for Business Studies, 1989; also Henry Neuberger, 'The Economics of 1992', report commissioned by the British Labour Group of Euro-MPs and published by the Socialist Group of the European Parliament, 1989.

26. Karl Marx, *Capital* Volume 1 (1867), London 1954, p. 714.

27. *Marxism Today*, October 1988.

28. *Guardian*, 25 August 1988.

29. See Eric Hobsbawm, *The Age of Capital 1848–75*, London 1975, p. 262, on the complicated hierarchy of the nineteenth-century railways.

30. Mark Abrams and Richard Rose, *Must Labour Lose?*, Harmondsworth 1960, p. 119.

31. The theory that higher living standards necessarily undermine class consciousness was dealt a severe blow by research among Luton car workers; John Goldthorpe, David Lockwood, Frank Bechhofer and Jenifer Platt, *The Affluent Worker*, Cambridge 1968-69.

32. February 1986 MORI survey for the Labour Party: 28 per cent of those questioned regarded themselves as middle class.

33. See in particular the assessment of the evidence in Karel Williams, Tony Cutler, John Williams and Tony Haslam, 'The End of Mass Production', and Ben Fine, 'Segmented Labour Market Theory: A Critical Assessment', Birkbeck College *Discussion Paper in Economics*, 87/12.

34. Eduard Bernstein, *Evolutionary Socialism* (1898), New York 1961.

35. Rosa Luxemburg, *Reform or Revolution* (1900), London 1968.

36. This approach was, for example, strongly promoted in the *What's Left?* series of television programmes screened by Channel Four in February and March 1989. A more serious analysis of trends in plant size and contracting-out in Italian production can be found in Fergus Murray, 'The Decentralization of Production – The Decline of the Mass Collective Worker?', in R.E. Pahl, ed., *On Work*, Oxford 1988, pp. 279–304.

2

The Challenge of Globalization

You know, capitalism is above the law,
It say 'it don't count 'less it sells';
When it costs too much to build it at home,
You just build it cheaper some place else.

Bob Dylan, 1983[1]

The early 1990s look set to be a period of uncertainty and far-reaching change in the world economy. The economic dominance of the US will come under continued and increasing challenge from East Asia – primarily Japan – and from the Common Market. A new phase of capitalist rivalry between these three major centres, which will be fought out by transnational corporations, is likely to dominate the period. Against this background stand the twin threats of international recession – from the US trade deficit and from the Third World debt crisis – at a time when globalized financial markets have introduced a rapid transmission mechanism for economic instability to spread throughout the international capitalist system.

At the same time Britain's role in the world economy itself hangs in the balance. It is being increasingly integrated into the Common Market, while still attempting to maintain the City of London's global role in international capital markets. And the flow of North Sea oil income, which has disguised the continued erosion of the country's manufacturing base, is now drying up – leaving a huge and dangerous balance of payments problem.

The End of National Policies?

In this unstable international environment, which will be the backdrop to any programme of political change in the early 1990s, many in the labour movement have come to believe that the growing integration of the advanced capitalist countries, the internationalization of production and the globalization of financial markets have now gone so far that a Labour government would no longer be able to implement a radical economic programme at national level. Since the failure of the expansionary strategy of the French Socialist-Communist government in the early 1980s, it has become a commonplace in Britain to regard 'go-it-alone' policies of 'reflation in one country' – or even straightforward national economic management – as a thing of the past.

On the right, such an attitude neatly chimes with the view that economic policy is now returning to normal after an unfortunate Keynesian interlude. After all, rightwing free-market economics has opposed national economic management throughout. Despite Margaret Thatcher's resistance to joining the European Monetary System's exchange rate mechanism, she does not envisage any attempt to run the British economy against the grain of the rest of the capitalist world. On the left, a range of individuals who were closely involved in the struggle for an alternative economic strategy during the 1974–9 Labour government – such as Frances Morrell, Ken Coates and Stuart Holland – have since given up any hope of a nationally-based strategy to tackle Britain's problems, pinning their faith instead on co-ordinating the economic policies of the governments of Western Europe. Under the banner of internationalism, they and many others in the labour movement have turned to the European Community as a long-lost friend of the left, even to the point of embracing the potential of the Single European Market and its elusive 'social dimension'. This sea change in the movement was revealed for all to see when the President of the European Commission, Jacques Delors, was given a rapturous reception at the 1988 Trade Union Congress.

Growing economic interdependence and globalization do indeed pose enormous challenges for any government wanting to buck the trend of the world capitalist market and carry out far-reaching economic and social reforms at home. Even more clearly, a move towards relative autarchy or a 'siege economy' is neither a desirable nor realistic option for a complex modern economy like Britain's. But there is also no doubt that some of the trends associated with globalization have been exaggerated; some actually create new opportunities for radical national policies; and the effects of all of them could be managed by a determined and innovative Labour government.

The Globalization Thesis

The 'globalization thesis' – the view that the internationalization of capital has now gone so far that radical national economic policies cannot work – rests its case on a number of separate developments, all of which reflect the growing importance of international economic relations. Four main strands can be picked out:

- Trade: the growth of international trade since the Second World War leaves economies like Britain's increasingly exposed to external shocks, such as the oil price rise of the early 1970s, as well as balance of payments crises if the government tries to expand the economy out of line with the rest of the capitalist world;
- Finance: the dramatic internationalization and computerization of capital and foreign exchange markets in the past fifteen years have given a colossal boost to the quantities of mobile cash buying in and out of different currencies and the speed with which it is transferred between the main international financial centres. With the abolition of exchange controls in Britain, these changes have dramatically increased the risk and potential scale of runs against the pound if a British government loses the confidence of international speculators;
- Production: the growing tendency of transnational corporations to divide up a single production process between plants in different countries puts serious obstacles in the way of any coherent national industrial policy, as even large domestic production centres only make economic sense as part of an international industrial and

marketing set-up controlled from outside the UK. Add to that the fact that rising economies of scale in many key industries – based on escalating research and development and design costs – are helping to create firms so large that even most medium-sized states cannot hope to maintain home-grown competitive firms across the whole industrial field;

- Investment: the growth of overseas investment – particularly between the advanced capitalist countries themselves – has helped to tie the economies of the capitalist world more tightly together and makes a country like Britain more dependent on the health of the others.

All these phenomena would present serious problems to any government carrying out a radical restructuring of the economy to reverse Britain's relative decline. But they are also trends which have been with us for some time, and they need to be seen in a historical context. For example, the British economy has certainly been becoming more dependent on trade in the last ten years. Between 1965 and 1975, the ratio of trade to Gross Domestic Product (GDP) averaged around 35 per cent; between 1982 and the 1985, the figure was more than 46 per cent. But in the years immediately before the First World War, the ratio was over 48 per cent. The same basic trend can be seen in the figures on capital flows, which were more than six times as large in relation to the whole economy in the early years of this century as they are now.[2] Throughout the capitalist world, economic integration reached fever pitch before the First World War, a process which was radically reversed in the inter-war years of slump. Since 1945, integration has again increased rapidly from low levels.

It is true that today's large capital movements and high trade levels exist in a very different financial and political environment from that of the beginning of the century. But it is important to realize that advanced industrial economies have in the past been at least as open as they are now. The doubling of trade dependence in the main capitalist countries between 1951 and 1979 effectively restored it to its earlier levels. The process slowed down in the early 1980s, as the threat of protectionism between the main trading blocs emerged, but has since shown signs of picking up again.[3]

Internationalization of production

One globalization trend which is clearly a new, post-war phenomenon is the growth of transnational corporations which organize a growing division of production between plants in different countries. The world's top two hundred transnational corporations now have an annual turnover of more than US$6 trillion, equivalent to about 30 per cent of the gross world product.[4] The computer industry, for example, has drawn states from all continents into its international division of labour: open the back of any personal computer and the country of origin marks of the different components read like a map of the world. Companies can relocate production internationally, wielding immense power over trade unions and national governments – a problem vividly illustrated by the 1988 controversies over closure of the Caterpillar earth-moving equipment plant at Uddingston and over a proposed new Ford factory in Dundee. In the case of Ford, management tried to have the new plant exempt from the company's national agreement on union terms and conditions as the first step in a strategy to break the overall agreement. When this failed Dundee was dropped in favour of a Spanish site.[5]

There are several factors driving in the direction of production globalization. Growing research and development costs are pushing firms to avoid duplication between different markets. The increase in optimum plant size in many industries means that production needs to be concentrated in large units, implying an increased international division of labour. At the same time, the flexibility that comes from reprogrammable capital equipment means that these large units can serve smaller, specialized niche markets. Standardization of components has been accelerated partly to take advantage of the potential savings from global production, though it has the contradictory effect of increasing the margin of manoeuvre available to national governments in their dealing with transnational companies. These developments have led companies like Ford to plan beyond the current division of production between its European plants, reviving plans for producing a global car whereby all Ford plants would contribute towards a single project: the new car, code-named CDW27, is to replace both the West European Sierra and the North American Tempo from 1992. To back up this move, Ford has created a global communications network of computers to link up its 20,000 engineers and designers in Europe, the Americas, Australia and the Far East. Such plans were tried unsuccessfully by most car firms in the early 1980s. But despite being written off as history by the theorists of Post-Fordism, they are now firmly back on the agenda.[6]

These trends have very different implications for different sectors, and create opportunities as well as problems for progressive national governments. Flexible specialization, as discussed in chapter 1, makes smaller batch production for more specialized markets economically feasible in some sectors. But it also allows existing production facilities in a country like Britain to be put to alternative uses if they need to be taken over from foreign-owned transnationals. Now British-based facilities have the potential to be reorganized to achieve a complete production cycle on newly-economic smaller batch production runs. Flexible manufacturing systems allow any particular factory to meet different production needs – including possible subcontracted production for other companies. While this does not mean that there is complete freedom to use any machine to make any product, the wider range of possibilities does increase the range of options open to an interventionist government, since each factory is no longer so tightly defined in terms of its place in the international division of labour.

Other new trends are giving nation-states more leverage over multinational operations. For example, the new emphasis on 'just-in-time' stock-reduction implies more use of local suppliers. And state-funded research and development programmes have now come to occupy an indispensable place in the ordinary product development and production cycles of big capital. Politicians and commentators who believe that the globalization of capital has weakened the power of the nation state overlook such increases in the economic strength of the state itself. The truth is that transnational companies have used the internationalization of production to serve their own purposes; nation-states have yet to take advantage of what, in some ways, is a greater room for economic manoeuvre.

Globalization of financial markets

By far the most destabilizing trend in the world economy in the last few years – and the most serious problem which would face a Labour government trying to carry out fundamental economic change in

Britain in the 1990s – has been the colossal growth in the level of international currency and capital transactions. The daily turnover on the main foreign exchange markets reached an astonishing US$400 billion in the late 1980s.[7] As much as a third of these foreign exchange transactions take place in London. Between 1964 and 1985, the size of the international bank credit market increased as a proportion of capitalist world trade in goods and services from 11 per cent to 119 per cent.[8]

These new and rapidly increasing financial flows, which are mainly a result of the breakdown of the international financial system based on fixed exchange rates in the early 1970s, dwarf the real flows generated by expanding international trade.[9] While trade growth does need an international infrastructure to finance and co-ordinate it, the massive hot money funds now sloshing around between Tokyo, London and New York have intensified the ever-present possibility of crisis at both national and global level. But ultimately more seriously, a permanent atmosphere of instability and uncertainty has developed in which long-term financial planning and investment are inhibited and distorted around the world. The April 1988 dollar–sterling rate was 72 per cent higher than it had been in February 1985. Interest rates have been even more unstable: in the year to May 1989 UK interest rates rose 87 per cent.[10] These fluctuations can turn one year's highly profitable project into the next year's white elephant. In this climate where dramatic and unpredictable movements in exchange and interest rates take place week by week, company decision-making on national and international investment can lay no claim to orthodox economic rationality.

As the world capitalist economy has become more unstable and profit rates in traditional Third World investment outlets have declined, investment in new plant and machinery all over the capitalist world has tended to stagnate and firms have gravitated towards paper and portfolio investments, spurred on by the international banking system.[11] Along with the closer integration of the major world stock exchanges, commodity and insurance markets, these were the trends which led the Thatcher government to legislate for the October 1986 'Big Bang' in the City of London. The simultaneous world stock market crash of the following year rather exposed the weak foundation of the argument that financial globalization reduces risk by spreading securities portfolios over more than one market.

In Britain, all large-scale commercial activity has become more insecure as it has become ever more dependent on this shaky global financial structure. Financial globalization therefore increases the need for a package of strongly interventionist policies organized around a public ownership programme. Such measures would mean diverting resources away from some of the City's current areas of activity, and would also probably involve losing some current earnings from international financial operations. But the restructuring of the economy onto a modern industrial basis demands such changes, and would more than offset any job and foreign exchange losses.

Britain's New Place in the World Economy

International trade represents a high and growing proportion of Britain's national income. Imports accounted for 27 per cent of Britain's GDP in 1987, against 23 per cent for the Federal Republic of Germany, 22 per cent for France and 11 per cent for the US. The continued expansion of the country's trade dependency puts its economy increasingly at the mercy of future world economic growth, which is threatened by the danger of international recession in the early 1990s. Such a slump could be precipitated by the Bush administration failing to raise taxes or cut arms spending enough to bring the US deficit under control. The risk would then be of a wave of protectionism, exacerbated by the expanding role of the European Community as a 'Fortress Europe' customs union. There are already signs of such an outcome, as trade is organized around the three blocs of Western Europe, North America and East Asia.

In all the advanced capitalist countries productivity has increased faster in manufacturing than in services, which has meant a relative decline in manufacturing employment. But in the case of the British economy – where there has been an absolute decline in manufacturing – the shift in output from manufacturing to services is mainly because it is producing fewer manufactured goods and importing more, not because demand has shifted away from manufactured goods.[12] The upward pressure of North Sea oil on exchange rates was an added factor in the loss of Britain's trade surplus in manufacturing during the 1980s. Between 1975 and 1986 EEC manufacturing output rose on average by 20 per cent in real terms; British industry managed an increase of 0.1 per cent.[13] Britain's manufacturing trade with the rest of the Common Market went from surplus at the time Britain joined to a deficit of £15 billion in 1988. There is no reason to expect an automatic compensating shift back to manufacturing once the oil runs out.[14]

In the international division of labour Britain has slipped down over the years. Other states, particularly in the Far East, are building a competitive industrial base. And although the rise of these 'newly

Figure 2.1
The Changing Pattern of British Trade

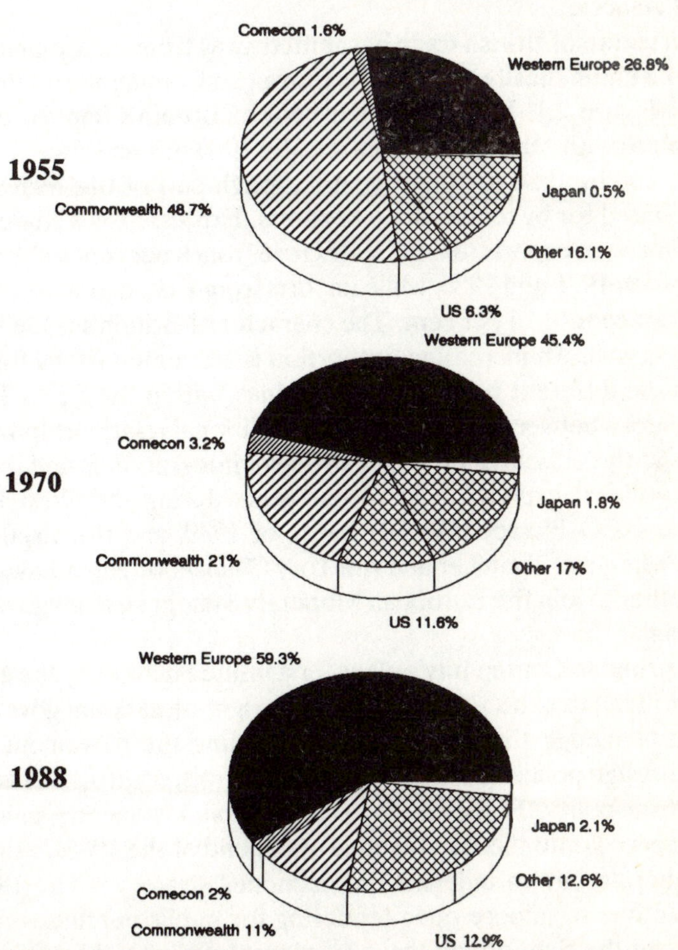

Source: *Financial Times*, 4 May 1989. Total trade turnover.

industrializing countries' constitutes a relatively small shift in terms of the world economy, British capital has signally failed to compensate by moving into hi-tech growth markets.[15] The danger for the British economy, and consequently for British living standards, is that these trends will combine to produce a continuation of Britain's relative economic decline, as a low-productivity, low-wage economy – particularly when the oil runs out. Globalization, combined with the 1992 developments in the Common Market, threaten not only to exacerbate Britain's drift towards becoming a low value-added assembler of high-value components produced elsewhere, but also to reproduce this division of labour within Britain itself in regional and local imbalances.

The structure of British trade has shifted away from the Commonwealth and emphatically towards the European Community, as illustrated in Figure 2.1. In 1970, 22 per cent of Britain's imports and exports were with other EEC countries. By 1980 this had risen to 40 per cent, and by 1988 to 50 per cent – though part of this increase was accounted for by temporary oil exports. Expressed as a share of national income, exports to EEC states rose from 8 per cent to 11 per cent between 1976 and 1986, while imports from EEC countries rose from 10 per cent to 14 per cent. The character of Britain's trade has changed as well. An increasing proportion is accounted for by trade between the different parts of multinationals within the EEC. The contradictions between British capital's traditional relationship with the US and the pressures of West European integration found their clearest political expression in recent years during the Westland affair, the GEC–Plessey takeover battle of 1989, and the disputes between Margaret Thatcher and the Tory Chancellor Nigel Lawson over whether to join the European Monetary System's exchange rate mechanism.

The European Community's plans for a unified market by the end of 1992 will mean extra restrictions on the right of national governments to challenge the 'free market', including the movement of capital, through policies such as exchange controls, controls on trade or industrial policy. Proposals for economic and monetary union, which emerged onto the EEC agenda at the end of the 1980s, would effectively rule out an independent economic strategy.[16] The 1988 draft directives to impose open tendering for public purchases further hamper the right of national governments to use public ownership in pursuit of social and economic goals, forcing such publicly owned industries to mimic and defer to the private market. They are also likely to lead to job losses and rationalizations for those firms that depend heavily on public contracts.[17] One recent study suggests that 1992 could attract disproportionate overseas investment to Britain because of the language factor and Britain's links with the US, but that its main effects within the country will be to aggravate the inequality between the North and the South and between rich and poor; and that Japanese companies could well have most to gain from the single market, since their comparative advantage lies in hi-tech sectors where the non-tariff barriers to trade that 1992 is supposed to sweep away are the greatest.[18] Leading capitalists are predicting that Western Europe's big firms are heading for an industrial blood-letting after 1992. Sir John Harvey-Jones, the former chairman of Britain's chemicals giant ICI, warned in 1988 that within ten years more than half of Western Europe's factories would close and half its companies would disappear or be taken over. Carlo De Benedetti, boss of the Italian computer company Olivetti, remarked: 'Despite all the singing and cheering, Europe's companies are marching off to war ... from which not everyone will come back a winner.'[19]

The drive towards the Single European Market is rooted in deep-seated economic forces which the left cannot ignore. Essentially it is about the tendency for the size of national markets to put a brake on the development of companies large enough to compete with their Japanese and American rivals in a world increasingly breaking down into protectionist trading blocs. The European Commission argues that 1992 will create the right conditions for firms large enough to hold their own in international markets while allowing continued competition at home. But even in the EEC big four (West Germany, France, Britain, Italy), firms on this scale based mainly on their home markets would be outright monopolies.[20] The Single European Market is the solution that suits the interests of the European-based transnationals: its completion will mean the realization of their original post-war dream of a Western Europe fit for themselves.

Policy Options

The dilemma of Britain's relationship to the European Economic Community would be the most difficult political problem in the management of Britain's international economic relations facing a

Labour government in the 1990s. The EEC exists to help organize the operations of big capital in Western Europe and the terms of the Treaty of Rome are framed for that purpose. The talk of a 'Social Europe', which won the hearts of the 1988 TUC and which Margaret Thatcher denounced as a form of 'creeping Marxism' in the 1989 Euro elections, is largely a smokescreen for the real aims of 1992: allowing capital to operate freely across Western Europe and further strengthening European capital's exploitation of the Third World.

To carry out a radical restructuring of the British economy in the interests of working people, a Labour government would have to use a variety of methods to intervene at home and to regulate Britain's relations with international markets which would be illegal under the Treaty of Rome and the terms of the Single European Act. Some of the most obvious are effective exchange controls, state investment subsidies and trade planning, but the range of potentially illegal measures is enormous. The Treaty of Rome, which is beginning to operate like a sort of written constitution for Britain and the other member states, aims to abolish 'obstacles to freedom of movement for ... services and capital' – Article 3c; it outlaws 'quantitative restrictions on imports' – Article 30; 'discrimination regarding the conditions under which goods are procured and marketed' by state monopolies – Article 37; and demands the 'progressive liberalization of movement of capital' – Article 61(1). Article 86, explicitly accepted in Labour's 1989 *Policy Review*,[21] clearly rules out contract compliance policies when it outlaws 'making the conclusion of contracts subject to acceptance by the other parties of supplementary obligations which, by their nature or according to commercial usage, have no connection with the subject of such contracts.' Even the Labour deputy leader Roy Hattersley's rather modest scheme to encourage the return of overseas investment by means of tax incentives that formed part of Labour's 1987 manifesto would have violated articles 3(c), 61(2) and 67(1) of the Treaty.

But a modern industrial economy cannot operate on a basis of autarchy or anything like it. Even taking account of the special effects of oil, the focus of Britain's trade has moved away from its traditional colonial markets towards the Common Market. Britain needs a strategy to allow the development of home-based industrial companies large enough to match the world leaders in terms of technological edge and cost competitiveness. This poses an enormous challenge, but not necessarily an insoluble problem. For example,

Sweden has been able to operate outside the Common Market, with large firms such as Volvo, Saab, Electrolux and Ericsson thriving mainly on production for the world market. It is also worth bearing in mind that none of the five advanced capitalist countries which have been most successful in maintaining low levels of unemployment since 1973 – Sweden, Austria, Japan, Switzerland and Norway – are members of the European Community. Several of the policies those countries adopted to head off mass unemployment, such as Norway's industrial subsidies and Sweden's competitive devaluation of 1982, would have been difficult or impossible if they had been members.[22] But the five are also the least integrated with and dependent on the rest of Western capitalism and none have economies that are as dominated as Britain's by foreign-owned transnational corporations. An approach which broke with EEC-determined policies would demand a sophisticated strategy for diversifying and expanding international economic relationships.

EEC: in or out?

There seem to be four basic policy options – which sometimes blur into each other – in the context of a radical economic strategy for Britain :

- immediate negotiated withdrawal from the EEC;
- renegotiation of Britain's relationship with the EEC, based on the repeal of Section 2 of the European Communities Act;
- implementation of radical policies regardless of the implications for relations with the EEC;
- carrying out the policy package in a way intended to be compatible with continued membership of the EEC.

The first option would mean the repeal of the European Communities Act of 1972 and the Single European Act of 1987 and the return of full legal sovereignty to the Westminster parliament. In view of the high proportion of Britain's trade with the Common Market, it would be essential to negotiate a new form of tariff-free relationship with the Community of the kind which has been, or is being, established with other states, including socialist countries like East Germany and Hungary. It has to be borne in mind that Britain would be in an extremely strong position in any such negotiations –

the other member states have enormous investment and trading interests in Britain which they have as much interest in maintaining as vice versa. This shared interest could well be enough to overcome policy differences, as shown by the existence of large-scale trade between the most unlikely partners: South Korea and the Soviet Union have moved to establish trading agreements and even Albania sells hydro-electric power to Greece.

The second alternative seems at first far-fetched, especially after the experience of the much trumpeted renegotiation by the 1974 Wilson government, which actually achieved very little. But organizations often have a more complicated life than is reflected in the treaties and agreements on which they are based. A Labour government setting out to pursue a radical domestic economic policy could make use of the reciprocal dependence of continental economies on Britain's. There is a tendency in debates about economic strategy to downplay the importance of the British economy and the consequent bargaining power of a progressive government. Britain is the world's third largest net creditor, and accounts for a high proportion of European research and development, as well as output in hi-tech areas such as aerospace and chemicals. There is no reason why a Labour government should necessarily adopt a take-it-or-leave-it attitude to the EEC. The repeal of Section 2 of the 1972 European Communities Act, which automatically makes European Commission regulations and directives part of British law, would give a Labour government the immediate powers it would need to begin implementing a radical economic programme and could form the basis for effective negotiation.

The third option of proceeding on a 'let them throw us out' basis has an appeal to some in the labour movement, but has hidden risks of being the most politically provocative. For a newly-elected government to set out systematically to break an international treaty without any attempt to renegotiate or draw up new agreements could make it even more difficult to maintain Britain's trade relationships with the other member states in present circumstances.

The final option is the one effectively favoured by the Labour leadership. But in reality it is only compatible with an economic strategy which stands no chance of dealing with Britain's underlying economic problems or delivering real benefits to the mass of the people the labour movement exists to represent. Of course, there are possibilities for some exemptions and derogations from EEC regulations. But although these are uncharted waters, it seems inconceivable that the other member states could stomach the scale of exemptions from the basic structure of EEC legislation that would be required.

The reaction of other member states and their scope for action would depend both on their own domestic situation and the international political climate. It is difficult to imagine the election of a radical Labour government in isolation from progressive developments in other parts of Western Europe. But to take account of the possibility of a favourable international balance of forces is quite different from opposing radical policies at home, as some sections of the left have done in recent years, with the 'internationalism' of a 'European' approach only viable on the basis of a speculative scenario of co-ordinated European class and government action.[23] The benefits of withdrawal or a renegotiated relationship would not follow automatically. But they would allow the possibility of policies which would not be permitted by the Treaty of Rome. And they could also bring immediate positive benefits, such as an end to the maintenance of Common Market food mountains in Britain and the costs of the Common Agricultural Policy.

If Britain left the EEC, a government aiming to build a modern industrial base at home would still need to realize the advantages of scale which are currently being extended through membership. Here again there are various options:

- Expanded co-operation and joint ventures with EEC countries and companies;
- Active upgrading of trade and other economic relations with non-EEC capitalist states, the socialist countries and the Third World;
- The gradual development of state-sponsored joint ventures, like the Airbus and Ariane projects, into new forms of international public enterprise and ownership.

The expansion and diversification of Britain's international economic links would allow a break with the recurrent tensions between dependence on a subordinate relationship with either the West European or North American trading blocs. The scope for expansion of trading and investment relationships with the socialist countries is enormous. Not only are there huge markets where British companies have hitherto made little headway, largely for political reasons, there are also far-reaching possibilities for co-operation in research and development, where access to the Soviet Union's scientific community could be invaluable. The scrapping of American-imposed Cocom restrictions on the export of hi-tech equipment to the Soviet Union would be an important step forward. Expanded economic co-operation with Eastern Europe could be the first step towards a real European Community.

Joint ventures with strong public involvement are already playing a role in Britain's industrial restructuring: both with other EEC states outside the Common Market framework and between British companies and foreign transnationals. Examples of the former include the highly successful Airbus consortium, which has taken a large slice of the international civil airliner market; and in research and development, the JET nuclear fusion programme. Private joint ventures between British and overseas companies are also expanding fast: the relationship between over Group the Rover Group and Honda and the GEC–Siemens link-up are different types of co-operation. A Labour government would want to encourage a new direction in joint ventures. But in general such forms of joint international enterprise offer a far more flexible international economic strategy than relying on an insecure role within the Common Market. In the longer run, the left will need to look increasingly to international social ownership and enterprise as economies of scale continue to grow.

Much current opposition to EEC withdrawal on the left treats the Community as an undifferentiated capitalist market which Britain happens to be part of and may as well remain part of until such time as the abolition of capitalism in Britain is feasible. This fails to take account of the specifics of the British economy. The alternative to withdrawal from the European Community – or a thorough renegotiation of the relationship – in the context of an overall challenge to monopoly capital in Britain would not necessarily be some equal share in the Common Market's 'progress'. It is more likely to be the continuing evolution of Britain into a low-productivity manufacturing base and a provider of financial and other services to transnational capital.

Socializing foreign trade

There are major uncertainties about future world trade levels. Growth in trade needs to be planned as part of any radical economic programme so that it would be compatible with an expanding economy at home. The technically optimal solution for such planning would be – in effect – the socialization of foreign trade, allowing a regulated increase in imports in line with reciprocally agreed increases in exports. That would mean multilateral as well as two-way, bilateral agreements. The relatively open nature of the British economy makes domestic economic developments that much more dependent on international changes. Without intervention in Britain's trading relationships, no Labour government is going to avoid the debacles of the 1960s and 1970s. Planning trade effectively would mean more than the import controls that are often advocated to protect this or that sector. It would involve the whole trading sector being brought under public regulation. But the problems in pursuing such a policy could actually be fewer than old-fashioned protection. Many of the political objections to import controls – particularly the fear that they would be used to reduce overall import levels – and the risks of retaliation could be avoided by ensuring that all trade was co-ordinated at national level.

The British economy in the early 1990s could face radically different problems depending on uncertain international developments. If a global recession is sparked off by the US trade deficit, the Third World debt crisis or any other shock to the system, then Britain would be particularly vulnerable to a bout of global protectionism. In such a situation the major task of a socialized foreign trade sector would be to rebuild trade levels, negotiating bilateral and multilateral deals for exports in exchange for imports. If on the other hand the international economy avoids a major recession, then the crisis facing Britain's balance of payments is likely to become even more severe as North Sea oil revenues run down. In this case the major task of the socialized foreign trade sector would be to hold down the growth of imports in line with the planned growth of exports.

The key point is that the aim of bringing trade under public control would not be to cut imports, but rather to increase imports at a planned and sustainable rate. Actual import levels should end up higher than under a free market policy whereby unsustainable rates of import demand lead to contractionary policies at home – such as increasing interest rates – aimed at reducing imports. The fact that the level of imports could be higher if the sector were properly planned and managed could prove a crucial factor in persuading other countries not to retaliate against such policies.

The major problems facing any such attempts to plan rationally for a growth in trade would be the Treaty of Rome and the possible need to replace any markets withdrawn by way of retaliation. A major diplomatic and political effort would be essential to explain and negotiate the policy abroad. But a danger of destabilization on political grounds would always exist with any attempt to challenge the power of international capital – whether in the form of its 'right' to control foreign trade, capital and currency flows, or to move production around the globe as it wishes. Globalization trends themselves, however, are tending to reduce the potential problems associated with planning trade. First, the number of potential trading partners is expanding. Second, the division of production processes between countries, and the greater use of contracting-out, make products from UK-based plants more important to firms' global production. They also increase the number of other firms which would be interested in buying in supplies. And finally, the growing intensity of inter-imperialist rivalry – both between blocs of capital, such as Japan and North America, and also between individual firms – increases the ability to play one off against the other in the event of attempted destabilization. Socializing foreign trade and developing multilateral trade agreements outside the European Community, North America or Japan would also represent a positive contribution to developing a new international economic order. Developing countries' trade is often tied directly to major industrial countries. By negotiating new multilateral trading arrangements Britain could help facilitate direct links between those countries with which it was expanding trade.

A Labour government in the 1990s would need to plan the restructuring of the domestic economy to retain and develop a capacity in the crucial sectors needed for economic independence. That is exactly the justification advanced by the US for its current 'Sematech' programme aimed at regaining a leading-edge capability in semiconductors, which has been lost over recent years to Japan, involving the US Federal government and leading firms in funding research and development in such areas as 'dynamic RAMs' – an important computer memory component. Intervention to promote hi-tech investment is clearly recognized, at least by the US, as a legitimate area of national interest, rather than a protectionist attempt to secure unfair competitive advantages. If an economic strategy defined its aims in terms of trade goals, and set out instruments, such as import controls, to achieve this by restricting imports and subsidizing exports, the General Agreement on Tariffs and Trade (GATT) and other countries might have some pretext for retaliation. But if the strategic aim is balanced trade, rather than a surplus, then a trade deficit over a decade or so could be planned for while goods and services needed to restructure the economy were imported – the deficit being financed by the return of previously exported capital. On the basis of such balanced trade, the economy could be restructured and planned to secure healthy research and development and production capability in both goods and services.[24]

Exchange controls

Every Labour government since the time of Ramsey MacDonald has been driven to change political direction by a run on the pound. That sobering fact should be enough to make it clear that without far greater control of the currency no government could hope to carry out any radical change in the way the economy is run. One of the first acts of the Thatcher government when it came to power in 1979 was the abolition of exchange controls, the signal for an outpouring of investment which continues to this day. The re-imposition of exchange controls would be essential for any significant degree of independent action to be open to a Labour government in the 1990s. It would also allow the added benefit of returning and investing at home the £150 billion-worth of overseas paper assets held by British companies and institutions.

What matters for the future prosperity of the British people are real productive resources rather than bits of paper – albeit ones representing claims on resources. But protection is needed against a flight of capital from Britain which would drive down the value of the pound and boost inflation by increasing the price of imports. The return of overseas assets would also help to offset downward pressure on the pound, as well as provide funds to compensate foreign holders of assets in Britain taken into public ownership. Arguments against the re-introduction of exchange controls focus on the idea that new technology and market developments mean controls are no longer technically feasible. Another claim is that they would be undesirable because they would lead to loss of City earnings or business. The two objections happily co-exist, despite being essentially contradictory: for exchange controls can only have undesirable consequences if they do in fact work.

Exchange controls could include a variety of different mechanisms and arrangements, some of which are set out in chapter 6. But essentially they would all be ways of regulating the market exchange of sterling for foreign currencies. Debate around exchange controls in the labour movement has focussed on two central concerns: would controls really be enforceable, and would the threat of their re-imposition lead to a collapse of the pound before a Labour Prime Minister even set foot inside Number Ten? If a radical Labour government seemed likely to be elected in Britain, capital flight would undoubtedly be a danger. And if the Bank of England tried to support the pound against panic selling, that would seriously deplete the reserves. The alternative, letting sterling fall, would make it increasingly expensive for speculators to switch out of the currency. The Labour Party could also make it clear that depositing sterling abroad would not be an effective way around the planned exchange controls. After an election victory the exchange rate could then be fixed at a suitable level and exchange controls put in place to protect it. The pre-election fall in the pound would be temporarily disruptive of trade, but would be unlikely to have had time materially to affect inflation and living standards. It would also create a political opportunity to highlight the 'dictation by overseas financiers' – which Harold Wilson threatened to call an election over, but never did – and the weakness of the foundations on which people's prosperity in capitalist Britain depends.

As to evasion, any laws and regulations can be broken. But new technology can be used to detect as well as perpetrate crime. The banks and financial institutions which might be tempted to break exchange control legislation hold large financial and other assets which could be subject to fines and sequestrations at a level which would offset losses. Other measures could strengthen exchange controls. For example, all private financial institutions over a certain size could be required to hold a proportion of their total financial assets in Britain – and a certain percentage of these in government sterling bonds. If the government varied these requirements, institutions would have to shift finance back to Britain and back into the Bank of England's reserves.[25]

Conclusion

The current trends towards the globalization and deregulation of international capital and currency markets are part of an attempt to reconstruct the conditions for profitable private capitalist growth as a new basis for long-term capitalist expansion. Such an alternative basis is still, however, far from having been achieved. The international economic situation is now far more unstable than it ever was in the post-war decades.

Major political changes would be required even to recover lost economic ground for Britain; and the difficulties for a Labour government legislating in the face of the increased power of transnational corporations and global financial markets have grown. But while in the past many on the left underestimated the enormous power of international capital, there is now a tendency to treat it as omnipotent. As Tony Benn puts it:

> The multinational companies will fight like tigers, but our powers of control over them are infinitely greater than we have ever admitted, if we choose to use them. They have huge investments and a big market here. The multinationals have got to come to terms with host governments.[26]

Recent technological and global economic developments not only do not rule out the possibility of nationally-based progressive economic policies, they make the sort of interventionist policies outlined in the following chapters more necessary than in the past. Capital and trade controls, a new relationship with the EEC, and public ownership to allow production decisions to be taken on criteria other than the global profitability of transnational corporations are all essential for a strategy for radical economic change. National economic management is only an anachronism if it is seen as operating in an international vacuum. Instead, the nation state should be recognized for what it is: the single most powerful mechanism of legal and organizational powers for economic intervention.

Notes

1. Bob Dylan, *Union Sundown*, © Special Rider Music, 1983.
2. Figures from S. Grassman, 'Long-Term Trends in Openness of National Economies', *Oxford Economic Papers*, Oxford 1980, also Jim Tomlinson, *Can Governments Manage the Economy?*, Fabian Society Tract no. 524, London 1988.
3. Organization for Economic Co-operation and Development, *National Accounts*, Paris 1969 and 1982; and GATT figures, cited in the *Financial Times*, 28 February 1989.
4. Susan George, *A Fate Worse than Debt*, London 1988, p. 12, quoting UNCTAD statistics. Updated from Mary Goldring, ed., *The World in 1989*, Economist Publications, London 1988.
5. See John Foster and Charles Woolfson, 'Corporate Reconstruction and Business Unionism: the Lessons of Caterpillar and Ford', *New Left Review*, no. 174, March/April 1989, pp. 51–66, for an excellent account and analysis of both cases.
6. 'The failings of Ford's global car strategy, an attempt to create worldwide strong power structures around common designs, have been well documented', wrote Geoff Mulgan in 'The Power of the Weak', *Marxism Today*, December 1988, p. 25. See also the repeated references to the demise of the world car in Charles Sabel, 'Flexible Specialization and the Re-emergence of Regional Economies' in Paul Hirst and Jonathan Zeitlin, *Reversing Industrial Decline*?, Oxford 1989, pp. 17–70.
7. 'The Corporate Dealer is the Star', *Euromoney*, May 1988. The magazine *Forbes*, 22 August 1988, estimated the turnover at US$420 billion, of which 90 per cent represented financial transactions unrelated to trade or investment.
8. Ralph Bryant, *International Financial Intermediation*, The Brookings Institution, Washington 1987, p. 22.
9. If daily turnover on the foreign exchange markets is around US$400 billion, then annual turnover is more than US$100,000 billion, roughly fifty times larger than the annual world goods trade of US$2,000 billion. See Margaret Reid, *All-Change in the City*, London 1988, p. 13.
10. Central Statistical Office, *Financial Statistics*, April 1989, tables 13.1, 13.8.
11. See Paul Sweezy and Harry Magdoff, 'A New Stage of Capitalism Ahead?', *Monthly Review*, New York, May 1989.
12. See Wynne Godley, 'Manufacturing and the Future of the British Economy', in Terry Barker and Paul Dunne, eds, *The British Economy After Oil: Manufacturing or Services?*, Beckenham 1988, p. 10.
13. Eurostat, *Industry Yearbook*, Brussels, 1988.
14. See Bob Rowthorn and John Wells, *De-industrialization and Foreign Trade*, Cambridge 1987.
15. See David Gordon, 'The Global Economy: New Edifice or Crumbling Foundations?', *New Left Review* no. 168, March/April 1988.
16. Delors Committee, *Report on European Economic and Monetary Union*, Brussels April 1989.
17. European Commission, 'The Economics of 1992', *European Economy*, Brussels 1988.
18. The Henley Centre for Forecasting, *The United Markets of Europe*, London 1988.
19. As quoted in Labour Research Department, *Europe 1992*, London 1989.

20. Cecchini Report, 1988.

21. '[W]e shall align our own law with the definitions of anti-competitive behaviour outlined in articles 85 and 86', *Final Report of Labour's Policy Review for the 1990s*, London 1989, p. 11.

22. See Göran Therborn, *Why Some Peoples Are More Unemployed than Others*, London 1986, p. 29.

23. A more plausible version of this argument is made by John Palmer in *Trading Places*, London 1988, p. 191, where he argues that the outcome of a battle between a progressive government and the Commission over interventionist policies 'would depend on the pressure which the European allies of such a government could mount in its support.'

24. For more discussion of trade socialization policies, see chapter 11.

25. The technicalities of imposing effective controls are set out and discussed further by Andrew Glyn in 'Capital Flight and Exchange Controls', *New Left Review*, no. 155, Jan-Feb 1986, pp. 37–49; and in 'A Case for Exchange Controls', University of Oxford Institute of Economics and Statistics, *Applied Economics Discussion Paper*, no. 36, 1987.

26. Interview with Seumas Milne, 26 January 1989.

3

Markets and Planning

There is no such thing as a free market.

Arnold Weinstock, chairman of GEC, 1989[1]

The impression is often given by politicians and the media that we are witnessing a global abandonment of planning and government regulation in favour of the market. From Bulgaria to Brazil, we are told, from Chile and China to the US and the Soviet Union itself, the whole world is involved in a sort of elemental embrace of private enterprise and the free play of market forces. Put like that, it sounds absurd. But there is a basis for the claim in reality.

In the advanced capitalist countries, there has certainly been an abandonment of the old Keynesian-style interventionist policies that were common in the 1950s and 1960s. While none of the other EEC states or even post-Reaganite America has matched the orgy of privatization indulged in by the Thatcher government in Britain, the trend is clear. Most strikingly, similar policies are followed by governments of both right and nominal left, and some of the most enthusiastic free-marketeers have been Labour or Socialist-led, such as David Lange's administration in New Zealand or Felipe Gonzalez's government in Spain.

Are We All Free-Marketeers Now?

In the Third World there has been a marked retreat from the radical, interventionist policies that were common in the early post-colonial years. More and more developing countries have succumbed to the demands of the World Bank and the IMF for economic policies which chime with the drive by Western capital to open up their markets and restructure the international division of labour. Nasser's Egypt has been turned into a speculators' and contractors' paradise, first under the former US President Jimmy Carter's unfortunate friend Anwar Sadat, and later under his more cautious successor Husni Mubarak. Rajiv Gandhi's India is moving more slowly in the direction of liberalization and the open door.

In the socialist countries, radical policy changes in the last ten years appear to be pointing in the same direction. China has performed a political somersault, turning from the attempt to abolish markets and commodities altogether during the Cultural Revolution into the complete opposite in less than ten years: the semi-privatization of the countryside, the encouragement of private business and plans to develop large parts of the coastline into a massive 'enterprise zone' for foreign capitalists and Western-owned transnationals.

The logic of market-orientated economic reforms in Hungary, Poland and Yugoslavia is pushing those countries towards far-reaching compromises with capitalist methods. In 1988 Hungary increased the ceiling on the size of private companies from 30 to 500 workers. Poland has abandoned all such limits, and has introduced a massive programme of economic rationalization involving the closure of scores of factories. Part of the Lenin shipyard in Gdansk, where Solidarity was founded in 1980, has now been leased to a Polish capitalist, who has threatened to sack any worker who joins a trade union.[2]

In the Soviet Union, the introduction of co-operative private enterprise and the move towards downgrading the role of central planning in favour of greater freedom for individual enterprises under perestroïka is often presented as part of this supposed global acceptance of the superiority of the market. When some Soviet public figures call into question the whole principle of planning, that has added to the impression that we are all free marketeers now. A leading Soviet commentator, Fyodor Burlatsky, could write in 1988, for example:

> The plan should be determined by the market, which is an objective social reality, because only the market links the producer with the consumer and determines the extent of social usefulness of labour input. Economics knows of no other means of fulfilling this purpose and all attempts to replace it by something else have so far failed.[3]

The idea that conscious social control over economic life must take the place of the anarchy of market forces has always been central to socialist thought. Socialists across a broad spectrum have argued for a century or more that the planned development of the major means of production, distribution and exchange under common ownership would not only allow the gradual dismantling of the class system, it would also overcome the recurrent crises of capitalist economies and release enormous new potential for rational growth. Socialist revolutions have tried to turn that conviction into a reality; in the capitalist world the same idea profoundly influenced industrial and economic policies for forty years after the beginning of the Second World War.

But the breakdown of social democracy and the return of a harsher form of capitalism to the industrialized West, combined with escalating economic problems in the socialist countries, have led large sections of the international left to question some of its most basic principles. The cult of the market spread so assiduously by the New Right since the mid 1970s has created an atmosphere where the assumption that economic planning – let alone public ownership – is inappropriate for modern societies has become commonplace. The emergence of this new orthodoxy poses a unique challenge to the credibility of socialist ideas and the possibility of carrying out a radical change of political direction in Britain and throughout the capitalist world.

Privatization, Deregulation and Capitalist Markets

The 'turn to the market' in the advanced capitalist countries – represented by the globalization of currency and other markets, fewer controls on international capital flows, privatization, contracting-out and deregulation – has been the result of an attempt to find a new way of creating the conditions for profitable capitalist accumulation and a reaction to the failed attempts of the 1970s to do so within the established rules of the game. It is part of the first sustained effort to change the fundamental regulation of capitalism since the post-war Keynesian settlement.

In the late 1960s, the basic conditions which allowed rapid and sustained economic expansion in the advanced capitalist world – notably large reserves of immigrant and agricultural labour, cheap raw materials such as oil, and a stable international financial order guaranteed by American power – had been exhausted. The re-emergence of economic stagnation and high unemployment combined in a new way with accelerating inflation in Western Europe and the US during the 1960s and 1970s to produce a prolonged period of social conflict. The working class, particularly in Italy, France and Britain, used its strengthened position inherited from the years of growth and social democratic corporatism to resist attempts to re-establish profitability at its own expense. The taxation which underpinned the welfare-state consensus was increasingly seen by capital not just as a burden – that had always been the case – but as a burden that could and should be shrugged off.

It was in that context that in the mid to late 1970s, a consensus started to emerge among the ruling classes of the major Western states that without the discipline of redundancy and mass unemployment on the workforce there was no possibility of overcoming the stagflationary crisis of the period and carrying out the economic restructuring necessary to meet the challenge from Japan and the Far East. In Britain, this ideology emerged in the form of monetarism which in due course turned into the free-market crusade of Thatcherism. In the US it started life as Reaganomics. In France it arrived in a dramatic form in 1983 when the Socialist government conducted a U-turn strongly reminiscent of the British Labour government's capitulation to the IMF seven years earlier.

The most striking feature of this political trend in Britain has been its promotion of privatization in the 1980s, a special form of the international capitalist offensive to 'roll back the frontiers of the state'. Privatization was stumbled on almost by chance, and was absent from the Tories' 1979 general election manifesto. But it has now become part of the general drive to force up profitability: both in the highly-publicized big sell-offs – such as telecommunications, electricity, gas and water – and in the vital but less visible form of compelling the National Health Service, national and local government to contract out work to the private sector.

The demands of technological change and economic restructuring throughout the capitalist world have provided the impetus for deregulation and privatization of industries and markets, as the new technologies require increasingly flexible behaviour from large public enterprises and private firms. As Tony Benn argues:

> Government in Britain had put a tightening noose round public enterprise, which effectively meant that publicly-owned companies couldn't grow or diversify until they were privatized. In those circumstances privatization became a liberation. As technology changes, you have to move into new areas, but public enterprise has not been allowed to.[4]

In the US, competition was introduced to the air transport and telecommunications industries, which were previously under a regulated private monopoly, and was therefore called deregulation. The term has been confusingly extended into Western Europe and Japan's different conditions, where nationalized utilities were directly owned by governments, rather than regulated by quangos. The US experience has been, however, that this deregulation has actually ended up requiring the devotion of more resources to regulation than ever before – in the form of what is known as 're-regulation' – to ensure that safety standards are met and monopoly does not re-emerge in an increasingly complicated and confusing market-place.[5] As one experienced American regulator put it: 'Theoretical formulations that assume that the competitive market will perform the regulatory function are, quite simply, wrong.'[6]

The turn to the market, which has in many cases meant a turn to different forms of government intervention rather than an abandonment of intervention, has been motivated by the interests of multinational companies, rather than any belief in markets as the route to social efficiency. The deregulation of television broadcasting is a case in point. Developing satellite and cable technologies opened up the possibility for the media monopolies to turn broadcasting into a free-for-all for private capital. Led by the Murdoch press, they launched a transparently self-interested campaign for deregulation of ITV and the break-up of the BBC, much of which quickly turned into government policy. The propaganda promoted 'choice' when all the experience, notably from the US, shows that the downgrading of public standards in broadcasting is the route to a proliferation of low-budget, low-grade programmes and the disappearance of coverage for specialized interests and needs.

Markets Under Socialism

The picture in the socialist countries and the pressures there for increased marketization are quite different. Despite all the ideological excitement in the West about where perestroïka is heading, the Gorbachev programme of economic reform in many ways represents a revival of the ill-fated 'Kosygin reforms' of 1965 – a parallel drawn quite explicitly in the Soviet Union. The Kosygin package also focussed on devolving economic power and decision-making to the enterprise level and upgrading the importance of profit-and-loss criteria. But at that time it would never have occurred to anyone that such changes were part of some international swing to the market, because the political and ideological trends in the contemporary capitalist world were in a quite different direction. In a period when most advanced capitalist countries were still enjoying a run of business cycles that involved relatively small fluctuations around historically high rates of economic growth, indicative planning and public ownership were still in vogue. In Britain, the Labour government was struggling to draw up its National Plan and supervise large-scale concentration and centralization of capital.

The Soviet economic reforms – then as now – are less a response to global liberalization than to the failure of earlier forms of planning to cope with an increasingly complex economy, and the resulting creation of an illegal double economy. The reforms do represent in one sense a retreat from planning to the market – though this should be qualified by the fact that as planning became increasingly ineffectual in the late Brezhnev years, illegal private enterprise was in the process of creating an embryonic mafioso capitalist class behind the screen of socialist orthodoxy. Insofar as there is a real retreat, it represents in part an attempt to exploit the country's untapped potential for market development – and this is even more obviously the case in China and some East European states – that was shelved at the beginning of the 1930s. The New Economic Policy of the 1920s, which allowed foreign investment, private farming and a limited internal capitalist market, was abandoned for political reasons. The assumption now – which can only be tested in practice – is that more than fifty years after the full expropriation of the capitalist class, the Soviet Union can afford to use markets for better gauging consumer demand and encouraging innovation without fears of capitalist restoration.

Current political and economic developments in the socialist and capitalist states, and even within the capitalist world as a whole, are the product of separate processes. The theory of a worldwide turn to the market today is no more firmly rooted in reality than the theory of a 'convergence' between capitalism and socialism was twenty years ago. Both are essentially based on little more than the association of simultaneous but distinct trends in East and West.

Nevertheless, despite the essential differences in motivation behind market-oriented reforms in the socialist countries and the privatizing, deregulatory gale blowing in the capitalist world, the globalization of markets does mean an important change in the international economic environment within which both socialist and capitalist economies have to operate. Just as important is the ideological effect that the coincidence of the two trends has had in creating the impression of the irresistible march of the market. Despite years of Cold War and relative isolation, the cross-fertilization between the two halves of Europe has always been strong. Among the intelligentsia in Poland and Hungary, for example, neo-liberal Thatcherite views, and even Thatcher herself, have become highly fashionable. Such attitudes are then given a bizarre image of respectability when Polish and Hungarian politicians claim that Thatcherite policies can usefully be applied in a socialist economy.

Meanwhile in the West, those in the labour movement who never had much appetite for socialism in the first place have borrowed models of 'market socialism' developed in Eastern Europe in the 1950s and 1960s and applied them indiscriminately to the very different social and economic conditions of the advanced capitalist economies – apparently as a way of trying to breathe some new theoretical life back into social democracy for the 1990s.[7] In such a confused ideological situation it is necessary to go back to the first principles of markets and planning to sort out what is essential for socialism and what can be discarded or modified, as well as to understand why the fashion for markets has become so powerful.

ABC of Markets

Markets are not specific to capitalism, nor are they its defining characteristic. A market is a forum – either physical or notional –

where goods and services are exchanged. Markets arose historically from the production of basic surpluses and the division of labour, and there is no country in the world – including Albania – where markets do not exist. There is also no doubt that they will continue to exist in one form or another for the foreseeable future. Markets persist in all planned economies and no capitalist economy, where the state and large monopolies are the dominant players in any major decision, can in any sense be described as a free market economy.

Capitalism is a social system where markets – or to be more accurate, production for exchange guided by private profit – become generalized throughout all spheres of economic life, and in particular, labour power itself becomes a traded commodity. The socialist case is that such a system by its nature is a system of class domination; that it produces and reproduces enormous social and regional inequality; that it thrives on waste, destruction and exploitation all over the globe; and that it suffers from endemic crises that manifest themselves in unemployment of resources and chronic social insecurity which experience has shown cannot be regulated away.

But the alternative that socialism offers is not based on the abolition of markets as such, but on the principle of direct production of goods and services for use rather than indirect production for exchange based on the criterion of profit. Direct production means economic activity that is planned on a social basis. Going beyond the profit criterion to a more rational and socially efficient way of regulating and developing economic life leads inescapably to the need for the socialization of the major sectors of the economy. But the argument runs that way round – public ownership is not an end in itself.

Of course it is easy to make such grand declarations, and far more difficult to turn principles into practice. The transition from profit-oriented capitalist society to a people-centred socialist or communist society represents an entire historical epoch, and we have so far only seen the early stages of such a process. But starting from the simple ideas just outlined, it becomes clear that the antithesis is not between markets and planning as such, but between privately-run economic activity carried out for profit and a socially-owned economy guided by democratically agreed goals. Naturally, the latter implies markets controlled and regulated in a new way; but it does not imply their disappearance, at least in the forseeable future.

Planning in Practice

A planned socialist economy is inherently neither more nor less centralized than a capitalist market economy. A capitalist economy can in theory involve either centralized decision-making by multinational giants, or decentralized decision-making by small businesses, or both. A planned economy can be run by imposing priorities from the centre, or by co-ordinating plans developed at all levels of society. The essential distinction between a socialist economy and a capitalist economy lies in the way the major decisions are taken: whether they are based on the narrow demands of maximizing financial profit, or whether they depend on broader social and economic criteria.

The association of socialism and planning with extreme forms of centralism has come about partly because of the history of capitalist planning, notably in Japan, France and war-time states, but mainly because of the commandist model of socialist planning first developed in the Soviet Union in the 1930s. In conditions of extreme backwardness, such a form of planning was highly effective in mobilizing resources for rapid industrial development – even putting on one side the wilder claims that were made for it at the time. A recognition of this earlier success is a condition for understanding more recent failures: planning saw the Soviet Union raise its share of world industrial production from 4 per cent in 1926–9 to 15 per cent in 1984, a period which saw Japan rise from 3 per cent to 8 per cent, the US fall from 42 per cent to 28 per cent, and the UK fall from 9 per cent to 3 per cent.[8] At the start of this process, the Soviet Union's level of economic development was on a par with that of India or Egypt.[9] To a less dramatic extent, the commandist formula was also effective in post-war Eastern Europe and other socialist countries like Cuba in concentrating investment on overriding social and political goals: the eradication of illiteracy, the provision of universal health care, the development of basic industry and so on. Even taking account of the make-up and quality of output, the success of central planning in organizing rapid industrialization cannot be disputed. The share of the whole socialist world in global industrial production increased from 8.4 per cent in 1948 to 25.4 per cent in 1984.[10] Growth in the socialist countries has in general also avoided the cyclical gyrations and instability typical of the capitalist states.

In the 1980s, however, weaknesses in the planning system became more serious. By 1982, income growth in the Soviet Union had stopped catching up with the US rate.[11] Elsewhere in Eastern Europe, political and economic problems have reached crisis proportions. In most socialist countries the advantages of exclusive reliance on highly centralized planning have now exhausted themselves. But it is also clear that the straightforward 'marketization' of planned economies has enormous economic and social costs: it is not an accident that the two East European states that have gone furthest down the market socialism road – Hungary and Yugoslavia – have also developed some of the most serious economic problems. The social upheavals in China in 1989 were in part directed against the corruption and profiteering that had accompanied the introduction of unregulated markets and private enterprise into the country's economy.

The pressing need in most socialist countries is for a planned shift from extensive to intensive, environmentally-sensitive and consumer-orientated growth. The mechanisms which suited the demands of what was called in the Soviet economic debates of the 1920s 'primitive socialist accumulation' must as a matter of urgency give way to more sophisticated, democratic, flexible and decentralized economic methods. That process is bound to be a complex and contradictory one. Effective socialist planning and self-management in the new conditions can only be developed in practice. But the potential exists for a powerful boost to the appeal of socialism in the advanced capitalist world, where the commandist model is clearly unsuitable except in time of war or national crisis.

Information, Computers and Market Failures

There is an old argument which says that centralized planning is impossible, because of the complexity of the problems it sets out to tackle. It is set out by the market socialist Geoff Hodgson:

> It is now realized in the Eastern Bloc that a complex economic system cannot be regulated by some computerized centre of control. This has been clearly demonstrated by a Soviet mathematician: a simple problem involving 2 objectives and 2 variants will have 4 solutions. With 5 objectives and 3 variants we already have 243 solutions. With 500 objectives and 10 variants (still a very simple economic planning problem) the number of solutions is 10 to the 500 (i.e. a '1' followed by 500

> zeros). This is much more than the number of atoms in the entire universe![12]

The argument usually carries on with the witticism that it would therefore take ten years to calculate every five-year-plan. Keeping the debate on this level for a moment, it happens that a calculation that took ten years on the Harvard Mark I computer of 1944 would have taken less than three days on the ENIAC of 1946 and less than an hour on the IBM 360/50 of 1964. On the latest top-end IBM 370 series machines, the same calculation could be completed in a matter of seconds.

But the difficulties of handling information are enormous. And the complexity of a problem – the number of calculations involved – remains the same whether it has to be solved by a plan or a market. If a plan cannot be calculated because consideration of all the variants for all the objectives would absorb too much of society's available resources, it would take just as long and still absorb too much of society's resources if the market were given the task. In the real world, markets take into account only a very limited proportion of the possibilities, just as real plans do. Markets do not process all available information. People going to one shop rarely have a full picture of the prices and quality in other shops. Likewise, companies cannot usually know the prices, quality and delivery terms of all suppliers. Some types of socially vital information are even systematically by-passed by markets, like pollution and congestion. Such omissions naturally simplify the calculation. At the same time, the processing of the information needed by markets is itself very expensive:

> The vast numbers of sales personnel, marketing experts, advertising executives, stockbrokers, etc. required to make markets operate has generally been ignored. ... Too often the claim for the superiority of market allocation has been based on a comparison between a market system with exogenously or costlessly given prices and a planned system with a multitude of visible administrative costs.[13]

The huge growth in expenditure on market research is a striking example of the fact that prices do not provide firms with the information they need to take decisions – otherwise why send employees out on to the street to find out what people want directly?

In an age of computer technology which has clearly extended the potential of economic planning, the emphasis needs to shift from the computational difficulties of planning towards the problem of how to make sure that economic decision-makers have an interest – and not merely adequate information – to act in ways that most benefit society. Running the economy on the basis of market price signals as the New Right wants is a bit like tailgating – accelerating and braking in line with the speed of the car immediately in front. It works fine when everything is going well. But when there is a problem, like a crash, involving more than the car in front and the car behind, the tailgating (or price-following) rule breaks down. The problem is then exacerbated because wider knowledge – in the case of the economy, of the social effects of individual actions – needs to be taken into account.

This type of instability, traditionally associated with financial markets, is starting to penetrate the real economy. Other markets are beginning to function as 'efficiently' and unstably as do the foreign exchange markets and stock exchanges. Already a futures market in D-RAMs, an essential component of computers, had been established in mid 1989. 'Just-in-time' stock control and the spread of electronic data interchange raise the spectre, in the absence of planning, of the rapid generalization of local instabilities throughout the economy, which could cause the same kind of damage to the real economy that the world stock market crash of October 1987 caused to the casino economy.

New Technology and Planning

A whole series of current trends in technology and the economy are, contrary to received wisdom, working in the long run in the direction of an increased role for planning and direct social control of the economy. Efficiency in the internal organization of information in large multinationals is now overflowing the boundaries of the firm. The private firm itself is beginning to be a drag on the need to exploit the growing advantages of closer co-operation and information flows between firms, which are reaching a level of complexity that cannot be handled by contractual relations.

Two conflicting trends are at work. On the one hand modern companies are increasingly obliged to share operational information and access to management systems with their suppliers and customers, so as to permit effective co-ordination and rapid response to changes in requirements. This trend is being accelerated by competitive pressure to adopt electronic data interchange between firms. On the other hand, a higher and higher proportion of a firm's assets are embodied in its knowledge – of markets, designs, production techniques and so on – which therefore cannot be given away lightly. Under capitalism there can be no final resolution of this conflict, which gives rise to increasingly roundabout strategies aimed at making knowledge unusable by competitors. One method employed is the effective balkanization of corporate knowledge through the use of non-standard technologies of information organization and communication. It still often proves impossible to localize the benefits of research and development. Apple Computers, for example, are reaping huge benefits from the 'user-friendly interface' of their Macintosh personal computers. But the system was developed by Xerox, who failed to benefit. This increased uncertainty for firms over whether they will be the ones to profit from their own efforts acts as a deterrent to research in the first place.

Another case is the US car industry. General Motors recently spelt out to its components suppliers its vision of the ideal future supplier, complete with specifications of the kind of electronic communication it wanted to be used. Within a few months the bulk of the suppliers had installed this technology, only to be successively forced by Ford and Chrysler to install equivalent but incompatible systems. The end result was rows of terminals in the components suppliers' offices, connected to the big three but not to each other, and data having to be re-entered by hand to bridge the different systems. The pursuit of strategic advantage by each of the major manufacturers has ended up by breaking down the efficient flow of information, and making it impossible to reap the potential benefits of this new technology.[14]

One of the biggest competitive advantages in Japanese industry is based on this move towards far closer relations between firms and their components suppliers, making possible 'just-in-time' organization of the flow of production between as well as within firms. But this process entails entering into the kind of long-term relationship between firm and supplier which erodes the supposed advantages of the market and competition as an incentive to high quality and low prices, by establishing semi-permanent relations between firms. To work properly, it means firms having full knowledge of each others' working practices, and even the staff of one firm being able to organize some aspects of work within the other firm.

The material impact of modern industrial production has also reached a stage where an increasing proportion of the results of any firm's activities have no effect on what appears in the firm's accounts, and it is the rest of society which enjoys the harm or benefits – most strikingly in the case of local or global environmental damage. So if it is society rather than a particular firm that bears the costs or receives the benefits, then the question needs to be asked whether it should not then be society which takes charge of the operations. These 'external' economic effects are not confined to ecological problems. Take the case of a public telephone by a remote village. Most people would be willing to pay a tiny sum, say one ten-thousandth of a penny, to keep it in existence, simply as a form of insurance against breaking down in the vicinity. But the information and transaction costs of organizing payment are too great for the market to arrange it. Democratic social organization can cut information and transaction costs by defining the practical political and social criteria of need and provision. In this sense, even by the logic of markets themselves, an expanding role for public economic intervention could be fully justified in a world of increasing external effects and interdependence.

Conclusion: Going with the Grain

Despite the passion for markets of all shapes and sizes that dominated the 1980s, real life is moving in another direction. The international market fixation is the result of the different problems of the established post-war economic systems in both the socialist countries and the capitalist world. Regulation by markets seems to provide an alternative in a period of uncertainty and flux. But in the longer term, as economies become increasingly information-based, there will be more and more need to work out ways of doing things which go beyond the market, because of the inefficiency and irrationality of the private appropriation of knowledge for profit.

The underlying technological trends favour democratic planning and social ownership, and it is socialism rather than free-market private enterprise which is going with the grain of society. Of course, planning a knowledge-based economy will have to be very different from the relatively crude, centralized planning systems developed in existing socialist countries. But even under capitalism, political attention in the 1990s is likely to shift away from markets as advanced economies try to grapple with the management of the new technologies and production systems. That can only increase the appeal of policies in capitalist countries which aim to tackle deep-seated economic and social problems on the basis of planning and public ownership.

Notes

1. *Financial Times*, 14 January 1989.
2. *Financial Times*, 18 May 1989.
3. Fyodor Burlatsky, 'Perestroika and Philosophy', *Soviet Weekly*, 6 February 1988, p. 10. Vasily Selyunin announced in *Moscow News*, 1 May 1988, that 'nearly 60 years of experience has failed to reveal any particular advantages of planning' and claimed that Western governments had used regulation 'very efficiently'.
4. Tony Benn, interview with Seumas Milne, 26 January 1989.
5. Kevin Morgan and Douglas Pitt, 'Coping with Turbulence: Corporate Strategy, Regulatory Politics and Telematics in Post-Divestiture America', in Nick Garnham, ed., *Proceedings of the Communications Policy Research Conference*, London 1989.
6. Edythe S. Miller, Commissioner of Colorado Public Utilities Commission, 'Potential Abuses in the Application of Social Contract and Incentive Regulation', privately transmitted paper, 1988, p. 18.
7. See, for example, Alec Nove, *The Economics of Feasible Socialism*, London 1983; Ian Forbes, ed., *Market Socialism: Whose Choice?*, Fabian Tract 516, London 1986; and Geoff Hodgson, *The Democratic Economy*, London 1984. A critique of market socialism can be found in Pat Devine, *Democracy and Economic Planning*, Cambridge 1988.
8. David Gordon, 'The Global Economy: New Edifice or Crumbling Foundations?', *New Left Review* no. 168, March/April 1988, p. 10.
9. Moshe Lewin, *The Gorbachev Phenomenon*, London 1988, p. 16.
10. These figures are taken from various issues of the UN *Yearbook of Industrial Statistics* and refer to all 'centrally planned economies'.
11. Fair comparison of Western and Soviet economic statistics is notoriously difficult, but between 1950 and 1980 Soviet national income as measured by 'national material product produced' grew from 31 per cent of US national income to 67 per cent, where it was still stuck by 1982. Interestingly, CIA estimates of comparative US and Soviet growth rates are generally favourable to the Soviet Union. See Trevor Buck and John Cole, *Modern Soviet Economic Performance*, Oxford 1987.
12. Geoff Hodgson, *The Democratic Economy*, Harmondsworth 1984, pp. 170–1.
13. Diane Elson, 'Market Socialism or Socialization of the Market?', *New Left Review* no. 172, November/December 1988, pp. 9–10.
14. Example supplied by Michael Borrus, deputy director of the Berkeley Roundtable on the International Economy, at the OECD in Paris, December 1988.

PART II

Crisis and the Road to Renewal

The collapse of the social democratic consensus in the capitalist world during the 1970s and 1980s was the result of the breakdown in the special post-war conditions for growth. That process has exacerbated Britain's own special chronic problems of relative decline. Far from being successfully tackled by the Thatcher governments, the underlying weaknesses grew more serious during the past decade. Long-term decline is set to continue unless there is a determined shift of the economy's priorities away from global financial speculation and towards investment in advanced production in Britain.

Chapter 4 analyses the economic record of the Thatcher administrations and the growth of social problems in Britain during a period of runaway profits and industrial restructuring on capital's terms. The special culture of short-termism is rooted in the economics of British imperialism and the dominance of the City of London, with disastrous effects on industrial research, development and investment, and the country's infrastructure.

Chapter 5 sets out the conditions necessary for a switch to 'long-termist' economic development: the planned development of the interlocking core industries of the future based on public ownership, research and development, investment and training. Such a strategy chimes with the way the new information and production technologies are evolving. Their development in the 1990s will depend on the national and global integration of systems, networks, compatibility and standardization – rather than the small-scale software houses and computing innovations whose time came and went in the 1970s and 1980s.

4

Relative Decline and False Dawns

I've worked myself up from nothing to a state of extreme poverty.

Groucho Marx, 1931

A class of film students was divided into two. Both groups were told to make a film about the same housing estate. One lot were told to present the estate as a thriving, bustling and happy community, while the other half were given the task of depicting it as a depressing, crime-wracked disaster area. Both teams succeeded in making very convincing films. Britain today is like that housing estate writ large, a country of paradox.

We live in a country where people die because hospital wards have been closed down; a country of rising crime, homelessness and insecurity; a country where the rich receive massive tax giveaways while petty economies are made at the expense of the old and the unemployed. Small or medium-sized riots break out from time to time in the collapsing inner cities. Scientific research is at an all-time low and basic research is being removed from many universities. The country's relative weakness in the economic sectors of the future is increasingly serious.

At the same time, Britain became in the late 1980s one of the fastest-growing advanced capitalist economies. Unemployment fell, albeit from record levels; inflation moderated for a time; wages increased rapidly for many sections of the population, and living standards rose in their wake. The proportion of households with central heating reached 72 per cent in 1987, up from 55 per cent in 1979 and 37 per cent in 1972. Households with telephones rose from 67 per cent in 1979 to 82 per cent in 1987.[1] Yet even these figures conceal huge class and regional disparities. Twenty-seven per cent of households in the North are without a phone, as against ten per cent in the South-east; one-quarter of households in the South-east do not own a car, as compared with half in the North. Two per cent of pensioners have a video recorder, as against over two-thirds of 'cornflake families' (one man, one woman, two children). Some parts of the economy and society are making it. Others are falling behind. This is reflected in people's attitudes, with 49 per cent saying in 1988 that they would prefer to live in a 'mainly socialist society in which public interests and a more controlled economy are most important', while 43 per cent wanted 'a mainly capitalist society in which private interests and free enterprise are most important'.[2]

We are told that Britain has been booming in recent years, because Gross Domestic Product per head rose quite rapidly during the 1980s. But GDP per head is an inadequate measure of living standards. Many are living through a puzzling experience at the moment: statistically they appear to be better off than before, there is more money in their pockets. Yet life does not seem to have improved. Part of the explanation is that public provision has declined and the overall social wage has been cut. For a scientist, it is frustrating to have research departments repeatedly cut back. For nurses, it is demoralizing to see the closure of hospital wards and the decay of facilities in the health service at the same time as government ministers claim to have massively boosted NHS spending. For millions, employment and daily life have become more insecure and the risk of poverty more threatening.

The contradictions of daily economic life are reflected in the paradoxical nature of the British economy as a whole. British capital has, since the end of the Second World War, continually lost out across the globe to US interests. Britain's share of world trade has fallen continually. Yet in terms of its global interests – overseas production, capital holdings and profits, financial transactions and the international role of the City of London – British imperialism remains powerful, whether measured in terms of overseas production, assets or its share of top transnational corporations.[3] The country's cyclical recovery from the depths of the 1981 trough resulted in eight years of economic growth up to mid 1989, yet unemployment remains at massive levels compared even to the 1970s, let alone the 1950s and 1960s. The government's attempts – through privatization and contracting-out – to open up new areas of the economy to private capital have taken place entirely during this period of economic growth and expanding profits. Since a higher proportion of the economy is now subject to the whims of private investment decisions, the potential devastation from a slump in capitalist profitability and production has also increased – rather like a driver who removes the indicators and steering wheel to save weight while on a straight road, only to come across a sudden bend.

Meanwhile the service economy on which the government pins its hopes is itself threatened by the disastrous failure to invest in the infrastructure in the 1980s. Even an official quango like the British Tourism Authority has been moved to warn that the growth of Britain's tourist industries is threatened by poor public transport and dirty leisure facilities.

The Post-War Breakdown: Good Evening America

The prospects for the British economy are closely tied up with the future of the international economy as a whole. In the next few years, the question of who or what might take over the role of the US as guarantor of the world capitalist order is likely to become pressing. Between 1945 and the early 1970s the international dominance of the US economy served to provide a relatively stable economic and trading environment, including a world monetary system with fixed exchange rates based on a US dollar convertible against gold. The final collapse of dollar convertibility was caused by the refusal of other capitalist countries to hold the dollars being issued by the US government to pay for the escalating cost of its war against Vietnam. And with the loss of dollar convertibility against gold, the international monetary system collapsed. The fundamental cause of this breakdown was the relative economic decline of the US and the rise of the defeated powers in World War Two – Japan, the Federal Republic of Germany and, to a lesser extent, Italy.

Crucially, the US was not succeeded by an alternative leader of the capitalist world – as America had replaced Britain – but rather by two new emerging blocs. The first was Western Europe, where Britain's relative decline was more than outweighed by the re-emergence of powerful economies in Germany, France and Italy. The second bloc is based around Japan's powerful economy and the 'Four Tigers' of South Korea, Taiwan, Singapore and Hong Kong. By the year 2000, Japan and these other East Asian economies will have a combined gross national product as big as North America's and greater than capitalist Europe's.

It is this lack of a single dominant economy capable of imposing or allowing a stable international monetary and trading order which represents the greatest obstacle to a renewed environment of stable international capital accumulation. Whereas the US could initially dominate the post-war international organizations, it has over the decades seen them slip from its grasp – first the United Nations General Assembly, then the General Agreement on Tariffs and Trade, and now even the International Monetary Fund and the World Bank – as Japan and Western Europe have grown in strength, and the Third World has increasingly gone its own way. Only in bilateral, one-to-one, relations can the US now bring its full economic and political might to bear, with the paradoxical result that the US which established the post-war multilateral financial and trading framework, is now itself challenging and tearing down this framework. In the 1970s the US abandoned the post-war financial system of the gold exchange standard. In the 1980s the US Trade Act signified a shift to bilateralism in trade as well. In high technology, the pursuit on a world scale of the new American industrial policy of extending state support for industry to non-military areas is reflected in the Sematech programme, the administration's efforts to impose the use of US semiconductors on Japan, the attempt to restore the US television industry through a programme of research in high definition TV, and the diversion of Japanese exports to Europe.

President Reagan's first term turned out to be an orgy of gung-ho American nationalism. The US was going to re-assert its place as leader of the Free World and stand up to Iran and the Evil Empire of the Soviet Union. It was going to be 'Morning in America'. Reagan enthused over Bruce Springsteen's 'Born in the USA' – an anti-war song, as it happened. This nationalistic revival clearly struck a chord in the wake of the humiliation of military defeat at the hands of the Vietnamese. But the reaction went far deeper than rhetoric. There was a real objective need for American capital to attempt to find some way of re-establishing stable conditions for profitable growth. A massive military build-up was launched which, along with personal tax cuts, gave a boost to the stagnant US economy and helped bring about a cyclical expansion in output and employment, while huge profits were diverted to the American military-industrial complex.

But already by the late 1980s, it had become clear that this attempt to regain past dominance was out of step with the country's economic foundations. The resulting trade deficit remains a destabilizing threat to the world economy in the 1990s, which could precipitate either a recessionary or an inflationary international crisis. The recessionary threat would materialize if the trade deficit led to deflationary economic policies and increased trade protectionism. But because of the continuing role of the dollar as the major international reserve and trading currency, the US also has the ability to pay for the deficit in the same way as it paid for the Vietnam war – by issuing dollars. In this way, the current US economic imbalance could just as well bring on an international inflationary crisis.

Britain's Relative Decline

As with the US, the relative decline of the British economy has not fundamentally changed the imperialist nature of the economy. It remains dominated by monopoly capital to a far greater degree than is the case even for most other advanced capitalist economies. Britain's economy is by far the most parasitic in the industrialized world: its net overseas assets represented 20 per cent of national income in 1987, compared with Japan's 8 per cent, West Germany's 12 per cent and a figure of minus 8 per cent for the US.[4] Its international interests are based on the import of materials, semi-manufactures and components, and the export of commodities; the export of financial and industrial capital and the repatriation or re-accumulation of profits; the pivotal role of the City of London in global financial markets, including the extraction of profits from financial involvement in overseas production; and the far-reaching transnational operations of British-based companies. Compared to rival capitalist economies, financial capital in Britain is far less closely involved in domestic industry, either in financing it or in forcing through structural change.[5] Financial capital dictates domestic government policy to a greater degree, and the state has not intervened significantly to restructure capital. The burden of military spending, particularly on research and development, is a far greater drain on resources than is the case in any of Britain's economic rivals with the exception of the US.

There is a glaring contradiction between the continuing strength of British imperialism and the weakness of the British economy. Indeed, the imperialist and parasitic character of Britain's economy exacerbates the problems of relatively low domestic investment, productivity and wage levels. The fundamental causes of the breakdown of the post-war boom and its associated social-democratic, welfare policies, were international. But in the case of Britain, there was the special problem of its chronically low rates of economic growth. Throughout this century, and especially since the Second World War, British growth has generally been slower than that of other industrial economies.

During the 1980s UK growth recovered almost to the level of the 1950–73 period, and was higher than in France, West Germany and Italy. This gave rise to talk, especially from the government, of a definitive reversal of the years of decline. But there are good reasons for a large dose of scepticism about this interpretation. First, such arguments often rely on figures which exclude the 1979–81 slump, which was particularly severe in Britain. In the period 1979–89, UK growth averaged barely 2 per cent a year. Second, Britain has always done relatively better, as in the 1930s, when the world economy is growing slowly – so current developments seem to be part of an old pattern rather than a new trend, and a return to high growth on the continent is likely to see Britain fall behind again. And third, it is already apparent that Britain is running into the same balance of payments problems as in previous periods of faster growth in the 1960s and 1970s. The large-scale destruction of British industry in the 1979–81 slump shifted the trade-off between unemployment and the balance of payments to the point where balanced trade can now only be achieved with three million unemployed. The fall in unemployment to an official level below two million coincided with a rapidly growing trade deficit, reaching the astonishing level of £14.7 billion in 1988 – far higher as a proportion of national income than in any other major country including the US.[6]

The underlying reason for the chronic problems of the British economy has been the low rate and quality of industrial investment in Britain. One way to account for this is by the lower output and productivity returns which investment led to in Britain, but clearly the connection between the two factors – rate of investment and rate of return – is a two-way one. Low rates of return will tend to lead to low investment, while low rates of accumulation are likely to result in a low productivity economy with low rates of return. Contrary to traditional economic theory, the higher the level of investment, the higher will be overall growth rates, productivity growth rates, and rates of return.[7]

For individual firms, relatively slow wage rises in the post-war period allowed British industry to continue operating old machinery. So for any comparable investment in modern equipment, the rate of return should have been greater in the UK than elsewhere. But that was not the case, particularly because of the lack of intervention by government or the financial sector to carry out the necessary restructuring of capital. By contrast, in competitor economies a combination of external intervention and wage rises forced the scrapping of old equipment and investment in new plant, with the consequent increased productivity allowing profitable production at the higher wage rates. For the economy as a whole, profit levels during the 1950s and 1960s were generally high enough to fund the welfare state and allow the system to function, partly due to profits from overseas investments and the international activities of the City. British capital's ability to tick over with a slow loss of world market share meant that the government was never compelled to restructure capital itself. While in competitor economies government intervention increased investment directly or indirectly, financial capital in Britain was happy to seek short-term profits abroad rather than compel domestic industry to change.

The burden of high military spending siphoned off resources and exacerbated this vicious circle of lack of industrial accumulation. For both the US and Britain the main factor behind their losses of world market shares seems to have been the unusually low shares of national resources devoted to productive investment in the civil economy.[8] This depressing effect on the competitiveness and world market share of British civil production seems set to continue through the 1990s as planned military expenditure remains much higher than in Britain's main economic rivals. This is, however, one area where a simple change in government policy could give a strongly positive boost to the economy. Both Labour Party and TUC policy has been to bring the burden of military spending down to the same share of national income as the NATO average – though Neil Kinnock fought and lost the 1987 general election on the opposite pledge of increasing conventional military expenditure above the levels reached even by the Thatcher government. Leaving aside the strong political arguments for a Labour government to cut overall military spending and contribute to general international disarmament, there is a strong economic need for such a commitment, as part of a package to diversify the product ranges of firms currently dominated by military contracts, and divert vital research and development efforts into the civil economy. GEC would be central to such a policy: its current reliance on military contracts is the result of a conscious decision to switch towards such safe, cost-plus contracts at the expense of its previous world market position in civil products.

Table 4.1

Comparative Living Standards in Major Capitalist Economies

	GDP per capita† 1986	Car production (millions) 1988	TV sets per 100 population 1985	Telephone lines per 100 population 1986	Motor vehicles per 100 population 1984
US	£11,491	7.2	80	50	54
Japan	£8,412	8.0	58	37	23
W. Germany	£8,336	4.3	37	43	41
France	£7,938	3.2	39	42	34
UK	*£7,872*	*1.2*	*33*	*38*	*30*
Italy	£7,555	1.9	25	32	37

† Gross Domestic Product at market prices per head (1986, at current prices and purchasing power parities).

Source: Eurostat, *Basic Statistics of the Community*, Brussels 1988; International Telecommunication Union, *Yearbook of Common Carrier Telecommunication Statistics*, Geneva 1988; European Commission, *European Economy*, Brussels, November 1988; DRI Europe.

Life Under Thatcher

From the snapshot of living standards in Table 4.1 it can be seen that Britain is slightly richer than Italy, but behind the other four major capitalist economies. This should be compared with the position forty years ago, when Britain was substantially richer than all except the US.

In one sense it is misleading to consider the Thatcher governments since 1979 as a separate period, since current economic policies were really adopted in 1976, when the last Labour government gave in to IMF demands to cut public spending – and did so with a vengeance. However, the ideological and practical assault on working class organization and the welfare state was stepped up dramatically after 1979, so the period since 1979 can reasonably be treated as a whole.

A greater source of confusion today in judging the economic record of the Conservative government is the choice of the statistical base year. This is illustrated in Table 4.2, which shows how the record

Table 4.2
UK Growth since 1979 and 1981

	GDP(A) 1980=100	Average Annual Growth (%)	Average Annual Growth since 1979 (%)	Average Annual Growth since 1981 (%)
1979	92.8	2.8	–	–
1980	90.7	–2.3	–2.3	–
1981	89.7	–1.1	–1.7	–
1982	91.4	1.9	–0.5	1.9
1983	94.7	3.7	0.5	2.7
1984	96.4	1.8	0.8	2.4
1985	100.0	3.7	1.3	2.8
1986	103.0	3.0	1.5	2.8
1987	107.6	4.5	1.9	3.1
1988	111.6	3.7	2.1	3.2

Source: Central Statistical Office, *Department of Employment Gazette*, London May 1989, table 0.1.

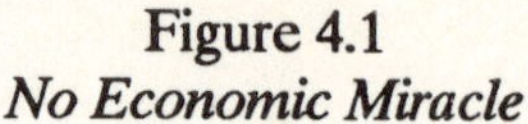

Figure 4.1
No Economic Miracle

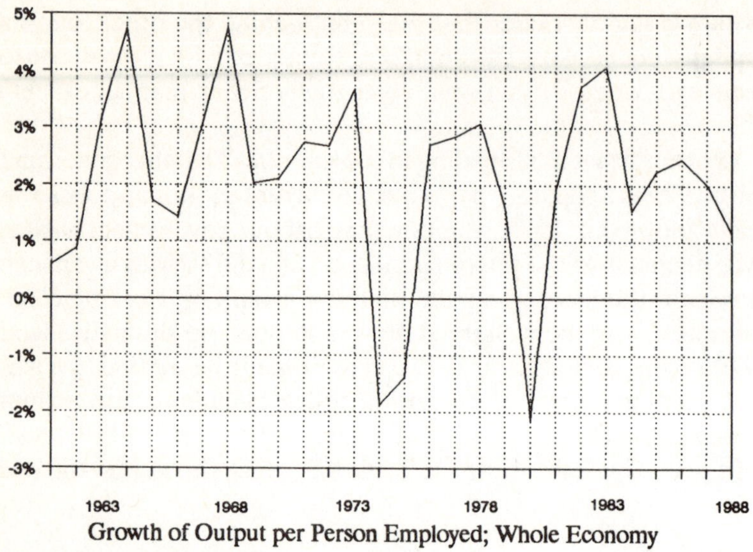

Growth of Output per Person Employed; Whole Economy

Source: *Department of Employment Gazette*, May 1989, table 1.8; *Economic Trends Annual Supplement*, 1988, p. 112

of the government can be dramatically improved (from 2.1 per cent growth to 3.2 per cent growth) if the 1979–81 slump is omitted, a statistical trick often used by government apologists. But by 1989, even government forecasts were for growth to slump back to around that 2 per cent rate.

The claims that the Thatcher years have seen a revolution in productivity, a break from the long-term relative decline of the British economy, are exposed in Figure 4.1, which charts the growth of output per person employed in the economy as a whole. It can be clearly seen that there is a trend rate of growth between 2 and 3 per cent, while the years since 1985 have seen a slightly below-average performance, slipping away from this trend.

As already argued, the immediate cause of Britain's economic under-performance lies in a lack of investment. Britain invests a lower share of GDP in fixed capital formation than any other member of the Organization for Economic Co-operation and Development

Figure 4.2
The Investment Squeeze

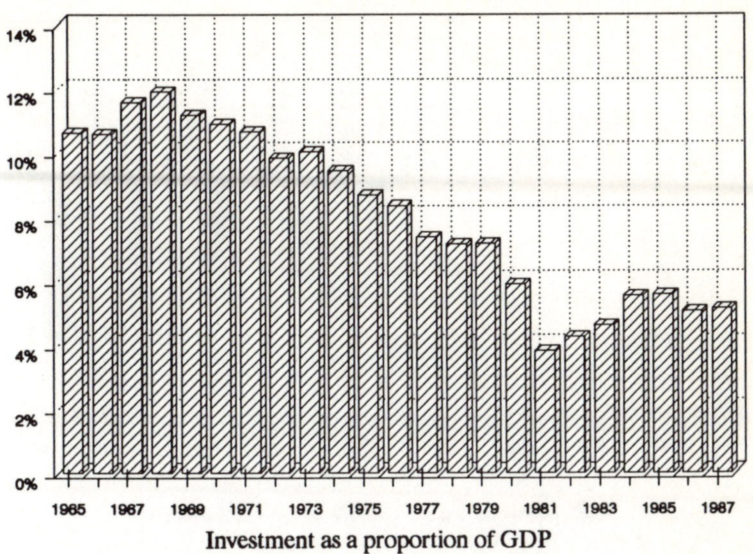

Investment as a proportion of GDP

Source: Central Statistical Office, *United Kingdom National Accounts*, London 1987, tables 1.1, 1.6; Central Statistical Office, *Economic Trends*, March 1988 pp. 6, 8. 1987 capital consumption estimated.

(OECD, made up of the richer capitalist countries) – except Portugal. The scale of the collapse of investment over the years – starting from internationally low levels – is shown in Figure 4.2, with less and less current output being devoted to investment in future output. And the recent recovery in investment levels is in no way adequate to ensure the recovery of the country's capacity to compete effectively.

Looking at Britain in isolation, these trends could be seen as part of an unpleasant, but bearable, pattern of decline. What turns them into a crisis is their trade implications. For years, low investment and sluggish growth weakened British industries until one by one – motorcycles, shipbuilding, consumer electronics, cars – they collapsed in the face of competition from rival capitalist countries. The scale of this trade crisis and its implications for the future are shown in Figure 4.3.

Figure 4.3
The Trade Crisis

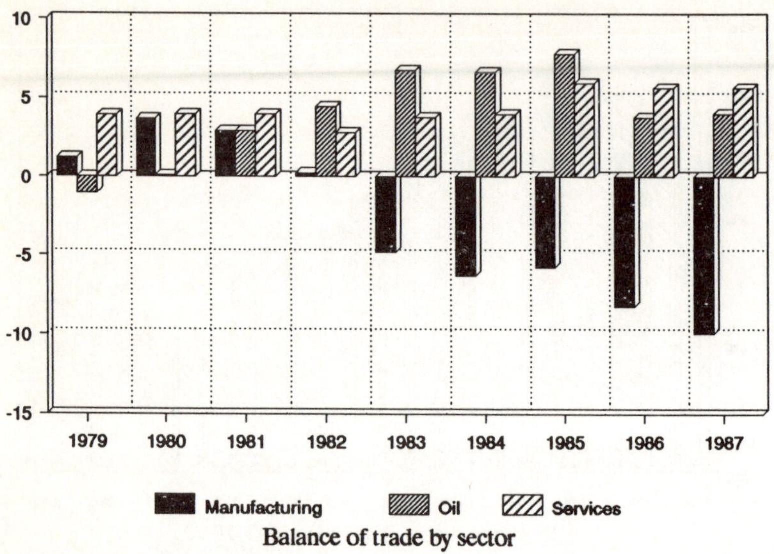

Balance of trade by sector

Source: Central Statistical Office, *Annual Abstract of Statistics*, London 1989, tables 12.3, 12.4, 13.1.

Manufacturing trade has now entered a state of chronic deficit. Trade in services cannot compensate. The surplus has only shown gentle growth over the recent period, which is generally seen as having been one of great success for British services. So there are no grounds for expecting a significantly better performance in services trade in future years. Even some service sectors that one would expect to help the situation have in fact been exacerbating it. The deficit on overseas travel and tourism doubled in 1987 to £1 billion, and redoubled in 1988 to a massive £2 billion.[9] Britain is less and less able to pay its way in the world. So far oil has kept the wolf from the door. But oil output probably peaked in the mid 1980s, and Britain will again be a net oil importer by the mid 1990s.[10] The fall in oil prices in the mid 1980s has already had the effect of sharply cutting Britain's oil income.[11] So an improvement of the trading balance in manufactures, at least to a position of near-balance, will be a necessity over the coming years.

Nothing in the current direction of government policy gives any indication that this will be achieved. Radical solutions to Britain's economic problems are often derided as ignoring the international context of an open economy. Yet it is clear that business as usual, carrying on as if there were nothing wrong with the economy, is the policy that is really open to the charge of ignoring the constraints of international trade – with the implication that British workers and consumers will again end up paying the bill when a slump is engineered to counter the resulting balance of payments crisis.

A conventional expansion of growth risks worsening the trade balance and increasing inflation, and is thus more of an option for other West European economies, since they have better trade balances and lower inflation. In the UK, worsening trade and rising inflation forced the government to step on the economic brakes from mid 1988 – raising interest rates ten times in less than a year to 14 per cent by May 1989 – to slow down the economy and cut growth. This signalled a return to the stop–go cycle which has characterized Britain through most of the post-war period. It was no miracle of economic policy that saved the economy from this cycle for a period, but largely fortuitous factors such as the cushion of North Sea oil. There has at the same time been a disturbing trend in the structure of Britain's imports which are increasingly concentrated on goods that require and embody a high degree of research (see chapter 5).

This tendency is already undermining Britain's capacity to sustain the level of research required to remain an advanced economy. If the country imports the kind of goods that require research for their development and production, there will be no rationale for carrying out the research in Britain. That means one more move in the direction of a low-tech Britain.

Social Effects of Thatcherite Restructuring

There has been a dramatic increase in inequality since 1979, as shown in Table 4.3, even though these figures do not take account of the massive tax give-away to the rich in the 1988 budget – the figures behind this revealing table having been removed from the 1989 issue of the government publication *Social Trends*. Tax changes since 1978–9 have taken £10 a week away from the poorest 20 per cent, while giving almost £40 a week to the richest 10 per cent.[12] At one

Table 4.3
Growth in Real Post-tax Income of Different Income Groups between 1978–9 and 1984–5

	Between 1975–6 and 1978–9	Between 1978–9 and 1981–2	Between 1981–2 and 1984–5	Between 1978–9 and 1984–5
Top 1%	2.7%	16.7%	14.3%	33.4%
Next 9%	6.4%	4.7%	10.6%	15.9%
Next 40%	4.4%	–4.5%	5.0%	0.3%
Lowest 50%	2.2%	–5.9%	6.1%	–0.1%

Source: Central Statistical Office, *Economic Trends Annual Supplement*, London 1988, p. 121; Central Statistical Office, *Social Trends*, London 1988, table 5.14.

extreme, directors' take-home pay rose 26 per cent in 1988.[13] And while 'the highest tenth of non-manual earners have seen their real take-home pay increase by 41.1 per cent between 1979 and 1988, the lowest tenth of manual workers have seen their real take-home pay increase by only 1.7 per cent.'[14] The clear message from these figures is that the economy is currently being run in the interests of these top 10 per cent and not, as Margaret Thatcher claimed in 1988, that 'everyone in the nation has benefited from the increased prosperity – everyone.'[15]

For the bottom 90 per cent of the population, there was no rise in real income between 1978–9 and 1984–5, as compared with a 33.4 per cent rise for the top 1 per cent and a 15.9 per cent rise for the next 9 per cent. Four out of ten households actually had lower real incomes in 1989 than in 1979. Even several years of reasonable rises would still leave the bottom 90 per cent, the vast bulk of the population, worse off than they could expect to be under almost any other set of economic policies. And taxation in Britain, while lower than in France or West Germany, is, at 44 per cent of GNP in 1986, higher than in the US, Japan or Italy.[16] The average family's total tax burden rose during the 1980s from 35 to 37 per cent.[17]

Public debate in Britain often implies that the Thatcher government has presented most people with a deal – more money in the pocket in exchange for worse social services and a greater chance of unemployment. But these figures show that the economy has been failing even to deliver more cash to most people – and there is no question that the social wage as a whole has been cut. Government statistics on the welfare state are less and less realistic, showing increases in provision where independent bodies find decreases. Between 1978–9 and 1988–9 real spending on education is claimed to have risen by 8 per cent and on health by 30 per cent to meet escalating needs. By contrast, the National Accounts give a very different picture for the period from 1979 to 1987, with increases in volume of a mere 3 per cent and 10 per cent respectively. What explains these differences? The National Accounts use an 'own cost' deflator. The government's Autumn Statement on public spending – which are the source of the above figures suggesting increased real expenditure – uses the GDP deflator, unjustifiably assuming that productivity growth is in line with the average for the rest of the economy.

Conclusion: The Price of Failure

The increased role of the state in the economy was thought at one time by capitalist ideologists and economic textbooks alike to be the source of post-war economic growth and relative stability.[18] The current turn to the market was not, therefore, a reaction against the 'bad old days' of state intervention during the post-war boom. It was a reaction to the collapse of those days, and an attempt to regain what had gone for capitalism.

Since 1976 – and particularly since 1979 – British governments have attempted to reduce the share of national income that flows through the public sector. This is a fundamental dilemma for all governments operating in capitalist countries. They determine the level of spending on a number of essential services. Demand for these services normally rises more rapidly than income, while their costs rise more rapidly than those in the rest of the economy. As society develops, an increasing share of employment and output is concentrated on providing goods and services which are most effectively provided collectively. But so long as capitalism continues, this development comes increasingly into conflict with the capitalist profit motive, squeezing out private capital, and requiring high taxes which dampen incentives.

These contradictions were at the heart of the global turn to monetarism. In Britain, after more than ten years of Tory monetarist policies aimed at rolling back the frontiers of the state, tax cutting and nursing the enterprise culture, public expenditure is growing in real terms and has only declined fractionally as a percentage of national income. This is true despite the breaking of the link between many benefits – notably pensions – and earnings. It is true despite a period of high economic growth which has cut the bill for unemployment benefit. The government's response is to continue with its attempts to offload essential public services on to the private sector. Even where such provision can be put out to the private sector – from pensions to health, from transport to education – it does not stop the increase in the share of society's output and employment which has to go to these areas; it merely splits this growing share between public and private sectors and increases social waste through duplication. Privatization of both electricity and water means shifting the financial burden of subsidizing nuclear power against coal and environmental provisions away from taxation on to increased prices and charges. This has the purely statistical effect of reducing both the tax burden and the share of GNP accounted for by government spending.

Tory policies during the 1980s helped to increase earnings for most of those in employment. But they did not solve any of the fundamental problems of the economy – despite having engineered a one-off increase in the intensity of work. In the 1987 general election Labour was the only party not to claim to be offering any radical policies; it appeared to propose only a return to the failed policies of the 1960s and 1970s. Its 1989 Policy Review is on the same track, but has made further compromises with Thatcherite rhetoric. Neither approach would stand much chance of making the fundamental changes needed to rebuild Britain's industrial base and provide a secure future for the majority of the people. Instead, the labour movement needs to look at the possibilities of going beyond the anarchy of the capitalist economy, and to campaign around a programme, which by challenging the power of monopoly capital to run the economy in its own interests, could begin to tackle economic decline.

Notes

1. Central Statistical Office, *Annual Abstract of Statistics*, London 1989, Table 15.4; *Department of Employment Gazette*, May 1989, p. 253.

2. MORI/*Sunday Times*/LWT opinion poll, conducted June 3–6 1988, *Sunday Times*, 12 June 1988.

3. 'Imperialism' is meant in the sense originally used by Hobson and Lenin, to refer to a system of monopoly domination at home combined with overseas expansion based on capital export, control of raw material supplies and foreign markets.

4. Figures from the *Bank of England Quarterly Bulletin*, 1988. Net external assets means direct and portfolio investment abroad minus inward investment. The negative proportion for the US is the result of its large and long-running deficit and means that the country is a net debtor. American overseas interests are nevertheless massive. It should also be borne in mind that Japan's net overseas assets are greater than Britain's in absolute terms – US$240 billion compared with US$160 billion – but smaller as a proportion of its much larger economy.

5. For a variety of industrial case studies illustrating this point see Ben Fine and Laurence Harris, *Peculiarities of the British Economy*, London 1985.

6. See the study by Terry O'Shaughnessy, Research Fellow in economics at King's College, Cambridge, reported in the *Financial Times*, 1 February 1989.

7. See the arguments in Karel Williams, John Williams, Colin Haslam and Andrew Wardlow, 'Facing Up to Manufacturing Failure', in Paul Hirst and Jonathan Zeitlin, eds, *Reversing Industrial Decline?*, Oxford 1989.

8. This is confirmed by Jan Fagerberg, 'International Competitiveness', *Economic Journal*, vol. 98, no. 391, 1988 who, like Ron Smith, 'Military Expenditure and Capitalism', *Cambridge Journal of Economics*, vol. 1, no. 1, 1977, includes shares of output devoted to military and non-military government expenditures (welfare state expenditures) in an investment function, suggesting that the main factor behind the low investment shares in these two countries is the high share of national resources used for military purposes.

9. *Department of Employment Gazette*, April 1989, p. S65.

10. Colin Robinson and Danny Hann, 'North Sea Oil and Gas', in Peter Johnson, ed., *The Structure of British Industry*, London 1988, p. 37.

11. See the argument in Campaign for Labour Party Democracy, *The Case for Public Ownership*, London 1986, predicting a balance of payments problem as oil income declined – which by the late 1980s had come about.

12. Child Poverty Action Group, *Changing Tax*, London 1989.

13. Remuneration Economics, *National Management Salary Survey*, Kingston-upon-Thames 1989.

14. Gabrielle Cox, *The Pay Divide*, Greater Manchester Low Pay Unit, June 1989, p. 4.

15. House of Commons, *Hansard*, 17 May 1988.

16. *Economic Trends*, London January 1989.

17. See *ABC of Thatcherism*, Fabian Society, London 1989.

18. 'In the 1930s the problem was to cure the slump, and the solution was the adoption of "Keynesian Economics". This managed the economy by controlling the total demand in the economy, for the slump was caused by insufficient total monetary demand. ... The result was a quarter of a century of prosperity ...' Geoffrey Whitehead, *Economics Made Simple*, London 1970, p. 317. This remark is to be found in the ninth [1979] edition!

5

The Long-term Economy

When the capital development of a country becomes a by-product of the activities of a casino, the job is likely to be ill-done.

John Maynard Keynes, 1936[1]

The original industrial revolution was based on the mechanization of repetitive physical operations; the current industrial revolution does the same for repetitive mental operations.[2] If the labour process is a combination of conception and execution, then the first industrial revolution was centred on technologies to make execution more efficient – such as the spinning jenny or the steam engine – while we are now seeing the introduction of technologies, notably the computer and the micro-chip, which make conception and control easier. The result is the word processor and the computer numerically-controlled machine tool.

The chip is the basis of an industrial revolution in a sense in which, for example, the laser is not. The laser is having a major impact on sound reproduction, data storage and surgery; but its effects are mostly limited to these uses. By contrast, every single sector of the economy has seen widespread new applications of information technology over the past decade, and this is set to continue.

Two Industrial Revolutions

The first industrial revolution initially transformed the production process in individual workplaces, whether through the introduction of industrial methods piecemeal into pre-existing workshops, or through the establishment of totally new factories. Attention then moved to transport between workplaces. Since materials were being transformed into their finished form at previously inconceivable speeds and in far greater volumes in each workplace, the transport network which had suited the old production system became a bottleneck. So attention was turned to putting the steam-engines on wheels, and to developing the new transport infrastructure to get rid of the bottleneck.

While factories had been set up on a purely private capitalist basis, such an approach could not support the rail and road systems necessary to link up the factories and transport people to and from work. After a period of haphazard and unco-ordinated experimentation with private provision of the new rail network during the nineteenth century – which led to duplication of services in some areas and neglect of others – there was a move in all countries to large-scale state intervention and planning to ensure systematic development. Public control was also able to eradicate the absurdities of private enterprise, such as different companies laying competing tracks between London and Scotland, and different regions using incompatible gauges of track.

Similarly, computers and micro-chips have been introduced into individual workplaces to improve the handling of information. After an initial digestion period, during which they probably absorbed as much time as they saved, they are starting to accelerate the flow of information and control of the production process within each production unit. Now the pressure is on to tackle the new bottleneck and develop information flows between units of production. This is the real meaning of the convergence between computing and telecommunications into a new sector, referred to as information technology.[3] As one new technology expert put it:

> Today the market for many new services depends on the development of the telecommunications infrastructure ... but its diffusion is hindered and its productivity potential is not realized because of institutions, management styles and market structures which are still geared to the old paradigm. The structural crisis of the eighties is in this

perspective a prolonged period of social adaptation to this new paradigm.[4]

These changes in technology are beginning to change the political horizon. Several years ago, when the micro-computer was first being introduced, the typical form of innovation, publicized by the media and right-wing ideologists, was the small-scale isolated start-up company. In a world of swirling technical change, it was easy to argue that the market should be allowed to decide which changes were beneficial and which were not, to allow maximum flexibility. Talk of planning raised images of stifling the dynamic changes sweeping through the production process.

Now the emphasis of technical advance is shifting back towards global efficiency, integration of systems, networks, compatibility and standardization. This material change is starting to influence economic and political debate in the same way that the previous wave of innovation around the micro-chip did over the 1970s. Information technology today is a far cry from the days when Steve Jobs was designing the first micro-computer in a California garage and setting up Apple Computers. That period reflected the early days of the industry, like the British motor car business at the beginning of the century, when Morris, the car designer and later magnate, was setting up shop in his Oxford bikeshed. The subsequent concentration and centralization of capital in computers has matched that seen in any other industry. IBM has reinforced its overwhelming dominance – which is greater than that of the largest company in any other sector of the international economy.

Missing the Point of New Technology

Such a process raises new political opportunities for socialists. Unfortunately this has not been grasped by Labour's current leaders, who are still fighting the battles of the last war. Thus Bryan Gould declared in 1988:

> The new terrain is that of high technology, of small firms, computers and information technology. It is a future of diversity and flexibility, of internationalization on the one hand and specialist production on the other.[5]

These sound uncannily like the views that led to British Telecom's market-led failure with its Prestel service, in contrast to the world-beating success France Télécom has enjoyed with its planned and supply-led Minitel strategy (see chapter 7). The full benefits of these new, integrating technologies can only be realized on the basis of a planned, state-led approach, since the current wave of new technology only delivers its full promise when the appropriate institutional arrangements have been developed to overcome the mismatch between the old forms of organization and the new technologies.[6]

A further characteristic of technological innovation is the need to experiment before the best uses of new technologies are found. For example, at the turn of the century the typical power arrangement was for one single steam engine to serve an entire workshop, with a system of pulleys distributing the power to each individual lathe or milling machine. Electric motors were first introduced to replace steam engines on cost and reliability grounds. Only ten to fifteen years later was the real advantage of electric motors brought into play by giving each machine its independent source of power, improving the flexibility of workshop organization and saving space. The potential of the new technology was enough to justify its introduction. But its full dynamizing effect could only be discovered after a period of experimentation.[7]

We are in a similar period of experimentation with information technology. There is clearly enormous potential for applying information technology throughout the economy. But no one can say exactly which concrete uses will turn out to be the most fruitful. The important task is to get the advanced networks and services in place, in a climate that will allow different types of users to create their own applications. By taking a planned lead at this stage of the introduction of advanced networks and services, at a time when most advanced countries have not yet adapted to the requirement for planning inherent in these technologies, Britain has an opportunity to secure a lasting strong position in leading-edge technologies.

Two features of the emerging information economy call for increased public intervention, as discussed briefly in chapter 3. First, information, design, research and development and software represent a growing proportion of the value of most products. Direct production costs are falling by comparison. While it may have been irrational to have three or four plants producing similar cars called Fords, Vauxhalls and Austins, at least each plant was doing a useful job – though savings could have been made by merging them. But today it has become absurd to have rival groups of scientists and engineers developing the same products in secrecy from each other, to have massive teams of scientists and programmers designing rival – and almost identical – micro-computers, word-processors, telephone exchanges or cloned drugs. Yet this is the only way that the market knows to develop today's and tomorrow's products, the cost of which is increasingly accounted for by design rather than manufacture, software rather than hardware. Three-quarters of the cost of a modern telephone exchange is software, whereas three-quarters of the cost of the previous generation of exchanges, just a decade ago, was hardware. Software has a special property: the first copy may cost millions or even billions, but the second copy is practically free to produce. This is the strongest possible form of increasing returns to scale, the classic justification in orthodox economics for social provision of 'public goods'. Over the past decade, right-wing theorists pushing for privatization and deregulation have seized on every case where technology has eroded increasing returns to scale – but the overall trend is in the opposite direction, requiring a sharing of research results and development efforts which only public provision can allow.

A second aspect of new technology which is pulling in the direction of greater social intervention and ownership is that as the importance of research and development rises relative to that of direct production, the purpose of labour is increasingly the production of knowledge, in the form of designs or production processes. But keeping such knowledge exclusive to the originating firm is difficult. If it cannot be kept secret for long, the generation of knowledge on the basis of pure private enterprise is less and less viable. Private enterprise would be a poor way to make steel bars if the bars could be effortlessly spirited from one firm's warehouse to another's without payment. But knowledge has just such a property, whether through the movement of staff with specialized knowledge, through 'reverse engineering' of competitors' products, or through simple industrial espionage. To have the key industries of the future under private ownership will result in an increasing proportion of society's resources going into ever more ingenious means of retaining the benefits of research within the originating company.

The Core Industries

Phases of successful economic growth, as well as phases of decline, can generally be traced to the performance of a group of core industries at the heart of the economy. The particular industries vary over time and geographical area. In the era of the industrial revolution, Britain's industrial pre-eminence was based on steam, textiles, engineering, coal and steel. Germany caught up and overtook Britain on the basis of some of those industries – notably engineering – as well as chemicals. America's development was orientated in the first half of this century around production lines, notably the car.

Production is the transformation of inputs into a form better suited to the satisfaction of people's final needs. As the economy becomes more advanced and complex, the chain leading from raw materials to final products becomes more and more complex. Increasingly, each sector is taking as inputs the transformed outputs of other sectors situated further back along the particular chain of production. Examples are *wheat >> flour >> bread >> sandwiches*; or *silicon >> chips >> computers >> factory control systems >> machine tools >> cars*. As production becomes increasingly advanced, and the development of new production techniques, products and services requires more use of science and high-level skills, success is less and less a matter of chance and more and more a product of conscious policy. Chance mainly affects the early stages of these chains. A sudden discovery of oil or change in climate will tend to make an impact at the start of a chain. Furthermore, as the processes in the middle of the chain are completely under human control and can take place anywhere, they tend to be carried out in many countries, and can be relocated. Oil refining occurs in all countries above a certain size, whereas oil extraction only occurs in the countries lucky enough to have oil. As the chains become longer, the area of chance diminishes and that of policy grows.

It is not surprising, then, that public policy and co-ordination have been central to the success of those countries that have emerged or are emerging in this century as advanced industrial powers with a capacity to develop and manufacture advanced products – typified by Japan, but also true for France and South Korea. In all three, the government identified key sectors of the economy in which the country could develop at least self-sufficiency and at best a leading-edge capability. It then set about organizing the establishment of these sectors behind protective trade barriers.

Strengthening the Core

Core sectors of the economy – such as basic metals, electricity, energy, railways, automobile production; or telecommunications, computing, electronic components – are characterized by a number of features, one of which is the provision of inputs for other sectors within the core. There are thus various overlapping core sectors of the British economy. These cores also produce the basic inputs for the whole range of goods and services needed by the rest of the economy. Any healthy and balanced national economy needs to have successful cores for several reasons:

- To make sure that the economy is not excessively reliant on imports in key areas. This would be particularly important for allowing Britain to pursue progressive political and economic policies independent from – and possibly at odds with – its main trading partners.
- To retain the capability to innovate. By embodying the key technologies and products that serve as inputs throughout the rest of the economy, developments and advances in core sectors can have multiple effects throughout the rest of the economy. Innovation is therefore particularly fruitful in these sectors, where it makes special sense for a country to spend large sums on research, whether in universities and polytechnics or in companies.
- To ensure that the rest of the economy can produce efficiently. The ability to make goods efficiently depends upon a reliable supply of high-quality inputs from the core sectors of both goods and services.

Rail transport, steel, coal and automobiles buy and sell a high proportion of each others' goods and services. Nationalization and planning of this core of industries could provide a firm basis for the less stringent planning of the rest of the economy. Much greater precision and conscious control would be possible in the planning of this core, as a result of its interdependence and relative autonomy from the rest of the economy.

It is often said that the old basic industries are out of date, and that we are increasingly becoming a service economy – indeed that the most materially advanced countries are becoming post-industrial societies. Closer examination shows, however, that the economies which have been in relative decline, such as the US and Britain, have shown the sharpest growth in the proportion of the economy accounted for by services – while Japan has actually shown a rise in the proportion accounted for by industry. The idea that there are stages of economic growth involving a march through the sectors – from primary (agriculture) through secondary (manufacturing) to tertiary (services) activities – is based on a number of misconceptions. The parallel between agriculture and industry is inaccurate, because agriculture is closely tied to the particular need for food, which is bound to decrease as a proportion of spending as living standards rise. The same cannot be said of industry as against services, since they can both satisfy the same needs. Cars (goods) are an alternative to public transport (a service); videos (goods) an alternative to cinemas (a service). And there is a systematic tendency for most goods to supplant the equivalent service over time, because the higher productivity growth in manufacturing makes goods cheaper compared with the corresponding services. So there is no reason to expect industry to diminish in importance over the long run.[8]

The Tory government's lack of support for the traditional basic industries is not simply a matter of opposition to what have been mainly state-owned sectors – though that was bound to be a factor for such a right-wing administration. The extra element is that the Thatcher government is especially strongly identified with the sectional interests of the City and the international interests of British capital, rather than domestic manufacturing capital. A litany of complaints about government interest rate and exchange rate policy has come over the last decade from the Confederation of British Industry (CBI), traditionally reflecting mainly domestic British manufacturing capital. Similarly, the House of Lords Select Committee on Overseas Trade stated in 1985 that:

> There has been a steady trend of deterioration in Britain's manufacturing performance. ... It is neither exaggeration, nor irresponsible, to say that the present situation undoubtedly contains the seeds of a major political and economic crisis in the foreseeable future.[9]

A conscious policy of promoting and privileging the development of advanced low-cost output from core industries is therefore a strong basis for securing allies in building a modern industrial base in Britain – even from outside the labour movement.

In three of the main constituent sectors of the high technology information industries – computing, electronic components and telecommunications – Britain has in the past shown great potential and then failed to develop that potential for lack of a coherent and planned policy. In telecommunications, it is arguable that Britain developed the first digital switch, the key technology currently revolutionizing the sector along with fibre optics, some of the most important early developments of which also occurred in Britain. The first prototypes of what we now call the electronic digital computer were developed in Britain at Bletchley during the war. In components, the same story seems to be repeating itself currently with the transputer, the first of a new generation of revolutionary cheap microprocessors, developed in Britain but being taken up in the US and Japan, while the public company that developed it, Inmos, has been privatized and since sold off to state-owned SGS–Thomson. German and French industry often talk of the 'not-invented-here' syndrome: a refusal to buy technologies invented somewhere else. Britain suffers from the opposite, an 'invented-here' syndrome: a refusal to buy technology invented in Britain.

This sorry tale shows up in the collapse of high technology capacity over recent years. In the so-called high research intensity sector – which includes data processing, electronics and instrument engineering – the ratio of imports to home demand rose from 29 per cent in 1975 to 54 per cent in 1985. In medium research intensity industries – such as rubber products and mechanical engineering – import penetration rose from 19 per cent to 28 per cent. Finally, in low research intensity sectors – such as food and textiles – import penetration rose from 21 per cent to 26 per cent over the period.[10]

Britain is now so far behind that there is no longer any question of simply providing incentives to existing companies to encourage them to take the actions needed to repair the damage. For the most part, such companies no longer exist. In computing, ICL is Britain's largest computer company. It is dwarfed by IBM (UK) and part-owned by the American ITT. In telecommunications, GEC–Plessey Telecommunications (GPT) is not generally seen as a leading player in the world compared with Alcatel, Siemens, American Telephone and Telegraph (AT&T), Northern Telecom, Ericsson or NEC. In electronic components, Inmos, founded in 1978, was a worthwhile attempt by the National Enterprise Board to establish a British presence. But the government discontinued support, selling it off in 1984 to Thorn EMI, which in turn sold it, despite being profitable, in March 1989 to SGS–Thomson Microelectronics, a Franco-Italian joint venture. Inmos itself was not consulted over the deal. Significantly, the partners in SGS–Thomson are the Italian state-owned IRI group and the French electronics group Thomson, also state controlled. Both the French and Italian governments have seen the strategic need for a national hold on the mainstream technology of mass-market micro-chips.

Planning the Core Industries

A crucial initial stage in the planning of these core industries would be to establish the scope of the movement of goods and services between them. There is a flow of goods or services between each pair of core industries – the Central Electricity Generating Board for example being the largest purchaser of coal in the Western world – which is potentially much larger than suggested by the statistics because of imports. Planning these flows could give strategic leverage over the whole economy. And the complexity and interdependencies involved in such a range of flows would allow planning to take advantage of economic externalities in a way that the market fails to do – for example, by ensuring long-term security of supply, rather than simply going for the short-term lowest price as competition forces firms to do. Competition blocks firms from buying the option of long-term security of supply, since by its nature it cannot be guaranteed by the market.

Private ownership is a notable failure in the area of the provision of skills, education, training and retraining, for the simple reason that – at least in a country like Britain where skilled workers tend not to stay with the same employer for long periods – employers are unwilling to pay for training and retraining when most of the benefit is likely to accrue to a different employer. Only under socialism, or in a capitalist country like Japan – and even then only in the large company sector where employees tend to stay with the same employer for life – is it viable to rely on the employer to conduct the training and retraining required.

A private employer in high technology currently needs to take into account the availability of skills when considering medium- or long-term investment. But there exists no way of properly integrating training decisions with investment decisions, whereas investment depends on the presence of trained staff. Attempts at integration that do exist – such as the work of the Training Commission, or pressure through the CBI – are ineffective partly because those making decisions about retraining do not have access to the investment plans of the other major companies, and vice versa. The result is that Britain has a shortfall in craft workers: an extra 50,000 would need to be trained a year to match France and Japan, and a further 80,000 would be required to reach German standards.[11] A survey of graduate employment in 1988 and 1989 showed that spiralling demand for new graduates is coupled with almost static supply from universities and polytechnics.[12]

Public ownership in conjunction with an integrated training policy offers a solution. Integrated planning of the core sectors would allow the identification of skill requirements in time to define new programmes and courses, in the confidence that the skills produced would feed effectively into the economy. Firms still outside the nationalized sector would then be able – indeed encouraged – to participate in this skills planning, which would involve them exposing and socializing aspects of their corporate plans, in return for gaining the assurance that the right skills would be available when they need them.

Long-Termism and Public Ownership

The short-term fixations of British capitalism, dominated as it is by the City of London, have become a cliché of political life. Everyone is against short-termism, few offer credible solutions. Short-termism is a chronic affliction of capitalism everywhere, but in Britain – where it is closely linked to the dominance of the City of London and its overseas interests – the disease has become crippling. At a time of rapid technical change such as now, the pursuit of short-term profit creates particular problems, because although it can allow the rapid adaptation of existing industries to consumer demand, it discourages the establishment of new industries until they are recognized worldwide as safe investments.

Short-termism in Britain has a long history. When German and American technical advance rapidly increased the importance of chemicals and electrical machinery, British capitalists were slow to adapt, so that even in 1913, textiles still accounted for just under 50 per cent of British exports.[13] The historian Eric Hobsbawm wrote of

British capital's failure to move into the new industries in the last century as follows:

> So long as satisfactory profits were to be made in the old way, and so long as the decision to modernize had to emerge from the sum-total of decisions by individual firms, the incentive to do so would be weak.[14]

Structural change in the world economy has characteristically been accompanied by structural decline for Britain, though it has often been masked by British capital's short-term ability to exploit available markets on the basis of the old industrial structure and its tendency to rely on earnings from overseas investments. Hence the period before the First World War, when Britain was already suffering rapid relative decline, was seen at the time as a period of growth and success.

The story is similar today. The failure during the 1980s to develop a long-term, integrated strategy for a new industrial structure with a cutting edge in information technology has been masked by the credit boom and overseas investment income. A few years' average growth are always enough for short-termist pundits to start claiming an economic miracle. 'British industry is in good shape', the CBI's David Wigglesworth announced in 1987. Sir Trevor Holdsworth, chairman of the engineering firm GKN, even managed to detect a 'permanent transformation' of British manufacturing under Thatcher. The scale of Britain's slump in the industries of the future is enough to puncture claims of a British industrial renaissance: trade in electronic and data-processing equipment swung from a surplus of more than £1 billion in 1979 to a deficit of over £1.5 billion in 1988.[15] The deficit in information technology and electronics reached more than £2.2 billion.[16]

This short-termist approach, previously the hallmark of private enterprise – and especially the City of London – has been turned into an article of faith by the Thatcher government, which insists that training, research and development and infrastructural investment should effectively be left to the market. This has been at a time when the establishment of viable new sectors demands the creation of pools of new expertise, which are not necessarily profitable in the short run. Take the example of computerization, where benefits often take years to outweigh teething problems of bad programming, management by enthusiasts and the gap between the theoretical and practical capabilities of computer systems; those years are not wasted for the economy as a whole, since they spread expertise among workers, who are then better able to use later, improved systems.

Market-led development of hi-tech sectors is increasingly seen as inadequate in other capitalist countries. The highly-developed industrial policies and publicly-supported training schemes of Japan and West Germany are well known. But even the US, which has traditionally avoided industrial policy outside the military sector, has now started to intervene in an attempt to regain its lost technological lead: government-sponsored programmes have been or are being set up in semiconductor design, high-definition television, opto-electronics and X-ray lithography.[17] If Britain is to re-establish a significant presence in new technology, more far-reaching intervention is needed.

Regulation, Incentives or Public Ownership?

The need for public intervention if Britain is to build up a successful economy based on long-term criteria is common ground throughout the Labour and centre parties in Britain. But the Labour leadership, the Democrats (Liberals) and the Social Democrats also believe that the behaviour of private companies can and must be changed without bringing them into public ownership. The measures they favour fall into two categories: financial incentives, such as tax allowances and investment and regional grants; and regulations, such as standards-setting or buy-British policies. Both have their place in an integrated approach, but they have fatal flaws that disqualify them from taking centre stage in a programme for modernization and social justice.

Financial incentives have a credibility problem, because they have to be financed. Some desirable goals of government are equally in the interests of firms, who are for example quite happy to absorb any amount of public money for research or training programmes. But essentially, subsidies and incentives amount to bribing private industry to do what is not otherwise most profitable, and this raises the problem of how to pay for the slush fund. Labour has continually laid itself open in the past to the question 'where will the money come from?' – and it has not always been able to give realistic answers.

Regulation, on the other hand, means leaving the private owners in charge, but using legal levers to try and make them act in a way consistent with wider interests. With secondary aspects of commercial policy, that may make sense. If a firm exists to make profits, it is realistic to pass laws saying it must not do this by cutting down rain forests or by using dangerous chemicals. But it is unrealistic and unreasonable to try and use regulations to make the firm pursue a quite different goal from making profits – such as satisfying social needs in a framework of sustainable growth – while leaving it as a private company with a management that can be sacked or taken over if it does not maximize profits. It also establishes an unequal contest between the regulators and the private management, who will always have a better knowledge of the industry than the regulators.

What is commonly understood as a worldwide advance of market forces can be seen more accurately as partly a revolt against regulation and outsiders telling insiders what to do, when the outsiders – or regulators – do not properly understand developments in a climate of accelerating change. But regulation was introduced in the first place to solve real problems. Leaving such problems to the market is unacceptable in an increasingly interdependent world, a point so obviously illustrated by the ecological crisis. Tackling red tape and interference in business can only be dealt with by moving on from regulation to direct control, through public ownership.

The real inconsistency in the policies favoured by Labour's leadership is in the complete mismatch between means and ends. The message is not lost on the labour movement or the public, who understand that no radical change in the orientation of the British economy is being proposed. To aim to reverse the secular decline of the British economy and change its direction through a combination of financial incentives and regulations is akin to trying to steer a supertanker with a tug-boat. It will simply carry on in its own sweet way. That, in a nutshell, is why a major extension of public ownership is essential.

Improving the quality of life for the majority of people is not simply a matter of boosting output and certainly very different from maximizing profits. There is a fundamental contradiction between a successful economy from the point of view of private firms and a successful economy from the point of view of the vast majority of the population – whether as citizens, workers or consumers. Eradicating unemployment is an urgent priority for most people; for capital unemployment is a useful downward pressure on wages and conditions. Regional development is a pressing concern in Britain in a way that is of no interest to firms which can only see the cost difference between production in Harrogate, Hounslow and Hong Kong. And economic growth has to be sustainable if it is to be real. There is no sense churning out cars and video-recorders if we are running up an unpaid bill in terms of the destruction of the environment. But once the central role of public ownership is accepted, it can then be seen how it could be supplemented with other policy instruments, including public procurement, contract compliance, compulsory planning agreements, tax and subsidy incentives, and standards requirements, to produce an integrated strategy.[18]

Conclusion: The Implications for Planning

If a Labour government is to implement a 'long-termist' strategy, it would need to have powers to change the behaviour of the largest few hundred firms that dominate the British economy. Ideally, that would mean the nationalization of all of them. But common sense dictates that even to carry out an extension of public ownership on the scale that the French government did in 1981–2 would be an enormous political and organizational struggle. The leverage necessary to plan the reconstruction of a modern industrial economy would therefore have to be partly based on statutory controls and agreements with the majority of the biggest companies that remained in private hands – as well as on the influence that could be directly brought to bear by a publicly-owned financial sector.

Planning, and the calculations upon which it is based, must relate to the real operations of firms and not to a shadow-play set up by firms to influence policy – the process the Americans call 'regulatory capture'. This is far easier where the state has a substantial presence, and is thus better placed to understand the market and technological position. And the presence of a major public firm can itself influence market conditions. For example, a high level of investment in skills development by a publicly-owned firm could help to bring about corresponding behaviour by private firms, afraid of being left behind.

The choice of how to control or influence any major company is broadly between financial incentives, regulation – including planning agreements – and public ownership. In the case of regulation, government efforts would be mostly aimed at imposing goals alien to the interests of private firms, through detailed rules and incentives. The problem is that such an approach builds a permanent conflict of interest into the central relation between public and private policy. On the basis of the historical record it is likely to absorb much of the energy of both the state and private firms, and result in neither achieving their goals – even where they are shared. Sometimes regulation is the best or the only way to ensure that policy is implemented, but two conditions have to be met. First, the organization making the rules must have sufficient understanding of the sector it is regulating; and second, it must have adequate powers to enforce its rules. In terms of both these requirements, nationalization of one or several firms in an industrial sector and effective statutory regulation of the rest are complementary strategies. Publicly owned firms are necessary to provide the information and practical clout needed to make regulations for the private sector stick.

A sectoral approach is needed to the extension of public ownership. In some sectors the key strategic issue is the scale of production; in others, investment in research and development; in others, employment. An effective public presence in a sector demands that the nationalized firm or firms should account for a substantial proportion of the total sector. But this proportion would need to be judged by different measure in different sectors: by output, investment, or employment, depending on their relative importance to the role of the sector in the economy as a whole. What constitutes a substantial proportion would also be bound to vary according to the different criteria employed, but in general it would mean at least 20 to 30 per cent of the relevant yardstick.

The next two parts attempt to apply these general principles in a concrete way to different industries as the basis for a new programme which could tackle the deep-seated problems of the British economy. But it would be misleading to pretend that these outlines could be interpreted as part of some sort of 'plan for Britain', with detailed targets and methods laid down for the development of the entire economy. Not only is this far beyond the scope of this book, but it is a task for the labour movement as a whole. The central aim of a socialist strategy is to increase people's power over their own lives; and technocratic solutions are no solutions at all. The proposals in the following chapters are meant, therefore, to be illustrative of a general approach and to show how current economic developments are increasing the need for social ownership and control. Formulating any full-scale programme for the coming years will have to be a wide-ranging and collective effort.

Notes

1. John Maynard Keynes, *The General Theory of Employment, Interest and Money*, London 1936, p. 159.

2. While a series of industrial revolutions are sometimes identified – including the industrial breakthroughs based on chemicals, electrics and the motor industry, for example – the current period of industrial upheaval represents a far more thoroughgoing change, as far-reaching in some ways as the original industrial revolution at the end of the eighteenth century.

3. The French call this new sector 'télématique'. The Japanese call it 'Computers and Communications' (C&C). The European Commission calls it 'Telecommunications and Information Technology' (TIT).

4. Christopher Freeman, 'Information Technology and Change in Techno-Economic Paradigm', in Christopher Freeman and Luc Soete, eds, *Technical Change and Full Employment*, Oxford 1987, pp. 61–2.

5. Bryan Gould, 'A Map of the Battlefield for the Left', *Guardian*, 25 August 1988.

6. As discussed by Carlota Perez, 'Structural Change and the Assimilation of New Technologies in the Economic and Social Systems', *Futures* 15, 1983, pp. 357–75.

7. See OECD, *New Technologies in the 1990s – A Socio-Economic Strategy*, Paris 1989.

8. See the discussion in Jonathan Gershuny and Ian Miles, *The New Service Economy*, London 1983; and Jonathan Gershuny, *Social Innovation and the Division of Labour*, Oxford 1983.

9. House of Lords, *House of Lords Select Committee on Overseas Trade*, Session 1984–5 (238-I), p. 56.

10. Midland Bank, 'The Output and Trade Performance of UK Manufacturing Industries', *Midland Bank Review*, Autumn 1986.

11. Sig Prais, *National Institute Economic Review*, February 1989.

12. Helen Perkins, *Graduate Salaries and Vacancies*, Price Waterhouse, London 1989.

13. Keith Smith, *The British Economic Crisis*, Harmondsworth 1984.

14. Eric Hobsbawm, *Industry and Empire*, Harmondsworth 1969, p. 188.

15. Phil Blackburn and Richard Sharpe, eds, *Britain's Industrial Renaissance?*, London 1988.

16. Treasury and Industry Select Committee, *Report on Information Technology*, London 1988.

17. *Financial Times*, 10 March 1989.

18. For a discussion of the range of measures that could be applied to information technology, see Phil Blackburn and Richard Sharpe, eds, *Britain's Industrial Renaissance?*, London 1988.

PART III
Planning for the 1990s

This part sets out to build up the case for an economic strategy based on public ownership and planning from an analysis of the problems of specific industrial sectors and the particular need for positive action to tackle racism, discrimination against women and the ecological crisis.

Chapter 6 looks at the City of London and the reasons why its activities must be radically overhauled if the underlying weaknesses of the British economy are to be overcome. A publicly-owned financial sector could play a decisive role in the planning and funding of a programme for social justice and the reconstruction of British industry.

Chapter 7 analyses the crucial importance of information technology for the sustainable development and independence of the whole British economy. Britain has failed to invest in the converging telecommunications and computing sectors. An effective strategy for the 1990s would re-integrate Mercury with a publicly-owned British Telecom on the basis of a monopoly of both traditional and new universal services. Any organization could then use this infrastructure of networks for the provision of additional information services. The importance of standardization for the computing and electronics industries is then explored.

Outline strategies for other major sectors are set out in chapter 8, including aerospace, the motor industry, public transport, energy, construction, and pharmaceuticals. Chapter 9 extends the analysis to argue that only large-scale democratic planning can ensure a strong regional and ecological dimension to sustainable growth; and the need to intervene positively to guarantee the economic rights of women and black people in the labour force is argued in chapter 10.

6

Taming the City of London

I said that we had now reached the situation where a newly elected government with a mandate from the people was being told, not so much by the Governor of the Bank of England but by international speculators, that the policies on which we had fought the election could not be implemented; that the government was to be forced into the adoption of Tory policies to which it was fundamentally opposed. The Governor confirmed that that was, in fact, the case. I asked him if this meant that it was impossible for any government, whatever its party label, whatever its manifesto or the policies on which it fought an election, to continue, unless it immediately reverted to full-scale Tory policies. He had to admit that that was what his argument meant, because of the sheer compulsion of the economic dictation of those who exercised decisive economic power.

Harold Wilson, 1971[1]

In its own terms, the City of London is a great success. Britain's financial nerve-centre has the greatest concentration of banks in the world, accounting for around a quarter of all international bank lending. It is the world's biggest insurance market with a fifth of the international insurance business. The City is also a principal international centre for trade in commodities. Its stock exchange has the world's largest listing of securities with a turnover of almost £400 billion in 1988 and the world's third largest government debt market with daily volumes at £4.5 billion – nearly three times larger than its equities market; investments in stock market companies and other securities such as bonds total £385 billion. Banking, finance, business services, leasing and insurance accounted for 16 per cent of Britain's total output in 1986. Together they accounted for 11 per cent of employment in 1987, though by far the largest number of workers are in the insurance business and commercial banking rather than the securities markets or international banking.[2]

But in terms of the performance of the domestic economy, and the living standards and life-chances of the British people, the City has for the most part been something closer to a disaster. Over more than a century, the City has failed to make the necessary long-term investments in domestic industry; its activities have seriously distorted the whole British economy; it has flourished on a parasitic relationship with the Third World; and its economic and political power has been wielded to block radical policies for change at home. On the basis of past experience, the City's continued existence in its present form would make impossible any serious attempt to use democratic political power to restructure and modernize the economy in the interests of the majority.

The Problem

The origins of the City of London's pivotal role in international finance and commerce and its effect on the British economy lie in Britain's grip on world trade in the eighteenth and nineteenth centuries and the evolution of British imperialism in the last hundred years. The City's power was partly built on Britain's industrial dominance, but its international importance has long outlived the decline of British industry and the City has undergone several radical changes to maintain its position.

The development of the City of London over two hundred years, its unique role in international trade and finance, and the importance of the London trade in commodities, stocks and shares and other financial assets have shaped the British domestic economy in a profound way. By its nature, financial capital always seeks maximum flexibility and liquidity, but the special position of the City has given British financiers an unrivalled degree of mobility and independence

– especially from British industry.[3] There are three main reasons for this. First, the City has always been as much about dealing and trading – in commodities, securities, insurance risks and foreign exchange – as about lending and investment. Its profits are made from fees and commissions as much as from interest and dividends. London has the oldest stock market in the world and the strength and size of its financial markets have traditionally allowed financiers to make money out of industry without being locked in to particular firms: they have been able to buy bonds and shares in the sure knowledge that they can easily be sold on the market. The result is that lenders have managed to avoid becoming involved in company management. By contrast, countries which industrialized later than Britain – such as Germany – did not have the developed financial markets to provide the necessary capital. So bankers had to make long-term commitments to the firms they backed and financial capital took on a strongly interventionist role.

The second factor which has given the City its special character has been its traditional reliance on financing state debt. In the post-war period, while the City was operating a profitable market in British government bonds – 'gilt-edged' stock – Japanese, West German and French bankers were financing the reconstruction of industry. All major capitalist economies have large government debt markets which soak up quantities of capital, but none is as well established as the City's. State bonds offer secure profits in a highly flexible form, and London's financiers came to impose the same terms on its lending to industry.[4]

The third characteristic of the City of London which has given finance in Britain a unique distance from industrial capital among advanced capitalist countries is its international orientation. The traditional strength of markets and trading in London encouraged banks to develop a strong taste for providing the short-term financial needs of trade, rather than the long-term capital needed for industrial growth. From the late nineteenth century until the 1960s, the City's international position was maintained on the basis of the Empire and the 'Sterling Area', whereby mostly colonial states held their foreign exchange reserves in sterling. When that system broke down, the City assumed a new role at the heart of the international Eurodollar market, based on borrowing and lending dollars held outside the US. London became the centre of this new international credit system because banks in Britain were less regulated than in any other advanced capitalist country, notably the US. In particular, the City had successfully seen off almost all government restrictions on borrowing and lending foreign currencies.

More than any other form of capital, financial capital is able to minimize risks by operating internationally; and the current globalization of financial markets has intensified that tendency. But nowhere has a financial system been guaranteed such a favourable framework for its international business as in Britain. The result can be seen in the global reach of the City's operations: London accounted for 27 per cent of all international bank loans outstanding in 1982, when its nearest rival – the US – had only 14 per cent. Between 1970 and 1982, the proportion of lending by London banks taken up by international loans rose from 46 per cent to 70 per cent.[5] Most of this international lending was by foreign-owned banks based in Britain, but even British-owned banks have traditionally directed an unusually high proportion of their lending abroad.[6] More recently, Tokyo has been jockeying for position as the leading centre for bank lending. But the City is the undisputed home of the enormous Eurobond market: a US$2.5 trillion market which raises US$200 billion a year – more than any stock exchange. In the words of *The Economist*: 'New York and Tokyo matter because of the domestic economies they serve. London, by contrast, serves the world community.'[7]

The Relationship with Industry

The ease of access to foreign investment opportunities has traditionally given the City a range of more profitable openings than were available at home. This results in an economic structure geared to foreign acquisition rather than domestic investment, as shown in Table 6.1. But as with the City's historic addiction to government 'gilts', the domestic effect has not been so much to starve British industry of funds, as to accentuate the tendency of British banks and other financial institutions to adopt an arm's length relationship with industry.[8] Just as the early development of sophisticated financial markets in the City and the easy availability of state debt encouraged the British banks' appetite for comparable short-term results in its industrial lending, so the flexibility afforded by the City's world role encouraged it to demand independence in its relationship with domestic industry.

Table 6.1
Ratio of Domestic Investment to Foreign Acquisitions 1988

Country	Domestic investment US $ millions	Foreign acquisitions US $ millions	Ratio of domestic to foreign investment
UK	128,969	44,530	2.9
Ireland	5,140	1,598	3.2
Switzerland	38,970	8,907	4.4
Canada	101,694	10,708	9.5
New Zealand	7,448	691	10.8
Australia	62,162	5,730	10.8
Sweden	30,978	2,134	14.5
France	176,525	11,162	15.8
Belgium	21,280	827	25.7
Norway	23,704	720	32.9
Netherlands	43,098	1,276	33.8
Finland	20,995	347	60.5
US	715,300	9,354	76.5
Japan	869,316	11,025	78.8
Denmark	18,825	224	84.0
Germany	231,096	2,752	84.0

Source: KPMG Peat Marwick McClintock, *Deal Watch 1989*, London 1989.

The most obvious way these trends have shown up in practice has been the tendency of the British banks to lend money to industry on terms which are completely unsuitable for long-term investment: in particular, in the form of short-term overdrafts. Until the 1970s – in contrast to the practice in Japan, France and West Germany – bank loans to British industry were made up almost entirely of overdrafts, reinforcing other characteristics of industrial firms and banks which have contributed to Britain's chronic under-investment and sluggish industrial growth. The flexibility of overdraft facilities allowed firms to avoid necessary strategic planning of investment, production and finance; while giving the banks maximum liquidity and flexibility of their assets, since overdrafts are repayable on demand. Many factors have discouraged British companies from long-term planning – such as stop–go policies, sterling crises and of course the short-term fixations of the stock exchange – but if bank loans had been available only to finance strategic production and investment plans, that would have acted as a strong influence in the opposite direction.

Another aspect of British banks' relationship with industry which has been a disincentive to long-term investment and closer involvement has been the traditional reliance on collateral in the form of charges on the borrowers' assets. While American banks, for example, tend to secure industrial loans by making agreements with borrowers on the firms' operations and cash-flow, British banks' main concern has been what happens when the firm collapses rather than how it operates when it is still up and running. That approach has been reflected in high UK bankruptcy rates.[9]

British industrial firms traditionally relied overwhelmingly on retained profits, rather than share issues or bank loans, for long-term investment. During the 1960s, for example, retained earnings were equivalent to 99 per cent of the funds British industry invested in new plant and machinery, compared with 60 per cent in France and 80 per cent in West Germany. The same phenomenon can be seen in British firms' low capital gearing: in 1972, the ratio of external debt to shareholders' capital in Britain was 55 per cent; in France it was 126 per cent and Japan 325 per cent.[10] The international economic crises of the 1970s and 1980s have brought about enormous changes in the City and the organization of the financial system, and the dramatic fall in profitability of companies operating in Britain in the 1970s led many firms to rely less on retained profits and more on bank credit.[11] But even so, in the period 1974–8, while bank loans to industry amounted to 15 per cent of the national product in Japan and 8 per cent in West Germany, in Britain they made up as little as 3 per cent.[12] A recent study of British industrial investment shows 72 per cent to have been financed by retained profits between 1970 and 1984. But if the accumulation of financial assets is excluded, all physical investment turns out to have been paid for from profits, compared with 62 per cent in France and 65 per cent in Japan. In other words, the stupendously competitive and efficient capital markets that the City likes to boast about made a zero net contribution to building up British industry in that period.[13]

During the 1980s there was a marked growth in lending to British firms by American banks and an expansion of medium-term loans with more reliance on performance conditions as security – 'cash-flow lending'. British commercial banks have followed the example of their American rivals and the dominant role of overdraft financing has to some extent been superseded. But the essential relationships have not changed. The new performance conditions used by the City do not in general involve the banks in a closer supervision of industrial capital and the conditions mostly cover the financial balance-sheet rather than the underlying production or trading position. There is still not much industrial lending for longer than five years, in marked contrast to the housing market, where pay-back periods are often twenty to thirty years. In Japan, the position is the exact reverse.

This is not to say that industry in Britain has suffered from an actual shortage of finance, as is often alleged. In the late 1980s, bank lending to British industry increased sharply to meet the growth in investment and the corporate bond market has been booming.[14] But even in the less recent past, there is little evidence that firms have not been able to lay their hands on the finance they need – either in the sense of unavailability at the going rate, or because of the disincentive of high interest rates. Despite periods of comparatively higher interest rates – such as during the 1980s – British interest rates have in general moved in line with those in New York, the Far East and the rest of Western Europe over the long run.[15] British industrial loans are usually more expensive than in other advanced capitalist countries mainly because they are short-term.

The central problem instead is that, as a result of its international role and historical evolution, City institutions have effectively played a blocking role in the development of modern industry in Britain. On the one hand, partly because of the intense competitiveness of the financial system, they have shown a chronic reluctance to become closely involved in industrial management; while at the same time they have kept industry on a drip-feed of short-term finance which has allowed firms to avoid having to turn to any other source of funds, such as the government, which could have imposed an external discipline and a strategic perspective.

The City and Government Policy

The negative effects of the City of London on the rest of the economy extend far beyond its direct lending relationship with industrial capital. The most serious and dramatic problem posed by the existence of the City in its present form is the way in which it has shaped state policies throughout the century and effectively writes the rules of the economic game for British governments. The mechanism through which the City exercises economic and thus political power is principally its control of two vital economic levers: the exchange rate and the interest rate – the price of foreign currency and the price of borrowing and lending money. Of course, the movements in these two rates are not engineered by cabals of City elders plotting in a backroom in Threadneedle Street. They are the outcome of decisions made by hundreds of dealers attempting to maximize profits in highly volatile markets.

Nevertheless, there is a clearly identifiable City interest. It is articulated politically by the Bank of England – effectively the City's representative in the state apparatus – and economically by financial institutions dealing in currencies, bonds or shares in line with rule-of-thumb indicators which reflect the constant drive by financial capital for maximum flexibility and liquidity. Short-term indicators for the health of an economy go in and out of fashion in the City. Sometimes dealers buy and sell pounds because of the state of the balance of payments; at other times because of the relation between US and UK interest rates; or because of the public sector borrowing requirement or the rate of growth of a bewildering variety of measures of the money supply. But the effect is always to force the government to toe the City's current line: if dealers believe that high public spending is a sign of economic weakness – and, crucially, think other dealers believe it – they will speculate against sterling, the exchange rate will fall, and governments then typically cut spending to restore confidence.

The underlying special interest of all City institutions is in protecting and strengthening London's role as a financial and commercial centre for the international economy. The City also has a secondary interest in ensuring that the domestic economy is regulated by financial markets rather than by planning or state intervention. But it is its pre-eminence in attracting international business that is the City's most basic objective. For much of this century, that has meant City support for high exchange rates and deflationary spending policies which have weakened Britain's industrial base and led to repeated bouts of closures, redundancies and mass unemployment. In 1925, the City ensured the pound was restored to the gold standard, heightening the problems of British export industries; in 1931 the bankers split the Labour government with their demands for more and more cuts to defend the pound; in 1947, the City saw off Labour's cheap money policy; in 1966, it forced the Wilson government into a damaging deflation to maintain an over-valued pound; in 1976, it led a run on sterling which ushered in the large-scale IMF-imposed spending cuts; and in 1979, the City found its greatest champion in Margaret Thatcher, whose abolition of exchange controls and imposition of high interest and exchange rate policies precipitated the collapse of almost a fifth of Britain's manufacturing industry in a couple of years.

Such a deflationary record has led many in the labour movement to believe that the City has an invariable objective of maintaining high exchange and interest rates. While it is true that banks generally favour higher interest rates because the greater 'spread' brings higher profits, the strategy of defending the pound has become less important since the late 1960s. The demise of the Sterling Area has meant that the international role of the City is no longer dependent on the confidence of foreign holders of sterling. During the 1970s, the focus of the City's business switched to the 'offshore' Eurodollar market which involves borrowing and lending in foreign currencies. The value of the pound is largely irrelevant to the City's dominance of this huge market. Instead, it was and is freedom from government controls, successfully fought for by the City during the post-war period, that gave London its edge in the Euromarkets.

The City's undoubted success in maintaining its position as the world's most important money market has been built on its ability to fight off any threat of government regulation or control. But that same success has given it enormous power effectively to dictate the basic economic policies of successive governments. From the beginning of the 1950s, the City made sure – in striking contrast to Japan – that interest rates were subordinated to foreign exchange policy rather than industrial policy: in other words, to short-term factors rather than a long-term strategy. Until the arrival of floating exchange rates in the early 1970s, the British economy was subjected to regular 'stop–go' deflations to defend the pound. And under the Thatcher government, the determination of policy by City concerns has been at its clearest and most damaging.

Big Bang, the Crash and the Euromarkets

The frenetic development of the City's activities during the 1980s added to the instability of the international financial system and increased the dangers and problems facing any potential Labour government – particularly one which thought it could get away with anything other than wholesale change in the way the City is run. Information technology was a major factor behind the intensified internationalization of financial markets, which was in turn the impetus behind the City of London's deregulatory 'Big Bang' of October 1986. Big Bang was essentially aimed at ensuring the City's continued dominant role in the world's stock markets and swept away many of the traditional City restrictive practices which were threatening to drive business elsewhere. Fixed stockbroking commissions were scrapped. The distinction between brokers, who bought and sold from the public, and jobbers, who traded stocks on their own account, was abolished. And outside firms – including foreign firms – were allowed into the hallowed portals of the London Stock Exchange. Before Big Bang, two companies controlled 80 per cent of the gilts market, with six others dividing the rest; after Big Bang, the total rose to twenty-seven.[16]

This latter-day 'bonfire of controls' was followed almost exactly one year later by the world's greatest financial crash since 1929. Much commentary since has stressed the continued health of the real economy – often from the same pundits who previously claimed that the financial markets were part of the real economy. But the depressive effect of the crash on the City was unmistakable. Trading in stocks and shares fell by 30 per cent in value between 1987 and 1988, and by 45 per cent in volume. 1988 ended with Morgan Grenfell, one of the City's leading merchant banks, shutting its UK securities business with the loss of hundreds of jobs following losses for the year of £4.5 million in its gilts business and £18 million in equities. That move cut the number of gilts market-makers to twenty-three, following the earlier withdrawal of giants such as Lloyds Bank and Citicorp and the Midland Bank's pull-out from the equity market. With the supply of British government bonds scheduled to shrink in 1989 and 1990 because of reduced borrowing, more firms are expected to drop out. During 1988, the Bank of England allowed two Japanese firms, Nomura Securities and Daiwa Securities, to break in to the gilts business. But it is likely that the four largest firms now account for nearly half the market, and the trend is clearly for increased concentration and centralization of capital in the City – a monopolization of power which would have to be neutralized if policies for progressive change were to be pursued seriously.

A further effect of Big Bang and the crash was an expansion of domestic consumer credit, which fuelled record balance of payments deficits. Credit expansion was given a direct boost by the sweeping away of restrictions epitomized by Big Bang – although many controls had already been lost after 1980. The removal of credit controls led to a speculative bubble around asset prices which was bound to burst sooner or later. The crash also had an indirect effect on the balance of payments problem, because it led the government to inject extra demand into the economy above the level which British industry was either willing or able to meet. This reaction was an attempt to prevent the 1987 crash bringing on a full-scale depression, as happened after the Great Crash of 1929.

The feverish speculative activity that was unleashed in the financial and securities markets by deregulation and financial globalization during the 1980s has created the most sophisticated and 'efficient' markets in the world, but it has done nothing for the construction of a modern and competitive industrial base in Britain and it has certainly increased instability in the world economy. An analysis of stock market activity and investment patterns in the most advanced capitalist countries shows that the world's most efficient stock markets – those of Britain and the US – contribute the least to their countries' investment in new plant and machinery.[17] The stock markets in New York and London were also those which were most gripped by merger-and-acquisition mania during the 1980s. British firms are highly vulnerable to hostile takeovers. Whereas, for example, in Holland majority shareholdings do not give predators the right to change the senior management, British companies have no protection and the stock market is a free-for-all. In 1987 the CBI asked the chief executives of 200 firms what factors might deflect their companies from taking investment decisions judged to be in their long-term interest. Fear of takeover was thought 'significant' or 'of major significance' by 12 per cent, with 23 per cent citing pressure from financial institutions or analysts, and 41 per cent saying they feared a weakness in their share price. The same survey revealed an increase in short-term criteria for evaluating investment projects, with the shorter investment horizons being caused in roughly equal proportion by the uncertain economic climate, high real interest rates and financial-market pressure.[18]

The influence of the stock market on industry has been a corrosive one. As one prominent industrialist put it:

> The market is such that fund managers are looking for undervalued stock to buy and overvalued stock to sell. That provides companies with little or no security. The only communication to management is through share price and p/e [price to earnings] ratio, which has proved not to be a reliable guide.[19]

The City has a further direct negative impact on the rest of the economy. Its appetite for skilled labour has 'caused severe scarcities, disruption and pay anomalies, benefiting job-hoppers and nobody else'.[20] Of 50,000 net new City jobs in 1984–7, 30,000 were filled by highly qualified experienced people, particularly experts in information technology sorely needed elsewhere in the economy.

The domination of the City's business by the Euromarkets, which first took off in the 1970s and are based on the unregulated borrowing and lending of foreign currencies outside their countries of origin, is a further source of economic instability and would pose a particular challenge to a radical Labour government. From a few millions in the late 1950s, the size of the total international Euromarkets had risen by 1988 to around US$5,300 billion, nearly a quarter of which is based in London.[21] The City is also the world's largest foreign exchange market. Much of this lending and dealing is carried out by foreign banks: there are now 500 in London out of a total of about 600.[22] But although this enormous business is not based on Britain's production or trade, that does not mean that it has no connection with the British economy.

There are a number of vital links between the Eurodollar markets and the British economy which would put them high up on the agenda for any incoming Labour government elected to carry out a radical programme of economic and social change. The expansion of the Euromarkets has massively stimulated the scale and speed of speculative dealing in major world currencies and provided a whole series of new instruments which make the import and export of capital easier. The effect on sterling has been to cause gyrations in the exchange rate – and thus the price of imports and exports – which may be unrelated to or wildly overshoot the underlying state of Britain's trade balance. The turnover on the world's main foreign exchange markets is now somewhere approaching fifty times as large as the value of international trade – and perhaps four or five times as large as it was in 1980.[23] Furthermore, 'domestic UK interest rates are bound by a golden chain, via Euromarkets, to the "world" rate of interest.'[24]

These features of the Euromarkets would cause problems for a Labour government whether they were based in London or not. But their presence in Britain causes an extra potential headache. Any attempt by a British government to impose the sort of financial regulation on sterling that would be necessary if it wanted to follow a policy of large-scale public intervention and economic restructuring would quickly undermine the attractiveness of the City as an unregulated financial centre. In this sense, the existence of the Euromarkets in Britain in their present form is incompatible with the scale of changes that need to be made in the British economy.

The First Hundred Days

The quantity of hot money daily changing hands in the international exchange markets is now not only a threat to the stability of the world economy, but has also intensified the kind of speculative pressures which have blown all Labour governments off course within a couple of years of coming to office. A radical Labour government committed to a programme of public ownership and planned economic growth would in itself be enough to send the markets into a frenzy. If such a government was also trying to reflate the economy – with or without compensating planning of the trade balance – that would be another warning light for the speculators. If there was an attempt to hold interest rates below international levels to underpin industrial restructuring, the rush from sterling would turn into a stampede. A major flight of capital from the UK would lead to a collapse in the value of the pound – cutting living standards in the process as imports became more expensive – and would ratchet up interest rates as banks struggled to stem the tide.

At the end of 1987, overseas investors in Britain owned £52 billion-worth of portfolio investments (mainly shares and government bonds) and held £44 billion in bank deposits and on the money markets in sterling, all of which could be withdrawn rapidly in a confidence crisis. Further pressure would come from foreign owners of British factories covering themselves in the 'forward' markets for exchange risk. And British residents could also be moving their money out. In the face of these enormous potential outflows, the government has foreign currency reserves of £23 billion.[25] Unless all elected governments are to accept that their main economic policies must be dictated by the financial markets, the only possible way round these problems would be through a sophisticated new package of exchange controls, as was suggested in chapter 2. Exchange controls would not be aimed at restricting in any way the balanced expansion of trade which would be a key part of any labour movement economic strategy; nor could they insulate Britain from the rest of the world economy, even if anyone was foolish enough to want to do so. They would simply be designed to regulate the country's relationship with the increasingly volatile international financial markets in a way that would make it possible to follow progressive economic and social policies at home.

There is nothing, of course, that could be done to control the probable run on the pound in advance of the election of a Labour government except to use it to demonstrate the political necessity of bringing the grip of the financial markets on the economy to an end. As Harold Wilson reported his discussion with the Governor of the Bank of England on the sterling crisis of November 1964: 'I warned him that if I went to the country on the issue of dictation by overseas financiers I would have a landslide. He said ruefully that he believed I would.'[26] It is also important to bear in mind that, as the slide in the pound continued, the cost of pulling out of sterling would escalate and eventually become self-defeating for the speculators.

But as soon as a Labour government was elected, it would have to move fast to put the new controls in place. The details of how such a system could operate are complex, but there would have to be three main building blocks.[27] First, there would need to be an end to new British portfolio investment abroad – direct investment would be treated separately – and a phased repatriation of the foreign exchange represented by existing investments. British holders of overseas securities – mostly financial institutions – could be legally required to liquidate a certain percentage of their portfolio each year and sell the proceeds to the Bank of England at the going exchange rate. The Thatcher government's abolition of exchange controls in 1979 led to a colossal outflow of funds. By the end of 1987 direct investment overseas by British residents – investment in branches, subsidiaries and associated companies – totalled £91 billion, while portfolio investments stood at £118 billion. Britain's identified external assets exceeded identified external liabilities by £90 billion.[28] Portfolio investments slumped in value by £25 billion during 1987 as a result of the dollar and stock market crashes – exposing the claim that capital export would spread risks. Control of these assets would allow compensation for nationalizing foreign capital holdings in Britain such as Ford UK or IBM, an orderly withdrawal of foreign investment from the UK, and the continuation of overseas operations in line with democratically agreed economic goals.

The second key element in an effective exchange regulation system would be legal controls on the release of both sterling and foreign currency from overseas accounts in British banks. This would involve a tightly defined separation between the 'commercial accounts' of overseas residents, which could be run up or down according to trade requirements, and 'investment accounts', which would be denied access to forward markets and would be the main channel for capital flows in and out of Britain. A dual exchange rate system could then be operated. Dealing in foreign exchange for trade purposes would take place on an official current sterling market, with the rate fixed or varied within a narrow band by government intervention. On the other hand, capital invested in Britain in marketable securities or in company subsidiaries could only be converted into foreign exchange and repatriated through an investment sterling market. Each year, the government could sell a certain quantity of foreign exchange derived from the liquidation of UK assets abroad to foreign investors who wanted to withdraw from Britain. The rate in this investment market would be freely determined by supply and demand from non-residents, and the premium on the official current rate for dollars or other foreign currencies would depend on how keen investors were to pull out.

Finally, foreign currency bank deposits by British residents would need to be restricted to trade commitments: other balances could be converted into sterling, providing the government with extra foreign exchange. The transfer abroad of either pounds or foreign currency by UK residents would also have to be shown to be for genuinely trade-related uses – as would covering for future exchange risk in the forward exchange and the financial futures markets. There would, of course, be plenty of technical difficulties about implementing a comprehensive set of capital controls. These are not principally the result of technological changes. The widespread belief in the labour movement that 24-hour round-the-world electronic exchange markets make controls impossible is wrong. In fact, electronic trading is no more of an obstacle to controls than the telephone. More serious are the spread of market innovations, such as swaps, futures and options, which make the purposes and origin of currency transactions much harder to define.[29] The fact that the Bank of England's exchange controls department was disbanded in 1979 and its 800 experienced officials dispersed also presents practical difficulties. But loopholes could be closed and teething problems overcome if the political will was there.

That would depend first of all on overcoming the fashionable view that the introduction of the sort of package of controls outlined above would somehow constitute the end of civilization as we know it. Many countries still have some form of exchange control despite the free-market fad and pressures from powerful private interests. In Sweden, for example, overseas portfolio investment was effectively banned during the 1980s. British governments operated exchange controls continuously for forty years until the arrival of Margaret Thatcher, and anyone wanting to invest overseas had to bid for a limited pool of foreign currency and pay a premium above the official exchange rate. Those controls did not prevent runs on the pound and a modern package of controls would need to be more far-reaching; while no system of exchange controls could prevent dealing in sterling by non-residents of Britain in other countries. But even Roy Jenkins, when he was Chancellor of the Exchequer in the late 1960s, agreed a secret emergency plan – code-named 'Operation Bootstrap' – which involved the compulsory acquisition by the government of all privately held overseas securities. Such a measure had only previously been adopted in wartime, but in 1968 the Treasury was ready to implement the plan at seven days' notice.[30]

There is no reason why a comprehensive system of exchange controls, which could only be a part of a much broader package of policies to regulate links with the world economy, would prevent the effective international operation of British-based companies. In fact, the only purpose of adopting them would be to allow a large-scale restructuring and modernization of the real economy free, as far as possible, from the destructive constraints of the international casino. Nor would there be any necessity for exchange controls to get in the way of foreign holidays and travel, as they did in the 1960s. Personal allowances could be made as generous as necessary, and the resulting deficit or surplus on tourism would have to be taken into account when planning levels of other imports and exports.

But such a thorough regulation of the operation of the exchange markets would mean a complete change in the relationship of the City to the international financial system. The imposition of controls would end the freedom of banks operating in the Euromarkets to switch currencies and investments as they pleased, and the likelihood is that the City's Eurodollar role would quickly be eroded. Despite some loss of dealing income, the rapid deflation of the foreign exchange balloon of foreign banks operating in London would be helpful, not least because effective controls would be easier the smaller the number of institutions involved in exchange transactions. From a broader point of view, a general withdrawal from the City's offshore role would be an essential part of the re-orientation of Britain's financial sector. Unless the Eurodollar business is explicitly run down, the City would continue to weigh its financing of trade and its lending to industry and the government against the rich management fee and interest pickings to be had from the Euromarkets. Their winding down might also help to defuse the opposition of those interests which currently judge every government policy in the light of how it affects the City's international role.[31]

Making the City Work for Society

Statutory exchange controls would essentially have to be operated on behalf of the government by the banks, as they were in the past. But whereas radical exchange controls in the 1940s were made possible by a burst of wartime patriotism and the post-war system was supported by a certain political consensus, that would hardly be the case if they were imposed by a government aiming to bring about a major shift in the balance of power and wealth in society. In such a situation, it seems highly improbable that the private banks would be prepared to act as government agents: more likely that they would be at the forefront of a City-wide effort to evade democratically-agreed policies. While a system of regulation might have been sufficient in the past, the conclusion must be that a system of comprehensive exchange controls could now only be implemented if the banking system was taken into public ownership.

But the need to bring the financial system under democratic social control goes far beyond the problems of exchange regulation. The central reason why public ownership of the banks and largest financial institutions would be an essential part of any radical programme for economic change and reconstruction is that it would be the only way to ensure that the necessary scale of investment funds are available to underpin a planned restructuring of the whole economy. Even a cursory examination of the City's relationship with British industry shows that its traditional methods of allocating funds would be hopelessly inadequate for the huge modernization programme necessary to change the direction of the British economy. The whole orientation of the City towards dealing and speculation is inimical to the needs of a major industrial investment drive. Just as Japan and many European countries took a crucial lead in co-ordinating finance and industry in their most successful periods of post-war growth, so a Labour government in the 1990s would need to guarantee that industrial planning was backed up by the necessary investment. A systematic link between long-term investment, production and financial strategies would have to be established.

But could the City perhaps be made to work for society through regulation rather than ownership? The Bank of England – itself under public ownership since 1946 – already has statutory responsibilities for banking supervision and a looser role for the financial services sector as a whole. The 1986 Financial Services Act, for example, makes it an offence to conduct investment business without authorization. Powers to give authorizations and attach conditions to them belong ultimately to the Secretary of State for Trade and Industry. But they can be delegated to the Securities and Investments Board (SIB) and the assumption underlying the Act was that the Trade and Industry Secretary would choose to do so.[32] The SIB is thus essentially a private organization with delegated statutory powers. But even if such powers were returned to government and the Bank of England's right to issue directives to the banking system were used to promote a long-term investment strategy, the giant private financial institutions have the greatest experience and most creative record of evasion of all large companies. The Bank of England is itself as much the creature of the private banking system as of the government which owns it.

The real problem is that privately-owned banks, insurance companies and independent pension funds exist to make a return on their assets for their shareholders or members, not to develop the economy in a way that benefits the majority of the people. They have no reason to believe that they will make a better return by taking the risk of a long-term commitment to an industry's development plans than by following their normal practice of maximizing short-term gains. No amount of government regulation can change that underlying reality. In practice private financial firms would anyway be unlikely to carry on as normal in an atmosphere of radical political change. At best they would want to move business to parts of the world where the interests of financial speculation were given a higher priority than producing wealth or improving the quality of life. At worst, they would deliberately undermine attempts by a Labour government to change the role of the City and by doing so inflict enormous damage on the wider economy. Of course such disruption would probably begin before the election of any progressive government took place, and legislation might therefore have to be retrospective, with the costs of past disruption paid by those responsible. But governments can move fast when they want to. The Bank of England's overnight takeover of Johnson Matthey Bankers – when threatened bankruptcy endangered the City – gave the game away as to how fast these things can be done when the will is there. The weekend of 30 September 1984 saw the Bank of England summon nearly two hundred bankers and advisers to the City. The Bank of England nationalized Johnson Matthey with the parent company being forced to pay the Bank £50 million for its trouble and twenty five other banks making £250 million available for the operation. It was all completed by 8.30 a.m. on Monday in time for the bank to open its doors with a reassuring statement for its depositors.[33]

Public ownership and control of the City is necessary both for political and economic reasons. Economically, the British economy is distorted by the size and nature of the City, even compared with other leading capitalist countries. Public ownership and control would allow a major shift of resources towards more productive uses. Politically, the City of London concentrates economic and thus political power in the hands of capital to a degree unmatched in any other part of society. Its key institutions are also in the grip of a narrow but highly influential upper-class stratum. If government policies are to be pursued in the interests of people's welfare rather than capitalist profitability, then a clash is inevitable. Negative controls – such as those applied during and after the war on new equity capital issues – could have a limited effect. But if financial institutions are to change their role fundamentally and long-term investment is to be directed in a positive way into particular industries in line with democratic priorities, then they would need to be brought under full social ownership and radically reorganized.

A common criticism of any proposals for public ownership and intervention is that markets are better than bureaucrats, and that there is no reason to think that planners could know how to pick winners. But although markets display a remarkable degree of impersonal anarchy – often wreaking havoc – they nevertheless use humans to do their dirty work for them. And while some financial dealing is now computer-controlled, causing even greater havoc, when the market decides whether to back a firm's billion-pound investment decision, it is actually individual brokers who take the decision in practice, by evaluating the proposal and advising their investing clients accordingly. It should certainly be possible for a national planning strategy – involving the workforce and consumers, local interests and public bodies – to be at least as well-informed as brokers.

Socialized Finance

Democratic ownership and control of the financial institutions could take a number of different forms. The ideal solution would be to take the whole of the City into public ownership: in other words, not just nationalize the individual firms, but the entire sector and the functions of banking and financial dealing themselves. This would actually be the simplest option. All compensation could then be handled by the newly-acquired sector itself, and progress could be made immediately towards establishing new relationships between the City and the rest of the economy. In a divided sector, effort would need to be focussed on defining the relationship between the publicly and privately owned institutions, and the newly-socialized institutions would be vulnerable to sabotage by the remaining private companies.[34]

Socializing the City would not necessarily involve the nationalization of every firm currently operating in the financial sector; nor would it simply be about the nationalization of firms. It would mean reserving the functions of finance for public enterprise. Private firms would not be allowed to operate in the sector on their own account any more than they can operate private police forces and law courts.

But just as private firms may be permitted to run police-like security services, or the law courts contract-out this or that service to the private sector, so a public financial sector would have countless connections to private firms. It is exactly such links – and the economic and political power they transmit – which are so important to have under social rather than private capitalist ownership and control. Such a proposal would certainly involve the nationalization of the big four banks – Barclays, Midland, Lloyds and National Westminster – and the major insurance and investment institutions. But some firms could be given the option of switching their operations to new areas, selling assets to the public financial sector and becoming one of the many private institutions through which the public financial sector would operate.

Foreign-owned firms would be in a special position, even if the whole financial sector was socialized. Some 520 overseas banks and financial institutions were represented in Britain in 1987 through branches, subsidiaries, representative offices and consortia. A distinction needs to be made between their strict banking business and their participation in the City's speculation on international currency and stock price movements. Foreign banks could continue with their normal basic banking functions, subject to new regulations to mesh with the new public banking sector. But most foreign banks are only operating in Britain because of its role of international casino and because of the free-for-all in the City's financial markets. The joint effect of exchange controls and bank nationalizations would be to close the casino and make Britain's financial sector more like those in most other capitalist countries. A public financial sector created from the takeover of British firms alone would be quite adequate for meeting the needs of British trade, industry and consumers. So there would be no real harm in all foreign financial institutions pulling out, and their assets could be bought by the public financial sector. The only conceivable situation in which compensation might be withheld would be if a firm had been involved in disrupting and destabilizing the economy, in which case confiscation of assets might be the only appropriate response – or, in view of the Thatcher government's requisitioning of ships during the Falklands crisis, any crisis caused by economic destabilization might be met with a similar requisitioning of assets.

Despite its attractions, nationalizing the entire financial sector is unlikely to be politically practicable in current conditions. A more plausible strategy might be to nationalize the four main clearing banks, the top British merchant banks and the largest dozen or so insurance companies. That would still leave the vast majority of financial institutions outside the public sector – which would have to operate under a new system of overall regulation of the financial markets – but it would allow the democratic control of the essential core of the financial system. It would also give the government indirect control of major shareholdings in some of the country's largest industrial companies. British commercial banks have insignificant direct shareholdings in industry. But through subsidiaries, nominee companies and control of pension funds, the Big Four, the merchant banks and the largest insurance companies control more than a quarter of the fifty largest manufacturing firms.[35] The very minimum required would be to nationalize a major company in each main component of the financial sector: one of the big four banks, say, and a major insurance company. In this case, the publicly-owned bank could link up with Investors In Industry to provide the services for which the TUC and others have advocated a British Investment Bank. But such a modest proposal could not hope properly to fulfil the main purpose of extending public ownership into the City, which would be to change its entire basis of operation and underpin a planned restructuring of British industry.

Compensation arrangements for nationalized financial institutions would have to be similar to those for other sectors, with government securities being exchanged for shares. The problem in financing public ownership is that people or institutions may not want to hold these securities, thus driving down their price, increasing interest rates and making further government security issues more difficult. If, however, a Labour government were to socialize major parts of the City, that would itself help to overcome this problem, since at least those financial institutions could no longer refuse to hold the securities issued. Although large-scale nationalizations of banks and insurance companies would be expensive – and it is always possible that the European Court of Human Rights would rule compensation insufficient – the government would not necessarily have to draw on other revenues to service the newly-issued bonds. Several of the largest insurance companies are 'mutual' organizations which means that, like building societies, they are theoretically owned by their policy holders or depositors. In practice they are run by self-perpetuating boards of directors. Socialization of such companies would therefore need some legal right for the government to nominate directors – who would be automatically elected unless a majority of the membership voted against – rather than compensation. Many large financial institutions own substantial shares in one another, and one estimate of the cost of nationalizing the fifteen top insurance companies, the clearing banks and main merchant banks put the net total in the early 1980s at £6.5 billion – or roughly two-thirds of the then military budget.[36]

Curious Accounting

A comprehensive programme of bank nationalization and controls on the City's role in capital markets would naturally provoke roars of protest from the partisans of wealth and privilege and dire warnings about the potential loss of foreign exchange earnings and the threat to the balance of payments. There is no doubt that some income would be lost, but it would be a small price to pay for the democratic control of investment and interest and exchange rates. Profits made on the international financial transactions of firms based in Britain register as invisible earnings in the balance of payments figures. Net overseas earnings of British financial institutions in 1987 were £9.4 billion.[37] The assumption that nationalizing the City would lose that sort of quantity of foreign exchange often forms the basis of arguments against a Labour government intervening in the operations of the City.

But there are a number of accounting oddities which mean that such figures need to be treated with great caution. First, the contribution from the City is inflated by a curious procedure which deducts from the earnings of City institutions their payments abroad but without deducting other payments to similar foreign institutions by companies and individuals. Thus the total of £9.4 billion is actually more of a gross than a net figure; while it is normally set against the net trade deficit in manufacturing of £6.5 billion in 1987, it is really more comparable in accounting terms to gross manufacturing exports at £62 billion in 1987. Second, the figures claim all interest, profits and dividends paid through City institutions as City earnings. But it cannot be meaningful to attribute the return on the savings of people throughout the economy entirely to the City. And while the alternative convention – used in the national accounts – of treating all City earnings as straightforward transfers might underestimate its contribution, it certainly should not be credited with the full £9.4 billion figure.

Finally, financial entries tend to dominate the invisibles section of the balance of payments – the catch-all category of financial and other services which recorded a £9.9 billion surplus for 1987 against a smaller surplus for services as a whole of only £5.6 billion.[38] Reference is therefore sometimes made to the importance of invisibles as if they only came from the operations of the City. But it is important to bear in mind that many industries which could be encouraged and expanded through public ownership also earn large invisible earnings. In 1987, for example, British shipping contributed £1.3 billion to the balance of payments in spite of the huge decline in the industry. In 1980 the industry was twice the size it was by the end of the decade, and the contribution to the balance of payments was correspondingly almost twice as large measured at constant prices. In 1987, the UK paid £1.6 billion net in foreign exchange to foreign shipping companies to carry freight and passengers to and from the UK. So invisible earnings are certainly important. But there are many sources for them other than accumulating interest payments from heavily indebted Third World countries and servicing the global financial markets.

A more accurate estimate of the level of foreign exchange earnings that might be at risk from a radical restructuring of the City's role would be the net overseas earnings of the banking part of the City's operations, which in 1987 stood at £1.4 billion – down from £2.3 billion as recently as 1984.[39] Most of this income, over half of which is made up of commissions and fees and the rest the margin between funds lent and borrowed overseas, would have to be replaced. But at less than 2 per cent of total exports, it should not be difficult to make up as part of a dynamic expansion and investment programme in the whole economy. Nor should it be forgotten that many services which are usually thought of as City operations – particularly in commercial banking and insurance – could continue to flourish and earn foreign currency under an entirely new system of ownership and regulation.

A publicly-owned banking sector could be integrated with a public information technology sector to provide a radically transformed level of bank services, including electronic fund transfer at the point of sale, 'smart cards' with built-in micro-chips, and home banking through Minitel-type terminals operating on a national integrated services digital network.[40] Much has been written about information technology and the City. Computers crashed at the launch of Big Bang – a sweet revenge for the computer industry against the City which has done so little over the years to provide finance for its development – and brokers refused to answer their telephones when the market was in free-fall. But there is a more serious connection. The City has played a retrogressive role in hindering the development of an integrated services digital network, putting pressure on British Telecom to concentrate instead on providing the City with its own personalized services. A publicly-owned financial sector could work to develop the information technology sector rather than ignore or distort it. Expanding banking services could help to ensure that the whole of the growing public sector core of industry and services is properly funded for research and development, training and other investment, and operates at the forefront of the new technologies in its dealings with consumers and other public sector organizations. And by fully using information technology to provide more advanced services, the publicly-owned financial sector could replace its parasitic role of exporter of capital and debt collector with one based on positive trade, exporting the know-how and equipment for modern banking services.

The International Debt Crisis

In 1988 the flow of capital between the advanced capitalist countries and the Third World amounted to US$43 billion. This figure does not represent a two-way flow. Nor does it represent a net flow of 'aid' or new loans to the Third World. It represents a net transfer of wealth from the Third World to the advanced capitalist countries – via their banking system. This was the fifth successive year in which net financial flows were in this direction, bringing the cumulative total since 1983 to US$143 billion transferred from poor to rich. It represents interest payments on loans, plus repayments of the loans themselves – the principal – minus new lending. The US$43 billion figure for 1988 was the largest net flow of resources away from the debt-ridden countries since the debt crisis first broke in 1982. But the money did not reduce indebtedness. On the contrary, those countries were further in debt after that net loss of resources than they were before, because for many their repayments did not even cover the interest due. So the total debt rose during the year by US$39 billion, to stand at US$1,320 billion by the end of 1988.

Despite claims during the late 1980s that the international debt crisis was under control, the schemes attempted so far have amounted to little more than re-arranging deck-chairs on the Titanic, and usually involving increased deck-chair charges in the process. In 1988 the Massachusetts Institute of Technology economist Rudiger Dornbusch argued that market-based mechanisms, such as debt-equity swaps or buy-backs, could at best be only a small part of the solution, and that instead some concession from lenders would be required. His policy proposal – for 'interest rescheduling', in the form of a debt-equity swap applied to interest payments rather than to the principal – represents little more than an alternative method of maintaining the debts. But a growing body of academic opinion is at least recognizing that free market approaches will not work and actually threaten to destabilize the free market itself. Even the US government – with its 'Brady Plan' for debt reduction to be financed by the World Bank and the IMF – has finally begun to move on the issue.

More radical measures were advocated by the Brundtland Report.[41] This was drawn up by a Commission put together at the request of the UN Secretary General by Norway's Prime Minister Gro Harlem Brundtland. The report put the debt crisis in a global context, recognizing the links between economic, developmental and environmental issues, and proposed new forms of international cooperation to tackle the whole crisis. While careful to base its recommendations 'on the realities of present institutions, on what can and must be accomplished today', the Commission highlighted the waste of natural resources which are not being used for development, but to meet the financial demands of creditors in the industrialized countries:

> To require relatively poor countries to simultaneously curb their living standards, accept growing poverty, and export growing amounts of scarce resources to maintain external creditworthiness reflects priorities few democratically elected governments are likely to be able to tolerate for long.[42]

Many Third World countries are being forced to sell off their limited natural resources to pull themselves out of debt and are in the process exacerbating the ecological crisis. The Netherland's Deputy Prime Minister Rudolf de Korte even proposed that Brazil's US$115 billion be swapped for an international project to save the Amazon rain forest.[43]

The Cuban leader, Fidel Castro, has long called for these debts to be cancelled, arguing that deteriorating terms of trade for the debtor countries, combined with rising interest rates and an overvalued US currency have added several tens of billions of dollars to the amounts due to be repaid. Creditor countries' governments could redirect resources away from military spending towards reimbursing their banks.[44] In his December 1988 United Nations speech Mikhail Gorbachev announced cancellation or a 100-year moratorium of the least developed countries' debts to the Soviet Union – along with the more publicized military cuts. These debts from twenty-two Third World countries run into several scores of billions of roubles. He argued that the accumulated debt could not in any case be either repaid or recovered on the initial terms. Third World debt to the Soviet Union is of course small in comparison with those to the capitalist states. But for developing countries in hock to Western banks, Gorbachev proposed a multilateral agreement to limit debt repayments according to each country's level of development, and the rescheduling of part of such payments; as well as the establishment of an international debt-takeover agency to buy loans at a discount.

The grinding indebtedness of developing countries is one of the greatest scandals of the late twentieth century. Debt has now taken over from direct investment as the most important way in which Western capital extracts surplus from the Third World. Bank profits are being swollen by hunger and misery in Latin America and Africa, and British banks have grown fat with the rest. There is wide international pressure to tackle the debt crisis. Concrete policy options have been developed. The problem is not, unfortunately, that Britain is not doing enough. Britain is already playing a highly active role – as a major debt collector, opposing those who are seeking solutions. If a Labour government were to succeed in simply neutralizing the role of Britain by taking the major institutions of the City into public ownership, that in itself would be a breakthrough in favour of those forces seeking progressive solutions to the debt crisis.

But a publicly-owned and controlled financial sector could also be used positively: helping to stimulate the international effort to construct a new international economic order, undertaking some of the technical work of debt assessment and cancellation or rescheduling, and participating in the establishment of an international debt-takeover agency. The question of how to cancel or radically restructure Third World debt to British banks needs, as Ken Livingstone has argued, to be brought to the front of Labour's agenda.[45] These outstanding debts represent, after all, book-keeping entries, and there are a variety of ways in which the bulk could be written off with government support. The French Socialist government's decision in the spring of 1989 to cancel £1.5 billion-worth of debt owed by thiry-five African countries to French banks is exactly the sort of imaginative move that could be taken further by a Labour government. Such a step would not solve the problems of the debtor countries, but it would have a highly positive political effect which could push other countries to act.

Conclusion

Proposals for the public ownership of the financial system have had a chequered history in the labour movement, but they have picked up some unlikely supporters over the years. Labour's deputy leader, Roy Hattersley, for example, is on record as supporting the nationalization of the banks.[46] Public ownership is not a panacea – for the financial institutions or any other company for that matter. When the Mitterrand government nationalized thirty-eight private banks in 1982, it was little more than a sop to the left and no effort was made to change the banks' role; nor was there any modification of the banks' legal duty to operate on a strictly commercial basis.[47] The only sense in nationalization is to change the way the financial institutions work in a fundamental way: and that would be its thrust as part of a radical Labour programme.

The City does not play as big a role in the real economy – in the sense of its contribution to jobs or national income – as is recorded by many of the official measures.[48] The role which it does play is widely recognized as being detrimental to the long-term development of British industry and obstructive to any government policies which reflect interests other than those of finance capital. The existence and character of the City of London is in no way an inevitable consequence or requirement of having a capitalist economic system. All countries require banking and insurance services. And all capitalist countries have some stock market arrangements. But no other country in the world has such a dominant financial sector, nor such a destructive stock market. Japan has built up a pivotal financial base, but Tokyo's role in international stock and currency markets involves nothing like the relationship between financial capital, industrial capital and government that exists in Britain. The only comparable case is the US, also suffering relative economic decline. But even there the financial sector could not be said to exert the same kind of overall dominance. Removing the problem of the City through policies of public ownership and control would not make Britain some sort of odd country out: it would remove one of Britain's major peculiarities.

Notes

1. Harold Wilson, *The Labour Government 1964–70*, London 1971.

2. Data from Central Office of Information, *Britain 1989 – An Official Handbook*, London 1989; Central Statistical Office, *United Kingdom National Accounts*, London 1987; and *Department of Employment Gazette*, May 1989.

3. The following argument draws on the analysis in Jerry Coakley and Laurence Harris, *The City of Capital*, Oxford 1983; and Ben Fine and Laurence Harris, *The Peculiarities of the British Economy*, London 1985.

4. In the late 1980s, activity in the gilts market fell dramatically as the Tory government used privatization proceeds to pay off debt.

5. Figures from Jerry Coakley, 'The Internationalisation of Banking Capital', *Capital and Class* 23, Summer 1984.

6. In the late 1980s, British banks scaled down their overseas exposure, mainly as a result of getting their fingers burned lending to Third World countries during the previous decade. For example, while 39 per cent of Barclays' profits in 1981 came from its international division, by 1988 – after its pull-out from South Africa – that had fallen to 15 per cent; and the comparable figure for National Westminster was down to 20 per cent. These lower proportions also reflected the strength of lending to the UK economy.

7. *The Economist*, 16 May 1987.

8. The main consumers of gilts are insurance companies and pension funds rather than the banks.

9. Overdraft financing secured by charges has mainly been characteristic of the 'Big Four' commercial banks, rather than the merchant banks, which have had a greater involvement with industry's financial restructuring.

10. Ben Fine and Laurence Harris, *The Peculiarities of the British Economy*, London 1985, p. 135.

11. See the 'Wilson Report' (*Report of the Committee to Review the Functioning of Financial Institutions*, 1980), which showed that whereas in 1958–62 10 per cent of investment funds came from bank loans, that had risen to 24 per cent by 1973–7.

12. Quoted in Richard Minns, *Take Over the City*, London 1982.

13. Colin Mayer, 'New Issues in Corporate Finance', Centre for Economic Policy Research, *Discussion Paper* 181, 1987. These percentages do not take account of other services provided by the financial sector.

14. Bank lending to UK industrial and commercial companies rose from about £12 billion in 1985 to £23 billion in 1988, while personal lending also registered large increases. See the *Bank of England Quarterly Bulletin*, May 1989.

15. See also the surveys in Laurence Harris, Jerry Coakley, Martin Croasdale and Trevor Evans, eds, *New Perspectives on the Financial System*, London 1988, showing that City margins are also not high by international standards.

16. See John Kay and John Vickers, 'Regulatory Reform in Britain', *Economic Policy* 7, pp. 286–343, October 1988; 'Changes in the Stock Exchange', *Bank of England Quarterly Bulletin*, 1985, and 'Changes in the Stock Exchange and Regulation of the City', *Bank of England Quarterly Bulletin*, 1987. Also Charles Goodhart, 'The Economics of "Big Bang" ', *Midland Bank Review*, 1987.

17. Colin Mayer, 'New Issues in Corporate Finance', Centre for Economic Policy Research, *Discussion Paper* 181, pp. 10–13.

18. David Goodhart and Charles Grant, *Making the City Work*, Fabian Society Tract 528, London 1988.

19. Ian Butler, quoted in the *Independent*, 24 February 1989.

20. London Human Resource Group and Institute of Management Studies, cited in the *Independent*, 22 September 1988.

21. *Bank of England Quarterly Bulletin*, May 1988.

22. Margaret Reid, *All-Change in the City*, London 1988.

23. See figures in Susan Strange, *Casino Capitalism*, Oxford 1986; Margaret Reid, *All-Change in the City*, 1988; and *Euromoney* magazine, May 1988.

24. Andrew Glyn, 'Capital Flight and Exchange Controls', *New Left Review* no. 155, January/February 1986, p. 37.

25. Central Statistical Office, *United Kingdom Balance of Payments*, London 1988, table 9.1; Central Statistical Office, *Financial Statistics,* London March 1989, tables 10.3, 10.4.

26. Harold Wilson, *The Labour Government 1964–70*, London 1971, p. 66.

27. The following proposals draw on the work done by Andrew Glyn reported in 'Capital Flight and Exchange Controls', *New Left Review*, no. 155, January/February 1986; and 'A Case for Exchange Controls', University of Oxford Institute of Economics and Statistics, *Applied Economics Discussion Paper*, no. 36, 1987.

28. Central Office of Information, *Britain 1989: An Official Handbook*, London 1989, p. 396.

29. See the argument in David Goodhart and Charles Grant, *Making the City Work*, Fabian Society Tract no. 528, London 1988.

30. Clive Ponting, *Breach of Promise – Labour in Power, 1964–70*, London 1989, pp. 373–4. Thanks to Ken Livingstone for drawing this story to the authors' attention.

31. See the argument in Jerry Coakley and Laurence Harris, *The City of Capital*, Oxford 1983.

32. For further details see the article by John Kay and John Vickers in *Economic Policy*, October 1988.

33. As described by John Plender and Paul Wallace, *The Square Mile*, London 1985.

34. The nationalization of the banking function itself was, roughly speaking, the strategy that was followed after the 1974 Portuguese revolution – with the difference

that the Portuguese banking system was a lot smaller and its banks owned key parts of industry.

35. See the detailed argument in Richard Minns, *Take Over the City*, London 1982, pp. 65–76.

36. Richard Minns, *Take Over the City*, London 1982.

37. Central Office of Information, *Britain 1989: An Official Handbook*, London 1989, p. 373.

38. Central Statistical Office, *United Kingdom Balance of Payments*, London 1988, table 3.1.

39. Central Statistical Office, *United Kingdom Balance of Payments*, London 1988, table 6.1; the appropriateness of this measure is argued in Andrew Glyn, 'Capital Flight and Exchange Controls', *New Left Review* no. 155, January/February 1986, p. 47. The figure includes the overseas earnings of the foreign subsidiaries of British banks, but is net of the earnings of overseas banks in the UK.

40. See chapter 7 for a discussion of both Minitel and the integrated services digital network.

41. World Commission on Environment and Development, *Our Common Future*, Oxford 1987.

42. World Commission on Environment and Development, *Our Common Future*, Oxford 1987, p. 75.

43. *Guardian*, 14 March 1989.

44. Fidel Castro, *Nothing Can Stop the Course of History*, New York 1986.

45. See Ken Livingstone, *Livingstone's Labour*, London 1989.

46. 'I have always been in favour of public ownership of the banks. I have always been in favour of a major revision of what we'll loosely call the City of London.' Roy Hattersley, interview with Chris Mullin, *Tribune*, 29 July 1983.

47. See Paul Fabra, 'Banking Policy under the Socialists', in Howard Machin and Vincent Wright, eds, *Economic Policy and Policy-Making under the Mitterrand Presidency 1981–84*, London 1985. The French banking system was already predominantly in the public sector before 1982.

48. The majority of jobs recorded by the government's *Employment Gazette* as being in 'banking, finance and insurance' actually turn out to be in property or a catch-all 'business services', which includes telephone sterilizers, market researchers, private detectives and architects. See David Goodhart and Charles Grant, *Making the City Work*, Fabian Society Tract no. 528, London 1988, p. 7.

7

Planning the Digital Economy

The same bourgeois mind which praises division of labour in the workshop denounces every conscious attempt to socially control and regulate the process of production.

Karl Marx, 1867[1]

The industrial challenge for a Labour government in the 1990s would be twofold. A progressive administration would be aiming first of all to establish a presence in the key new sectors where private enterprise and the market have left the country without a strong enough base to build an advanced economy of the future – such as consumer electronics, computing and electronic components. But it would also need to concentrate on regenerating and modernizing the traditional core of British industry which has been systematically eroded, including the motor industry and engineering. These two strands are far from being alternatives, as they are sometimes presented. On the contrary, a domestic base in advanced electronic technology and equipment is essential to the modernization of the traditional core of British industry in a way that does not create a strain on the balance of payments.

It is not necessary to have a presence in every industrial sector regardless of strategic importance or cost. But it is essential that Britain have a broad industrial base if living standards and employment are to be secure in the future. The strategy followed by the

Thatcher governments of relying on financial services and high value-added niche markets in what is left of industry was already coming unstuck by the end of the 1980s.

Telecommunications

Telecommunications is a key to Britain's future capacity in high technology and a major employer, with 300,000 people working in the sector. It accounts for around 3 per cent of Gross Domestic Product (GDP), a figure likely to rise above 5 per cent over the coming decade. Government policy, based on the 1981 and 1984 Telecommunications Acts, has been geared towards maximizing the role of the market in the industry. This has had disastrous effects for British telecommunications, in terms of equipment, trade and services to ordinary users. In the late 1980s a marked deterioration in the quality of service was only reversed after a public outcry at the number of phone-booths not working, wrong numbers, delays in repairs and installations forced stronger – albeit still weak – regulatory intervention. These problems were in great part a consequence of the cuts in the workforce rushed through to please shareholders, and of giving priority to the demands of the City for specialized telecommunications, at the expense of the majority of users. This policy hit the regions especially hard. While public sector monopoly provision in Europe has always benefited less developed regions, the shift as a result of deregulation and privatization has been most marked in Britain where the provision of new telecommunications services in the peripheral, less favoured areas of the country is increasingly in doubt.[2]

The pursuit of short-term profit by a privatized British Telecom (BT) has also led it systematically to choose to buy in technology – either in the form of imports or from foreign-owned transnational corporations operating in Britain – rather than develop it in-house. While in the 1970s BT offered several thousand apprenticeships a year, by 1988 they had been cut back to a few hundred.[3] Britain's trade position in telecommunications suffered a dramatic collapse during the 1980s. The attempt to justify the privatization of BT by pointing to wider share ownership looks increasingly threadbare. The stock market crash of October 1987 took the shine off share ownership in general. More strikingly, share ownership of BT had already fallen from 2.3 million at the time of privatization in 1984 to 1.3 million by March 1988. At the same time, 84 per cent of the company was owned in blocks of shares of 1 million or larger – hardly people's capitalism!

The old consensus and the changing technical base

Traditionally, telecommunications consisted of the provision of a very limited range of services – principally telephones and telex – on a general and uniform basis throughout a given territory. In all countries this was organized as a monopoly: though there might be several different companies or organizations covering different parts of the country, as in Denmark or Portugal, only one would have the monopoly in each region. This was because, even from a capitalist point of view, it was accepted that telecommunications could be provided more efficiently as a single national network than by allowing competition. The irrationality of having several companies digging up the roads to install identical cables was obvious, as was the need to avoid the construction of parallel networks. This logic was seen to apply to telecommunications in the same way as it does to railways. So the concern to provide telecommunications to users on a cheap and efficient basis overrode the pressure to allow companies a free share of the profits to be made in the sector. Apart from the US – where the company AT&T was granted a private monopoly, subject to government regulation – all major countries went further and nationalized telecommunications.

From the sixties onwards this consensus began to be undermined, first in the US and later in Europe and Japan, under the influence of technical changes. The first change was the increase in the number of possible services. Over recent years a large range of terminals, networks and services have been developed. The most widespread new terminals are answering machines and fax machines. An example of a new service is electronic data interchange, or EDI. This involves replacing paper documentation with electronic messages for communications between different organizations, typically covering orders, bills and customs declarations. The rationale is that these are now usually handled by computer within each firm, and then sent by post, or at any rate on paper, between firms. By establishing standards for this kind of communication, it is possible to link up the computer systems of the different firms, leading to major savings in speed and cost. In Britain around 1,600 companies were using EDI by late 1988, an increase of 100 per cent on the previous year. The implications of EDI run deep. If near-instantaneous ordering of raw materials and components becomes possible, this makes it possible for firms to keep very low levels of stocks, provided they are sure of their suppliers' reliability; and it encourages a much closer and tighter integration of production throughout the whole economy. The information flows between firms grow dramatically, in extent and detail, and come to rival the flows within firms. The boundaries of the firm are thereby called into question. The management of the integrated production process of the economy by a series of independent firms – under separate ownership – becomes increasingly irrational.

The second and associated technical change affecting the telecommunications sector has been its increasing convergence with computing. The last decade has seen the accelerating introduction of a new kind of telephone exchange. These digital exchanges are really large computers which are assigned the specialized task of connecting telephone callers to each other – 'switching' calls. All the information is stored and transmitted in digital form. At the same time more and more users of the network are handling information in digital form in computers outside the network, and are hooking up these computers to each other through the network to operate many different kinds of communications service. The new telecommunications services which are developing involve computing as an essential part of their functioning. They lie in a sense in between telecommunications and computing. This means that it is becoming, and will continue to become, ever more difficult to distinguish between the two sectors of telecommunications and computing. They now use the same basic technology, and more and more functions can either be performed inside the telecommunications network, or outside it by computers, as a matter of user choice.

So two sectors – computing and telecommunications – are converging to become a single sector of information technology. Computing has traditionally been competitive in the sense that any firm can produce and sell computers without requiring the state's permission; whereas telecommunications has traditionally been a strict state monopoly. As the borderline between the two sectors has been eroded, decisions have had to be taken as to whether to extend the state monopoly to include areas of computing, or to extend the area of competition to include areas of telecommunications.

This question has been raised for modern capitalism over the past decade, during a period of resurgence of right-wing market ideology, especially in Britain and the US. This matter of timing has determined the answers given in these two countries, and has had a great influence over the solutions adopted elsewhere as well. Britain has adopted the most extreme solution, of allowing competition between BT and Mercury right down to the level of provision of service to local subscribers, so that the companies actually lay competing sets of cables, reminiscent of the competing railroad companies laying competing tracks side by side in the last century. No other country has gone down this road and Britain looks increasingly out of line in this respect. Many other solutions have been proposed or adopted in other countries, but two general points are crucial. First, the option of returning to the previous situation – state monopoly for telecommunications but private competition for computing – no longer exists, since the two sectors cannot now be disentangled. But second, the tendency to opt in favour of competition owes more to the international right-wing offensive under way at the time the decisions had to be taken, than to the nature of the case and the imperatives of technology. As the hi-tech consultancy Logica acknowledged:

> Liberalization is not just a neutral response to new technology, but is driven also by political changes which favour private as opposed to public provision, and competitive rather than monopolistic, as basic principles.[4]

Convergence essentially creates two possibilities – the extension of the strengths and weaknesses of monopoly and planning to the computer sector, or the extension of the strengths and weaknesses of competition and the market to the telecommunications sector. On the one hand, it has become increasingly important to make advanced telecommunications available throughout society, to small as well as large organizations, in the home as well as in the workplace. This is important in order to bring the whole economy and society into the information age and prevent the development of two nations: the information-rich and the information-poor. At the same time, there now exist a range of sophisticated telecommunications services whose use can only be envisaged in the short and medium term by large, advanced technology organizations. It is important that these should also be made available if productivity is to be enhanced in the economy as a whole, and especially in such sectors as publishing and financial services.

Large users already understand the new communications technologies, and want maximum flexibility in access to the network. It matters less to them if network integrity and end-to-end compatibility of services are subverted by this freedom, because they will still be able to ensure these goals within their own internal, coherent communications plans. And if their smaller competitors have their communications strategies thrown into disarray by the resulting chaos in public networks and standards – of the kind that has emerged recently in the US – so much the better. It is these large users who are the main political force behind telecommunications deregulation. Their relative preponderance in Britain, particularly in the City of London, has ensured that the Thatcher governments have deregulated telecommunications further than any other country.

As far as the majority of users are concerned, however, the importance of network integrity, standards and compatibility cannot be overstated. Technology would allow a dramatic improvement in the speed and convenience with which information can be exchanged in society. Yet typically, even firms and organizations which have computerized their internal operations rely on the post or talking on the phone to communicate with other organizations. Messages and documents prepared at the speed of light are then delivered by post at five or ten miles an hour. This is because it is usually extremely difficult, prohibitively expensive and unreliable to get a computer or software supplied by one company to talk to a computer or software supplied by a different company. A public standards policy could tackle this sort of problem, permitting rapid linking-up of the different systems being installed in all the different work-sites.

While Britain has been privatizing and creating a confusion of different systems and standards in telecommunications, France has taken the lead in the size and the quality of its telecommunications network, on the basis of planned, state-owned development. The size of the French network overtook Britain's in 1983 (see Figure 7.1); and it now embodies the highest proportion of modern, digital exchanges of any country in the world.

A 1989 survey by the British regulatory agency Oftel showed that France has the cheapest telephone service of the four major West European countries. The cost of the service to residential subscribers in France is 78 per cent and to business users 85 per cent of the cost

Figure 7.1
France Overtakes Britain in Telephones

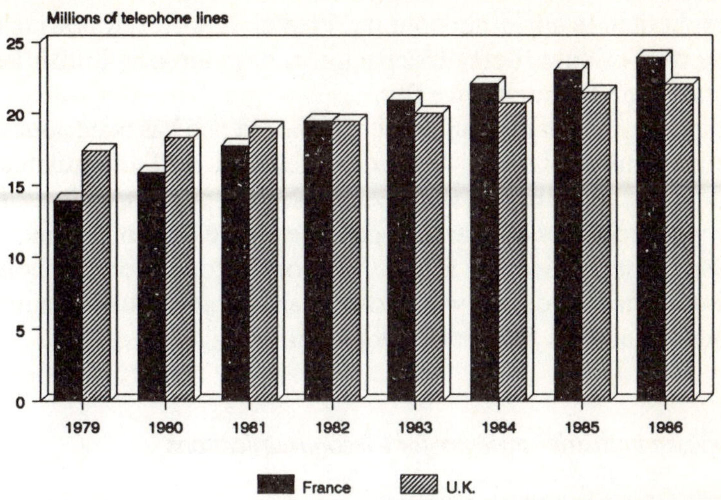

Source: ITU, *Yearbook of Telecommunication Common-carrier Statistics*, Geneva 1988. Size of telephone network measured as total number of connections.

in the UK. As *Telecommunications* magazine notes: 'It is significant, perhaps, that prices closely followed the level of digital exchanges and transmission equipment, but did not follow the level of deregulation. France has the most modern digital network in Europe.'[5]

A central aspect of the successful French approach has been the policy of provision of advanced communications to the general public. The Télétel service, often called Minitel after the name of its terminals, is on the technical level the French equivalent of the British Prestel. They are both versions of the videotex service, which makes it possible to receive and send information from a cheap computer terminal along telephone lines, and to use this possibility for electronic mail, home shopping and banking, and consulting databases.

Technically the systems may be equivalent, but their introduction strategies have made Minitel a resounding success, while Prestel has been a failure. By early 1989 France Télécom had already installed over 4.5 million Minitels (more than half the videotex terminals in the whole world) free of charge in French homes. Initially they were meant to replace telephone directories, but they immediately gave access to a wide range of services – over 10,000 by early 1989. Eventually they are likely to be in the majority of homes, giving the French an access to information incomparably more comprehensive and rapid than in any other country. Prestel, however, following the commercial-oriented demand-led approach favoured by British Telecom, has been a comparative flop.

Ironically, this planned approach by the French has been a success even in commercial terms – the extra telephone traffic stimulated by Minitels has amply repaid the free distribution of the terminals. But this commercial success was only possible on the basis of a monopoly of telecommunications by France Télécom. Information technology has thus reached the stage where state planning and public ownership will be crucial to its further development.

A proposed industrial structure for telecommunications

The telecommunications sector is made up of three distinct kinds of organization:

- the network providers (principally British Telecom, plus Mercury, Cellnet, Racal Vodafone, and the City of Kingston-upon-Hull, which was never brought under the post office monopoly): with around 250,000 employees;
- the new and very international 'value-added service' providers (such as the British Reuters, and the American GE Information Systems[6] and IBM): employing about 15,000 workers;
- the equipment industry (GEC–Plessey Telecommunications – GPT; Standard Telephone & Cable – STC; Ferranti; plus various smaller manufacturers): with 40,000 employees.

In spelling out a possible structure for the public development of the telecommunications sector, separate considerations would need to apply to the network providers, to the value-added service providers and to the equipment industry.

The network It seems natural and makes economic sense to be able to send information through the network in digital form – 'end-to-end digital connectivity' – and the network must allow a wide range of different kinds of equipment to communicate with one another. This requires the definition and imposition of common rules. A large number of essentially arbitrary decisions about exactly how the data is to be coded and transmitted have to be standardized, which means that a standard for a digital network allowing the integration of services has to be defined. And this standard must be the same, even internationally, if smooth and efficient communications are to be possible in the future. In railways it was this realization that led to the standardization on four foot eight-and-a-half inch gauge track, and the eventual abandonment of, for example, seven foot track on the Great Western Railway. For digital telephony, a standard has been developed internationally and is still being refined. It is called the integrated services digital network (ISDN), and is currently being introduced, at least in pilot stage, in most advanced countries. Defining such a common form of access to new services benefits all but the very largest users of telecommunications, such as large banks or IBM, who would prefer to have their own customized but incompatible standards.

The most important change, as the National Communications Union urged in a submission to Labour's 1988–9 policy review, is that BT:

> must be brought back into social ownership and control. We need strong central direction of telecommunications in the public interest. Profits should be ploughed back into developing a modern, efficient service, playing a full role in an integrated European digital system.... The way BT plc uses its profits in terms of research and development, social policy and regional development will have significant effects on British society. Telecommunications and information technology must be viewed on a world scene so that the way that British Telecom responds to this world challenge will, in a number of very important areas, determine Britain's overall position within the world economy. In short, British Telecom is too important to be left in private hands and subject to private control. BT must be brought back into social ownership and control immediately on the return of the next Labour government.[7]

For the provision of basic network functions, Mercury should be reintegrated with British Telecom. There is no economic logic in having competition in the basic network. This is evident from the fact that the Office of Telecommunications (Oftel, the official regulatory body) has had to step in and change the rules in Mercury's favour every time that it has proved unable to compete with the dominant BT. This monopoly of basic network and service provision should also extend to the basic services of voice, dedicated data networks, telex, and, in time, the ISDN and still more advanced broadband telecommunications networks. A new category of 'new universal services' should also be defined for general provision. This would refer to services such as videotex or – with far greater ultimate significance – ISDN. They will be critical to the adoption of advanced production and communication methods throughout the economy, and at the same time essential to avoid the development of two information nations in Britain – the information-rich, plugged into the new networks, and the information-poor, forced to rely on older methods of communications and increasingly excluded.

These new universal services should be provided exclusively by British Telecom, with targets defined for national and regional provision of these services, with the fulfilment of these targets a condition for the retention of the monopoly by BT in each area:

> BT brought back into social ownership would be in a unique position to extend significantly the availability of information throughout the community. In particular it should be required to develop a comprehensive public information system which would be operated at local level so that it would be nearer to the community it serves. By being outward looking, BT would also be able to encourage new forms of consumer representation, for example, through pensioner groups, tenants' associations, the unwaged, child action groups etc., and not rely solely on existing consumer groups which tend to be middle class dominated.[8]

In an age when electronic access to information is becoming increasingly important for all, these will be the electronic libraries of the future, and should be provided on the same basis of need as libraries are today.

Value-added service providers Other value-added services – over and above what is covered by new universal services – would typically include the provision of information services, databases and electronic publishing, ticket reservation systems, remote medical diagnosis, home banking, electronic data interchange (EDI). Since most value-added services are transformations of functions currently carried out on the basis of older technologies, it makes sense that they should continue to be performed by the same organizations – the NHS, banks, theatres, industrial companies – using information technologies. This will in different cases imply their provision on a monopoly or a competitive basis, by public or private organizations.

A policy such as this should at the same time allow an increase in the coherence and interoperability of different systems, through the integration of Mercury into BT as a single network provider, a strict standards policy, and the extension of uniform provision up through the layers of the Open Systems Interconnection (OSI) model[9] to the point where divergent needs apply. Diversity should be encouraged at the higher (service and application) levels of communication, where needs and requirements really differ. But diversity descends into fruitless chaos when it is dogmatically imposed at the lower, purely telecommunications-orientated layers of communication.

An example of the type of diversity which should be encouraged would be the viewdata services increasingly offered by local authorities, and promoted by the Local Authority Viewdata Association. The information side of the service can perfectly well be run at local level and there is no reason at all why it should be the prerogative of any single organization such as British Telecom. But the network should be run by British Telecom. The only reason why local authorities and others are being pushed to try and establish their own networks is the current strategy of British Telecom, which designs its tariffs and service provision to capture the large business market at the expense of its service to the rest of society.

A strategy for the 1990s would be based on an overall planned approach, with large-scale investment required before these services have any adequate networks to run on in the first place. But it would also allow a multiplicity of organizations – including British Telecom (incorporating Mercury); local government; nationalized, co-operative and private firms; public libraries; universities, polytechnics and other colleges; community and voluntary sector organizations – to offer a wide range of information and telecommunications services on the new networks.

The equipment industry The merging of the telecommunications interests of the two major British manufacturers into GEC–Plessey Telecommunications (GPT) in 1987 was long overdue. In a sense it occurred too late. Under present circumstances GPT is not seen as a credible world-scale supplier of the core business areas of telecommunications – notably digital switches, meaning System X in the case of GPT – where it is estimated that 'the new digital systems need to secure 8 per cent of the world market in order to break even' and justify the huge outlay on research and development involved.[10]

To reverse this situation, GPT should be brought into common ownership – whatever the outcome of the attempted takeovers as of the summer of 1989 – and set the key strategic task of developing a British capacity in the development and production of the primary coming technologies: broadband switching for the short to medium term, optical switching and processing for the medium to long term. This should leave open the possibility of collaboration with overseas switch manufacturers if GPT is shown not to be large enough to finance the development of future generations of switches alone. A publicly owned sector stands more chance of participating on equal terms in such collaboration.

The nationalization of GEC and the full use of its research resources would be a key element in the revival of Britain's high-technology capacity. First, the preponderance of GEC within the sector in Britain means that any strategy must give it a central role – with the implication that a strategy of public ownership to develop state-funded and planned acceleration of research in high technology areas must involve its nationalization. Second, the negative strategies hitherto pursued by GEC – diverting resources to its huge cash mountain, developing production abroad if anywhere, and switching resources from civil to military production – mean that a drastic reorientation of its capacities should be a top priority. That could most efficiently be achieved by bringing it under direct social ownership and control. The convergence process means that it is impossible to draw a hard and fast line between research and development in electronics, in computing and in telecommunications. This adds to the importance of bringing into public ownership a firm which already integrates two of these three converging sectors.

Integrated broadband communications

A still more far-reaching development is on the horizon – one which will transform the network, services and equipment industry and whose effects will extend far beyond telecommunications: broadband communications. Just as telecommunications has been converging with computing, it is now starting to converge with broadcasting.

Telecommunications has always been about narrowband, interactive communications, and broadcasting about broadband, one-way communications. But technical change – digitization and fibre optic cables – means that telecommunications is becoming broadband, while new cable TV systems, installed mainly to distribute TV, are capable of interactivity. Both telecommunications and broadcasting are thus developing into broadband, interactive networks. It makes clear economic and technical sense for both to be provided over a single network – integrated broadband communications.

In 1988 the MacDonald Committee reported to the government with recommendations on *The Infrastructure for Tomorrow*, concluding that 'the government should not make the installation of a national broadband grid based on optical fibre a keystone of policy.'[11] Yet the consultant's study on which their report was based had shown that the option of establishing a national grid promises higher output and employment than the other two options considered – laissez-faire or lightly regulated competition – and furthermore that the national grid would have dramatically more balanced regional effects on employment, creating far more jobs in the North than the other options.[12] Investing in such a grid would imply an increased public role in the economy, and would offer benefits throughout the economy rather than to big business alone. The MacDonald Committee clearly knew which answer the government wanted, but the study they commissioned provides valuable information about the benefits to be gained from a public investment push for advanced telecommunications networks. BT would be better placed spending its massive profits – in 1988–9, the company made £2.4 billion on turnover of £11.1 billion – on a national grid than on dubious acquisitions in North America or dividend handouts.[13] But in Britain BT has been forbidden to provide TV over its main network. This policy is a major block on innovation, and the clearest example of how the government's obsession with competition is blocking technical advance. Their pretext for the prohibition is the fear that BT would dominate the new market, and stifle competition. This amounts to sending the strongest player off the field in order to ensure a fair game.

The government has followed the MacDonald Committee in rejecting the idea of a 'national grid': an integrated development towards a broadband network, led by BT. The way in which the fixation with creating 'free markets' prevents social and technical progress has been highlighted by Tony Young, the National Communications Union's General Secretary. As part of the union's campaign, he picked out seven reasons for a policy in favour of a national grid, including the fact that 'this would eliminate the need for duplicate investments and obviate the need for two cables to be buried in the road or the use of unsightly television aerials and satellite dishes.' It would also be 'a "future-proof" network capable of meeting all service demands that can currently be foreseen. The alternative is a "patchwork quilt" of local networks deploying different technologies in different configurations, making at least partial replacement at some time almost inevitable.'[14]

The Labour Party's 1989 policy review prescriptions for telecommunications start with a bang and end with a whimper. It rightly notes that 'just as the railways and highways of the past were the product of public investment, so the development of "electronic highways" cannot be left to the free market either.'[15] It goes on to propose a national grid, and draws the sensible conclusion that 'this investment is most appropriately carried out in the public sector. We shall therefore take BT back into public ownership.' But a later section shows that things may not be quite what they seem. 'If the public stake in BT's equity remains at 49 per cent, we shall buy sufficient shares at a fair market price to take that stake to 51 per cent and we shall make it clear that we intend to use that majority shareholding in the public interest.'[16] The problem is that buying 2 per cent of the shares would be unlikely to change BT's market-driven low-investment approach, or its bias towards serving big business at the expense of the ordinary consumer. Under section 459 of the Companies Act, a business must take full account of the interests of minority shareholders. A Labour leadership serious about using a majority BT shareholding to serve wider social interests, even at the expense of the shareholders, would need to take powers to over-ride that section of the Act.[17]

The fear of the Labour leadership, of course, is that a newly-elected Labour government could not afford to buy back BT. But this is to misunderstand the problem, as will be discussed in detail in chapter 11. Selling BT did not make the public sector richer, and buying it back need not impoverish the public sector. The Labour leadership's mistake lies in ignoring the annual £2.4 billion stream of profits which the government would gain after buying back BT, enough to pay off the compensation bonds. The irony is that this error has left the Labour leadership with a strongly free market programme for telecommunications by comparison with most advanced industrial countries. Almost throughout Western Europe, for example, BT's counterparts are in one hundred per cent public ownership. This free-market approach was never intended, but follows inevitably from the basic decision not to mount any major challenge to the power of capital in any part of the economy.

Technical trends are pushing in the opposite direction to free markets and competition. Conscious planning and network integration is already developing to an extent even in countries and institutions with a mainly market-driven perspective. In the US several major firms, such as Merrill Lynch, which had established their own networks in the early 1980s, are now going back to the network operators to provide cheaper and more effective solutions, enabling them to concentrate on their own primary business, which is not telecommunications. In the EEC, the European Commission is proposing the acceptance of monopoly for network infrastructure and basic services.

There can be no doubt that the most important immediate task for a genuinely renationalized BT would be the development of a fibre-optic national grid. Public ownership and planning of telecommunications makes sound economic and social sense. The benefits from such a policy would be widespread throughout industry and society; and these benefits are crucial to the development of an advanced and internationally-competitive economy.

Computing

Computing has become increasingly integrated with the rest of the economy, not only in the obvious sense that other sectors depend increasingly on computing for their day-to-day operations, but also in that a successful computing sector now requires industrial strength in other fields, notably electronic components. After many false starts, computing is spreading rapidly through the economy, and transforming production. In engineering, computing equipment worth £2 billion had been installed by late 1988, double the value of two years earlier.[18] The turnover of the UK's 300 largest computing services companies rose to £2.2 billion in the year to June 1988, three times the figure for 1981–2. Over the same period the number of staff employed by Computing Services Association members almost doubled, reaching a total of 48,870 in the middle of 1988.[19] Even the backward book distribution system is modernizing, with a third of bookshops linked into the computerized 'Teleordering' system by the beginning of 1989.[20]

This rapid growth is beginning to reach a phase of relative maturity. There were 197 significant mergers and acquisitions worth £3.6 billion in the British information technology sector during 1988, a rise of two-thirds over 1987.[21] These included major takeovers such as the £164 million acquisition of Hoskyns Group by Plessey, the £94 million spent by Sema-Metra of France to buy CAP Group and the purchase of IBM Science Research by Maxwell Communications for £86 million. The emphasis is increasingly on systems integration – the ability to put together computer hardware and software to provide a solution to a customer's requirements. To take prime contractor responsibility for such projects, a systems integrator needs both size and financial stability. Consequently, there has been a rush to reach critical size quickly enough through acquisitions. In Britain, however, the piecemeal approach to computer use is hampering its successful introduction – a 1989 study showed that Britain has a less systematic and therefore weaker corporate culture for the successful use of information technology than West Germany, France or Italy.[22]

The free market in Britain has responded to this rapidly growing industry by failing to develop the training that it needs. By 1988 there was a shortage of over 30,000 data processing staff.[23] A National Computer Centre report broke down the shortfalls by skill sector and blamed employer resistance to training for the problems. The reply offered in 1988 by one minister, John Butcher, was that 'government does not have an exclusive obligation to remedy all information technology skills deficiencies. ... There needs to be a strong element of self-help in this area.' Computing is an industry with exceptionally high labour turnover in Britain. It therefore makes no sense to appeal to the private sector to step up training as individual companies have little interest in doing so. The training they pay for is just as likely to benefit the next employer as themselves. The only kind of training scheme they are likely to endorse is one that produces qualifications which are not fully transferable. This was the case, for example, with a non-graduate software engineering qualification proposed by the Engineering Industry Training Board in 1988. Focussing on courses organized by colleges and polytechnics to meet the needs of local employers, it is unlikely to be recognized outside its town of origin.[24]

Private solutions, here again, offer only a balkanization of skills and knowledge when what is needed is their integration.

Standards in computing

In terms of hardware, computers are generally divided into three categories: mainframe computers, mini-computers, and micro-computers. But in terms of usage, they can more usefully be considered in two categories: personal computing and specialist computing. Personal computing covers the use of computing by those not specialized in the sector, typically for word-processing, databases, graphics, spreadsheets and CNC (computer numerically controlled) machine tools. Roughly speaking, these replace and enhance the respective functions of typewriters, card indexes, hand-drawn graphics, calculators and conventional machine tools. Their common point is that the users are not computer specialists. Specialized computing, on the other hand, ranges from running a department's local area network up to organizing the computer systems handling the production line of a factory or the cash machines in banks.

It is easiest to see the importance of standards from the perspective of personal computing. Here the important thing is that a document written on one word-processor should be usable on another, that a filing system created with one database should be usable by another database. Generally, they are not. This is why different firms, different local authorities, even different departments within the same organization, often lose the advantages of computerization as soon as they have to communicate with each other. They have to get the data out of one computer system, and often actually type it back into the other system.

This is the price that is paid for having free competition in the computer market. There are numerous ad-hoc attempts to get round this problem:

- by buying whatever the market leader – generally American and often IBM – supplies, even when it is more expensive as is usually the case. That still does not guarantee that your correspondents will use the same equipment; even less that they will use the same software, and in the same way;

- by defining standards for interchange of data between different systems – absurdly, there are many such interchange formats, and none of them is standard. Furthermore, to operate this kind of interchange itself requires a degree of specialist knowledge and acts as a barrier to the use of computers by non-specialists;
- by adopting the system proposed by a leader in the same sector. As described in chapter 3, in the US automobile industry, components suppliers are forced by General Motors, Ford, and others, to adopt a different – and totally incompatible – system to communicate with each manufacturer. As a result they have up to five unconnected terminals in their offices, and have to re-key the information into their own systems;
- by agreeing with others – within trade groups or under the auspices of local authorities – to use the same system. But this may cause conflicts when, for example, an organization's suppliers use different systems from its customers.

The problem with all these solutions lies in the lack of credibility and generality of the standards adopted. The only level at which it is possible to challenge the market power of American multinationals to define computer standards is that of the state or supranational institutions. The closest governments have come is the IBM disclosure agreement, by which the EEC compelled IBM – the largest multinational in the world – to publish details of its computer interfaces in advance.

There would thus be a need for a Labour government to carry out studies in each of the important areas of software and hardware, to investigate the cost of non-standardization as well as possible costs of standardization. Where appropriate, the government could then set binding common standards, with defined introduction periods, to ensure compatibility in Britain. These standards would need to build on existing international standardization work, to ensure maximum compatibility with overseas systems. Such a policy proposal would meet an immediate reaction of outrage from the computer industry, and especially from the largest suppliers within that industry. They would raise arguments about freedom and flexibility, and claim that such a strict standards policy would suppress innovation. But these protests would be nothing more than special pleading. The very firms most vociferous in using this kind of argument – producers such as IBM and large users such as financial institutions – themselves operate strict standards policies internally. IBM uses its own standards – such as Systems Network Architecture (SNA) and latterly Systems Application Architecture (SAA) – as strategic tools to tie customers to their often second-rate technical solutions. Banks run their own data networks, with their own standards, in order to gain competitive advantage.

The example of Apricot Computers is instructive. They almost went bankrupt by developing technically excellent but non-standard systems, only retrieving their position by coming back in line with the industry standard. In this case the standard was that dictated by IBM. But since then some international non-proprietary standards, such as Open Systems Interconnection (OSI) and Unix, have made enough headway to form the basis of a public policy which could provide compatibility of British manufacturers and users. International compatibility would also be guaranteed to at least the extent that would otherwise be possible, with the additional advantage of not being at the mercy of the likes of IBM. The savings in money and efficiency would be substantial. But as soon as these kinds of policies are proposed for a country, these computer companies who profit so much from the fragmentation of the market are the first to cry foul. And the power and influence of major corporations is such that governments have rarely had the courage to stand up to them consistently on the issue.

Electronics

The British market for information technology and electronics is larger than the home market for the motor industry. In 1987, it was worth around £17 billion – half for equipment and half for software and services.[25] The British electronics industry is a case study of how not to run an industry, and encapsulates all the main failures and weaknesses of post-war British capitalism. Without radical changes, the chances of survival of a UK electronics industry in any form now look poor, according to a 1988 report by the consultants McKinsey's. Britain has neither invested enough nor researched enough, with three major consequences:

- a large and growing trade deficit in electronics. From a rough balance of trade in electronic goods in 1970 – ranging from computers to industrial, medical and office equipment – the country had moved by 1986 to a deficit of £2.8 billion, contrasting with the West German surplus of £1.7 billion. This UK deficit swelled to £3.4 billion in 1987 and £3.9 billion in 1988;

- a shrunken electronics sector. In the US and Japan the output of the information technology industry amounted in 1987 to an average of more than 16 per cent of total manufactured output; in the UK, it came to just 6.5 per cent;
- an increasing concentration of UK electronics production in the hands of foreign-based transnational corporations in the areas of computers, semiconductors and consumer electronics; the surge in UK television production over the last few years is mainly traceable to new Japanese plants.

A strong electronics industry requires the depth of a healthy components sector, as in Japan where close relationships of firms with their suppliers underlie a powerful components industry. The UK, by contrast, is weaker in the field than most of Europe. As a result the trade deficit in the electronic components sector leapt from £77 million in 1980 to £604 million in 1986. Table 7.1 gives an overview of production and trade developments in the different parts of the electronics sector. It shows a general pattern of rapid market growth met primarily from increased imports, notably in data processing and consumer electronics. The only remaining area of relative strength is that of electronic capital goods.

The British electronics industry has registered slow growth over past decades, not because of any lack of demand but because, typified by GEC, it has preferred to put its large profits anywhere but back into the British electronics industry. A recent study of British research and development identified GEC's effective withdrawal from development of image and sound equipment as the basis for Britain's loss of strength in this area, with the deterioration in semiconductors and computers also traced to the decisions of a handful of firms – GEC, STC/ITT and Plessey.[26]

UK demand for electronics goods and services increased in real terms by 9.4 per cent a year between 1976 and 1988 – growth as rapid as in any of the world's major markets except Japan. But sales by British electronics firms rose only 2.6 per cent a year over the same period.[27] The beneficiaries of that market growth were overseas suppliers and foreign multinationals operating in the UK. Foreign

Table 7.1
The UK Electronics Sector

		Output (£m)	Imports (£m)	Exports (£m)	Market size (£m)	Trade balance (£m)
Telecoms	1970	241	12	38	215	26
	1980	908	70	96	882	26
	1985	1578	318	242	1654	–76
	1986	1617	365	219	1763	–146
Data Processing	1970	208	144	82	270	–62
	1980	1013	1082	938	1157	–144
	1985	3099	3919	3314	3704	–605
	1986	2899	3918	3094	3723	–824
Electronic Capital Goods	1970	250	56	116	190	60
	1980	1418	314	479	1253	165
	1985	2444	819	1162	2101	343
	1986	2558	867	1240	2185	373
Consumer Electronics (Brown Goods Only)	1970	193	37	27	203	–10
	1980	505	504	149	860	–355
	1985	778	1196	356	1618	–840
	1986	831	1284	448	1667	–836
Total Electronic Equipment	1970	892	249	263	878	14
	1980	3844	1970	1662	4152	–308
	1985	7899	6252	5074	9077	–1178
	1986	7905	6434	5001	9338	–1433

Source: *Mullard*, cited in *Financial Times*, 24 November 1987.

firms now have two-thirds of the market, compared to less than half in 1976. The fact that British firms have not even held their home market position is in great part because of lower investment. By the end of the 1980s announcements of major closures by British firms like Ferranti and ICL were regularly alternating with announcements of new Japanese investments.

Over-concentration on military business, in research and development as well as in production, has been the other main cause of the growing weakness of the sector. Military sales account for 40 per cent of GEC's total output, and 35 per cent of Plessey's.[28] Even the Ministry of Defence's 1987 defence estimates said that the government 'shares the underlying concern of those who fear that necessary investment in research and development may crowd out valuable investment in the civil sector'. But it is government policies which have led military research and development to pre-empt a high proportion of the engineers and scientists who could otherwise be used on civil electronic research and development. About 45 per cent of electronics research and development is government-financed, with the great bulk of government funds coming from the Ministry of Defence. Around half of the total government research and development spending in 1986–7 of £4.6 billion went on military work, against a third in France and only a tenth in West Germany. Thus:

> Part of the reason for Britain's poor performance in the information technology sectors derives from these defence commitments. At a time when Britain should have been concentrating resources on meeting the challenges and opportunities presented by these new technologies, which involved both developing new industries and updating the design and performance of equipment in older industries, we have seen an increasing proportion of our manufacturing resources, and particularly our highly trained manpower, pulled into the defence sectors. With their protected markets and guaranteed profit margins, the defence sectors inevitably attract all the resources they need. At the same time, in the civilian sectors of the engineering industry, firms have been under severe cost pressures and have skimped on research and development, training and retraining, running down rather than strengthening Britain's capacity to innovate. As a consequence, Britain today is less capable of competing in the civilian high technology sectors than it was five or ten years ago.[29]

Furthermore, while military work used to be at the leading edge of technology in most areas, this is no longer the case. On the contrary, electronics is now seen as the key military technology and mass produced integrated circuits (ICs) the key electronics technology.[30] But these mass produced ICs, notably dynamic memories ('DRAMs') are for the commercial, not the military, market.

Military orientation will be still less appropriate as a strategy for electronics in the future. Military budgets in the West have stopped growing at the rapid rates of the early and mid 1980s, at the same time as important developing countries, especially in the Middle East, are cutting back their defence spending. Thorn EMI, Plessey, GEC and Racal all had to shed labour in 1987 and 1988, largely because of falling demand for military communications in the Middle East. This trend can only be reinforced by decreased international tension. The British electronics industry has gambled on a continuation of superpower confrontation and regional conflicts – and lost. It is time to turn the industry towards worthwhile civil applications, for which a market exists.

A rapidly growing sector such as electronics should be drawing in resources from outside to finance this growth. Indeed, a good test of the City's relationship with British industry is to examine its financing of fast and slow growing sectors. From 1949 to 1982 all physical investment in the electrical and electronics sector was financed from retained profits – with the City providing no net finance to the sector.[31] The pursuit of short-term profits, which the City lives by, does not make it worthwhile for financial institutions to develop the kind of lasting relationships with their lenders which are required to justify lending in such a specialized sector as electronics. This City short-sightedness means that Britain in particular needs state intervention geared to the long term, to ensure a productive economy.

In this vacuum of long-term thinking, overseas firms show a greater understanding of the need for strategic investment than do their British counterparts. NEC of Japan, for example, has a semiconductor manufacturing plant in Scotland; and Fujitsu have decided to follow with a £400m plant in Newton Aycliffe, including the key diffusion stage of the production process.[32]

The need for a strategy

Britain stands alone in having no overall industrial strategy for electronics. The economy urgently needs one in which 'consistency and continuity of policies over time' is essential.[33] The 'rush to hands-off' has been more marked than in other nations, with the result that UK policy lacks cohesion and consistency. In Britain state support for the electronics industry is lower than in America, Japan, France or West Germany. It should then come as no surprise that our electronics industry is weaker than in those countries.

A strategy for the 1990s would need to include as a key element a programme of collaborative research. The £350 million, five-year publicly-financed Alvey programme ended in 1988; yet despite the warning from the government's chief scientific adviser that Britain's electronics industry spends too little on research and development to stay competitive internationally, and despite being warned that 'the delays and uncertainties' in launching a successor to Alvey 'could yet undermine the achievements of the programme', there has been no adequate follow-up.[34]

A report by the National Economic Development Office (NEDO) on education and training in the late 1980s made the point that in electronics the UK has been at a disadvantage from an inadequate supply and use of graduates; that in other countries industry itself contributes more to training; and that Britain has, by comparison, failed to plan for rapidly shifting skills requirements.[35] Britain is the only country to have had persistent skills problems in this sector. The government and the CBI have for years exhorted industry to pull its socks up and take responsibility for more training. This has proved quite inadequate. Training in electronics is a strategic need for the country. The necessary resources could and should be supplied through the state educational system – through universities and vocational institutes. Especially in a country like Britain with a high labour turnover, the efficiency benefits of education and training accrue to society as a whole, and not just to the firm or organization in which the trained person works. It is logical, then, that training should be provided publicly and that the public should reap the benefits from that investment.

The elements of a solution to the problems of Britain's electronics industry must therefore rest on:

- Increased investment. There is a clear necessity for publicly-led investment since the lack of investment has been a major cause of Britain's relative decline in the sector, especially in the case of GEC which has instead accumulated a massive cash mountain.
- Stepped-up research and development. This should include collaborative research in the area of information technology. For the rest of the electronics sector, civil projects, involving international collaboration where appropriate, should be developed to take the place of the large-scale military projects that have dominated government funding for research and

development in the past. Collaboration on new computers, consumer electronic devices or electronic factory control systems can be envisaged on the scale hitherto reserved for such irrelevancies as the Tornado fighter aircraft.

- Removal of the military bias of research. As military expenditure is reduced as a proportion of GDP, an automatic link should be introduced to ensure that this leads, not to a reduction of government support for research, but to a redirection of this support to where it is really needed.
- Nationalization of GEC. GEC is the appropriate vehicle for the stepped-up state investment in the sector. On the one hand, it has shown its unwillingness to invest. On the other, it has sufficient size, in international as well as national terms, to be able to serve as a channel for a planned strategy of expansion for the sector. Initial injections of public funds for additional research would be amply recouped later in the form of repayments as well as additional taxes from the resulting extra output. GEC symbolizes the negative, low-investment, cash-rich, short-term, no-growth approach of modern British capitalism.

Only a radical public intervention can steer Britain's electronics flagship into positive growth. The alternative is continued relative decline until it becomes a tidy enough morsel for Siemens, Alcatel, General Electric or NEC to bite off and swallow up.

Notes

1. Karl Marx, *Capital*, Volume 1, Lawrence & Wishart, London 1954 (1867), pp. 336–7.
2. See Andrew Gillespie and Mark Hepworth, 'Telecommunications and Regional Development in the Information Society', Newcastle Studies of the Information Economy *Working Paper* 1, CURDS, University of Newcastle upon Tyne, 1986, p. 23; and Jeremy Howells, *Economic, Technical and Locational Trends in European Services*, Aldershot 1988, p. 147.
3. *Financial Times*, 1 March 1989.
4. Logica, *European Communications Systems*, London 1986.
5. *Telecommunications*, March 1989, p. 14.
6. Formerly known as Geisco.
7. National Communications Union (NCU), *Submission to the 'Labour Listens' and the Policy Review*, London 1988.
8. National Communications Union (NCU), *Submission to the 'Labour Listens' and the Policy Review*, London 1988.

9. The OSI model was established on the basis of work in the International Standardization Organization, in order to lay the basis for communications between computers in an open way, not dominated by IBM, by defining speeds, shapes of messages and so on, in a way that allows the products of different manufacturers to communicate provided they adhere to these standards. The model comprises seven layers. The lower levels cover the more physical and telecommunications-related aspects of standardization, while the higher levels are more orientated towards applications and the definition of the kinds of messages that can be sent.

10. Herbert Ungerer, *Telecommunications in Europe*, Brussels 1988, p. 114.

11. Department of Trade and Industry, *Communications Steering Group Report: The Infrastructure for Tommorrow*, London 1988, p. iii.

12. PA Consulting Group and PA Cambridge Economic Consultants, *Evolution of the United Kingdom Communications Infrastructure*, London 1988, p. S.9.

13. Such a national broadband network could also take advantage of other technologies as appropriate including microwave communications, cellular systems, satellite technology and narrowband cable with data compression – as discussed in Asu Aksoy, Ian Miles, Kevin Morgan and Graham Thomas of the Science Policy Research Unit, 'The Changed White Heat of Technology', *Guardian*, 8 June 1989.

14. National Communications Union, *The Network of the Future* Conference, May 1989.

15. Labour Party, *Final Report of Labour's Policy Review for the 1990s*, London 1989, p. 12.

16. Labour Party, *Final Report of Labour's Policy Review for the 1990s*, London 1989, p. 15.

17. Thanks to Lord Wedderburn, Professor of Company Law at LSE, for his clarification of this point.

18. Benchmark Research Survey, *Engineering Computers*, November 1988.

19. Computer Services Association, *Annual Report*, London 1988.

20. *Financial Times*, 14 February 1989.

21. Regent Associates, cited in *Financial Times*, 28 February 1989.

22. Amdahl Executive Institute, *Clues to Success: Information Technology Strategies for Tomorrow*, London 1989.

23. Salary Survey, *Computer Users' Year Book*, London 1988.

24. The failure of British industry to finance either adequate training or research and development is well documented in Kevin Morgan and Andrew Sayer, *Microcircuits of Capital: Sunrise Industry and Uneven Development*, Polity Press, Cambridge 1988.

25. Trade and Industry Committee, *Information Technology* vol. 1, HMSO, London 1988, p. ix.

26. Keith Pavitt and Pari Patel, National Institute of Economic and Social Research *Quarterly Review*, November 1987.

27. McKinsey's, *Strengthening the Competitiveness of UK Electronics*, London 1988.

28. McKinsey's, cited in *Sunday Times*, 15 January 1989.

29. Mary Kaldor, M. Sharp and W. Walker, 'Industrial Competitiveness and Britain's Defence', *Lloyd's Bank Review* no. 162, 1986, p. 48.

30. Axel Pavillet, 'Integrated Circuits for US Defence – and the Defence of US Integrated Circuits', *Military Technology*, May 1988.

31. Colin Mayer, 'New Issues in Corporate Finance', *Centre for Economic Policy Research*, Paper no. 181, London 1987.
32. *Financial Times*, 13 April 1989.
33. University of Sussex, *Government IT Policies in Competing Countries – Report for the National Economic Development Office*, London 1988.
34. University of Sussex, *IT Report for NEDO*, London 1988.
35. NEDO, *Comparative Education and Training Strategies*, London 1988.

8

Linking up the Sectors

It is inconceivable that we could ever transform this society without a major extension of public ownership and control.

Neil Kinnock, 1983[1]

The years 1979–81 saw a drastic loss of manufacturing capacity in Britain and it took until 1988 to restore the 1979 level of manufacturing output. This process was accompanied by a drive to restore 'management's right to manage' and enforce more 'flexible' working practices. At the beginning of 1989, for example, Ford was trying to introduce round-the-clock three-shift working for the first time in Europe.[2] Rather than modernization based on the introduction of genuinely more advanced work practices, increases in the intensity of labour – making workers work harder – have generally been the order of the day. This reflects itself in low overall levels of investment and training. British average productivity remained in 1986 about 30 per cent lower than in the US and about 25 per cent less than on the continent. As the organization of the richer capitalist states, the OECD, commented at the end of the 1980s:

> stronger labour productivity growth has not been linked to capital investment, which, in fact, has remained lower relative to GDP than in earlier recovery periods. Rather it seems linked to changes in work organization, with inflexible and outdated job demarcation giving way to more rational job allocation.[3]

Britain effectively abandoned many areas of manufacturing in the 1979–81 slump, and there is little sign of their being replaced. Crude steel use in 1988 was down 23 per cent on 1978, as against a fall of only 13 per cent for West Germany, while Italian use – 23 million tonnes against Britain's 15 million – rose by almost a fifth. In the case of machine tools, West Germany installs three times as many as the UK each year. Engineering is an essential base for the whole manufacturing sector, producing as it does much of the equipment needed for all other production. It represents almost 40 per cent of manufacturing output and about 10 per cent of total GDP.

The idea, propounded by the Tory government, that the reduced weight of manufacturing in the British economy is a sign of progress, of a transition to a modern service economy, is put into context by the veteran critic of de-industrializing free-market policies, Professor Wynne Godley:

> The reason for the decline of British manufacturing output has nothing to do with any preference for services; it is simply that a rapidly rising proportion of our supplies has come from abroad while foreign demand for our exports has not risen commensurately. ... Manufacturing output is now 10 per cent lower absolutely than it was in 1973. Yet imports of manufactures have more than doubled over the same period.[4]

'Manufacturing matters' is the name of a best-selling American book. It is also a fact. As the book's authors argue: 'a substantial core of service employment is tightly tied to manufacturing. It is a complement and not, as the dominant view would have it, a substitute or successor for manufacturing. Lose manufacturing and you will lose – not develop – those high-wage services.'[5]

In chapter 7 the requirements for a planned strategy for the new technology sectors in Britain were examined in detail. In this chapter the aim is to begin to flesh out proposals for the modernization and restructuring of the British economy – based on the interventionist approach outlined earlier – using the examples of a number of key industrial sectors.

Aerospace

Aerospace is the most electronics-orientated of manufacturing industries. At first glance, Britain's aerospace sector is a picture of rosy success. Turnover, estimated to exceed £8.5 billion in 1987, makes the British industry the second largest in the capitalist world. In 1988 exports outstripped imports by £1.7 billion. In real terms the industry has more than doubled the value of its exports, rising from £1 billion in 1977 to £4.7 billion in 1986. Over the same period, productivity doubled.[6] In 1988 British Aerospace secured a record 137 aircraft orders worth US$1.5 billion.

Yet the aerospace industry is famous for its violent swings between excess demand and overcapacity. The markets are civil and military. Civil airlines in the late 1980s were going through one of their periodic rounds of re-equipping, which boosted aerospace sales around the world. In 1989, Boeing forecast that airlines would buy 8,417 jets of all types from all makers by the year 2005. But such an optimistic assumption supposes stable prices for aviation fuel and no economic recession. An oil price rise or a trade slump could throw these calculations out dramatically, since 70 per cent of the expected new purchases would be to meet a growth in traffic, and only 30 per cent to replace ageing aircraft.[7] At the same time, the 1980s saw a phase of rapid real growth in NATO arms expenditure, stimulating demand for military aircraft and missiles.

With both of these trends highly unpredictable and the second set to go into reverse as East–West relations improve and real cuts in armaments are for the first time in prospect, the medium-term picture is a great deal more worrying for the industry.

The two largest aerospace firms operating in Britain are:

- British Aerospace: 130,000 employees in the whole group, including Rover, and about 87,000 in aerospace; 1988 sales £5.64 billion;
- Rolls-Royce: 40,000 employees; 1988 sales £1.97 billion.

Together these two companies account for over half the sector. Both have been privatized, and the danger of these privatizations for the future of the industry have already become apparent. The terms of privatization for British Aerospace set a maximum 15 per cent foreign ownership limit. But in the spring of 1989, that condition was being challenged: under EEC law, member states must give each others' citizens the same treatment 'as regards participation in the capital of companies' unless essential security risks are at stake. Privatization has thus opened the way for a total loss of British control of the company. Furthermore, the private strategies of British Aerospace threaten to lose British strategic control of the sector: the French electronics giant Thomson (which, incidentally, is state-owned) has been negotiating with British Aerospace about opening up the British civilian and military aircraft market to Thomson's systems.[8] On the jobs front, British Aerospace is cutting back the workforce of its guided weapons subsidiary from 16,000 to 13,500 and closing two out of six factories, in Berkshire, by the end of 1990 – 'stripping the heart out of the dynamics business'.[9]

All these are the problems and dislocations of a boom period. It is not hard to see how they will be magnified as the boom inevitably comes to an end. The last time the industry was in trouble, in the 1970s, it was trade union pressure on government that rescued it. The industry and services union MSF records the part played by the trade unions in 'retrieving the BAe 146, after Hawker-Siddeley threatened to pull out in 1974. The aircraft, a leader in defeating noise pollution, is now an unqualified success. ... Had it not been for the faith of the workforce in their project, and the organization that the trade union movement was able to bring to bear, the BAe 146 simply would not exist.'[10]

In the case of Rolls-Royce, the product was the RB–211 engine, now a mainstay of the fleets of many of the world's major airlines. Problems in financing its development led to the bankruptcy and nationalization of the company. This injection of public money was not, however, accompanied in the long run by any public industrial strategy. Sir Austin Pearce, the Chairman of British Aerospace, regards this as symptomatic of a more general problem of government policy towards manufacturing industry:

> The real problem is the Treasury. The Treasury happens to operate on a one-year basis, and our twenty-five year programme is something that is very difficult to bridge. You'll find this with many industrialists, that the problem area is with the system the Treasury operates, a system which is inconsistent with industry.[11]

The need for a longer-term public commitment to aerospace demands an extension of public control over the industry. That would have to take two forms. Most obviously, British Aerospace – along with the Rover Group – and Rolls-Royce should be brought back into public ownership. An integrated aerospace policy could then be developed whereby air transport;British AirwaysBritish Airways places orders which provide work for British Aerospace and Rolls-Royce rather than their competitors.[12] At the same time, a public aerospace components combine needs to be built up, supplying different manufacturers at home and abroad. The Thatcher government has only been willing to put cash into public aerospace firms in order to privatize them. As Short's, the Belfast aerospace company, was dressed up for sale, the government undertook to write off £300 million losses and inject an extra £200 million equity. The company's chairman remarked: 'I find it difficult to come to terms with the fact that a business owned by the British taxpayer should have been starved of government aircraft and aerostructure contracts for a quarter of a century.'[13] It was eventually sold to the Canadian firm Bombardier.

Avionics – the name given to the part of the electronics business producing aviation systems and components – is the basis of an important link between the electronics and aerospace industries, as the electronics-intensiveness of aerospace continues to rise. Firms such as GEC, Plessey, Lucas, Ferranti and Dowty are the key players. Of the 330,000 workforce in the electronics sector, around 100,000 are engaged in aerospace projects. This tightly defined industrial link-up provides a strong basis for bringing aerospace into the planning of the core sectors of the economy.

One of the first strategic tasks for public policy in a restructured sector would be re-orientation away from dependence on military contracts, and especially the arms trade. The problem is how to reconcile opposition to high military spending with the prime union task of defending jobs. The contradiction can only be solved by a planned restructuring of the industry's product base, using the skills and techniques already available, a campaign for which is currently being co-ordinated by the National Trade Union Defence Conversion Committee and supported by the major union in the sector, MSF.[14]

The uncertainties hanging over the industry – notably the twin threats of oil prices rises and international recession – are not natural calamities, but the normal hazards of the international capitalist market system. Only a planned economic environment can shield aerospace from these dangers and allow the forecasting of demand which is a condition for stable growth in the civil part of the industry. Hitherto, the military side has been the only planned part of the sector and the result has been that firms have been inclined to rely on it, partly to ensure stability. Now that new international conditions are developing to cut back the waste on arms spending, the challenge must be to create the same kind of stability on the civil side of the business.

One helpful factor in that direction could be the development of international public enterprise. As argued in chapter 2, private firms have long had the freedom to exploit international economies of scale, while public enterprise has either been confined within the borders of the nation-state or forced to mimic the behaviour of private transnational corporations. In the long run such confinement condemns public enterprise to increasing relative technical backwardness; and it is imperative to find the appropriate institutional forms which could allow public enterprise to enter international markets on a par with the private multinational giants. The possibilities for international co-operation in aerospace have been shown by the successful European Airbus consortium, which has gone from nothing to become one of the big three world passenger aircraft suppliers, alongside Boeing and McDonnell Douglas, in a matter of a few years. British Aerospace has a 20 per cent stake and makes most of the wings for the growing number of airliner designs in the Airbus family, securing 7,000 jobs in Chester and Bristol. At the same time, airport congestion is increasingly a constraint on the growth of air traffic. According to Airbus Industrie's vice-president, it 'could easily choke the air transport system long before the end of the century.'[15] The clear interdependence of aircraft development and production, airline operation, and airport and air traffic management, highlights the need for an integrated aerospace policy covering all these areas – as a key part of an integrated national transport system.

Aerospace stands at the forefront of the globalization of trade unionism. In 1988, Airbus Industrie unions announced the formation of a transnational works council covering British, French, German and Spanish unions. As the organization of firms is increasingly international, the organization of workers needs to follow suit – and the Cold War divisions in the international trade union movement are becoming more and more of an anachronistic drag on these trends. Where companies have integrated international production strategies, as is the case with Airbus, a legal condition of their activity in Britain should be full recognition of any international joint union committee representing their different national workforces.

A prime candidate for international public enterprise in the aerospace industry is the revolutionary space plane, Hotol. This design is for a machine which takes off and lands like an ordinary aircraft, uses air to help burn fuel until it reaches five times the speed of sound and a height of eighteen miles, when it switches to liquid oxygen carried on board. In principle it could reach Australia in less than four hours. The patents are owned by British Aerospace – which has kept a team of a hundred working on the project – and Rolls-Royce, but development has been blocked by the Thatcher government. It will neither provide £6 million towards demonstrating the technology – full development could cost £6 billion – nor declassify the engine technology, as would be needed for a move towards commercial development. While it is impossible to be certain that the technology will be effective, a publicly-owned British Aerospace and Rolls-Royce should certainly continue the project into a demonstration phase; and overseas governments and state enterprises should be encouraged to participate, as several are known to be keen to do.

The Motor Industry

The motor industry is already going down the road opened up by aerospace, by incorporating an increasing proportion of electronics inputs in its products. There is therefore a certain industrial logic in the link-up of British Aerospace with Britain's only surviving home-based volume car producer, the Rover Group – which came about as part of the Thatcher government's privatization strategy in the late 1980s.

The UK motor vehicle and components industry employed 289,000 workers in 1987, of whom 139,000 were in the components sector.[16] The overall figure fell by 45 per cent from 1980. Although it has been run down over the years, vehicle production still accounted for 5 per cent of GDP in 1987 and 1.5 per cent of total employment directly, rising to 3.4 per cent of total employment if indirect employment – particularly in components – is included. The industry's position in the world market can be seen from Table 8.1, showing that Britain has slipped to seventh place.

In 1988 UK car production recovered significantly, rising to 1.23 million, an increase of 7 per cent. This was the highest level since 1977, though still well below the 1972 peak of 1.92 million.[17] It is an industry in which a long-term view is perhaps even more important than in other areas of traditional manufacturing, since the economies of scale and scope available from the long-term pursuit of market

Table 8.1
World Vehicle Production by Country (millions), 1988

	Cars	Commercial Vehicles
Japan	8.0	4.2
US	7.2	3.7
West Germany	4.3	0.3
France	3.2	0.4
Italy	1.9	0.2
Spain	1.5	0.3
UK	1.2	0.2
Canada	0.8	0.8

Source: CAITS/MSF, *The Motor Industry Today and Tomorrow – A Report for Motor Industry Representatives*, London 1988; DRI Europe.

share are far more advantageous than are the gains from using it as an instrument for demand management and fine-tuning of the economy. The Japanese, West German, French and Italian governments have historically understood this much better than the British. There are no longer any British owned enterprises producing on a major European scale. In Italy, France and West Germany, by contrast, there are domestically owned enterprises with sufficient volume to operate as serious volume car producers. In 1988 Western European registrations included Fiat's 1,929,000; Volkswagen's 1,930,000; Peugeot's 1,672,000; and Renault's 1,325,000; with Rover Group (formerly known as BL and Austin Rover) trailing at only 448,000. Rover registrations in Western Europe are barely in excess of Mercedes (445,000) which is a specialist producer only operating at the top end of the market.

Arguments about the significance of scale economies in the modern car industry have carried on over the years, but given the development costs of modern cars it remains imperative to have high output to produce volume cars economically. Designing and developing a new model is now reckoned to cost more than US$1 billion, and is expected to rise to US$10 billion by the end of the century.[18] In production, while the increased use of automation has actually raised the optimum scale for assembly plants from 200,000 units per year to 300,000, more flexible equipment does permit the assembly of a greater variety of models and a fall in the length of the model-specific assembly runs needed for optimum scale economies.[19]

Optimistic arguments were put forward in the early 1980s – when Michael Edwardes was in charge of BL – that the company could survive by the use of flexible automation as an independent volume car producer. But they have proved completely misplaced. And while UK market share targets set in the Edwardes era were around 22 per cent, the actual figure for 1988 was barely 15 per cent. As well as being too small, the company suffers from a poor mix of models. Its relatively most successful model, the Metro, is in the small car class where profits per unit are very low. Rover's performance in the crucial medium car segment is lamentable. The result has been a downward spiral and there are now problems in generating the resources required for new models. The Maestro is to be replaced by a model developed jointly with Honda, but there are no plans for a replacement for the Montego in the vital upper-middle range, which is the mainstay of the fleet car market. In reality, any attempt to operate as a significant volume car producer has been abandoned. It has been argued instead that Rover should attempt to emulate the major European specialist producers. The Rover Sterling was to be the product, but in the key US market, sales in 1988 amounted to fewer than 10,000 units – compared, for example, with Volvo, which usually achieves sales of around 100,000 units a year in that market.

The multinationals in the UK

Given the current weakness of Rover, the UK car industry is crucially affected by the American-owned multinationals, Ford and Vauxhall, but also by Peugeot, Nissan and Toyota. Toyota's 1989 decision to invest £700 million in a car plant near Derby – the largest Japanese investment ever in Western Europe – and Nissan's expansion plans, show the opportunities in Britain that Rover has been failing to take up. With the exception of Nissan, the multinationals import a large proportion of the cars which they sell in the UK. These are generally referred to as tied imports. In the first seven months of 1988, 43 per cent of Fords sold in Britain and 36 per cent of Vauxhalls were imported. In 1987, a relatively good year, Ford sold 580,119 cars in

Table 8.2
UK content (per cent of ex-factory price), 1987

Vauxhall	Astra	55	
	Cavalier	50	
Ford	Fiesta	75	
	Sierra	75–85	
Rover	Metro	97	
	Montego	95	
Nissan	Bluebird	54	
Peugeot	309	66	(diesel, 50)
	405	55	

Source: CAITS/MSF, *The Motor Industry Today and Tomorrow – A Report for Motor Industry Representatives*, London 1988, p. 22.

the UK but produced only 386,698. For Vauxhall the figures were 270,778 sold with 183,857 built locally; for Peugeot, 101,264 sold with 45,549 manufactured in Britain. Thus even in a good year tied imports make up almost 20 per cent of the UK market.

Although car sales in Britain rose by 10 per cent in 1988 to a record 2,215,574, sales of British-built cars actually fell to 965,883, giving a drop in market share to 43.6 per cent. In addition to the problem of the scale of imports – tied or otherwise – of motor vehicles, the other key issue is their local content. Vauxhall and Peugeot's major models are effectively kit cars: in other words, they are assembled from imported components. The UK content of Ford models built here is a good deal higher, as shown in Table 8.2.

Naturally, the lower the UK content, the higher Britain's trade deficit in motor vehicles and components. In addition, there is an erosion of the British technical and skills base when sophisticated components such as gearboxes are not produced at home. The volume of British components firms' output also drops as a result, becoming insufficient to compete effectively. In addition, there is no significant compensation in the shape of exports by the multinationals. Ford exports from Britain are down to about 15,000 per annum. They were running in a range between 100,000 and 140,000 in the second half of the 1970s. Britain's weak export performance is creating a mounting motor trade deficit. In 1987 the overall motor trade deficit was £3.99 billion, but the 1988 figures were much worse. In the first nine months alone the overall deficit was £4.65 billion, up 50 per cent, and while all parts of the industry trade balance deteriorated (cars, commercial vehicles and components), the picture for cars was particularly bad. In the first eleven months of 1988, imports captured 56.5 per cent of the market compared with 51.7 per cent the year before. Again, export performance is poor so that while the value of car imports rose by 33 per cent, the value of car exports fell by 3 per cent.

Ford

Ford UK's globalization strategy risks using Britain as a low value-added, low-wage assembly point for components produced elsewhere. This danger was reinforced by the company's 1989 decision to transfer production of the Sierra from Dagenham to Genk in Belgium. It is becoming increasingly difficult to influence such decisions – or even get access to the relevant information – through any policy short of public ownership.

Ford's plants could be put to completely new uses. Joint ventures or contract work with other firms are one possibility. The alternative would be to develop the company's capacity to undertake the complete production cycle, though on smaller batch runs than those to which the plant currently contributes. Of course, one of the options for co-operation or a joint venture would be with Rover itself. The tie-up between Volkswagen and Seat in recent years has shown that the possibilities of integrating different car producers are much greater than previously thought.

It cannot be said in advance whether continuing to participate in Ford's world car project would be preferable to the other two strategies – joint ventures with other firms, or developing an independent production capability. That would depend on the relative terms agreed. However, the potential advantages of taking Ford into public ownership would be to prevent the rundown of the company, which might otherwise ultimately result in the physical transfer of the capital abroad; to open up options for the productive resources involved other than participation in the global Ford car; and to divert profit flows from Ford to the national exchequer.

These goals would depend on negotiations with Ford. If the company pursued a disruptive strategy which was not simply based on profit-maximizing, but also on political motives, then the plant and equipment could be put to new uses, because of their flexibility, without Ford's agreement. Greater benefits could probably then be extracted in terms of cash, with all the future profit streams returning to the public purse, and with the government also having greater freedom to determine compensation levels, since there would no longer be the requirement to buy the company's co-operation.

The vital importance of components

The relative importance of different parts of the British motor industry has shifted over recent years. It is a shift that provides a possible basis for the revitalization of the British industry. A high proportion of the value of cars and other vehicles is bought in from component suppliers, and this proportion is higher in Britain than elsewhere – around 65–70 per cent for Rover and Ford, 70 per cent for Peugeot UK and 85 per cent for Vauxhall. As developments in cars are increasingly linked to sub-systems of the vehicle – fuel supply, exhaust, electronic control systems – the components suppliers are often becoming more important than the manufacturers themselves, who come to play a role closer to that of assemblers and distributors. The importance of information systems and electronic components will continue to rise as a proportion of the value of vehicles, possibly overtaking such basic parts as transmission or even engines. By the late 1990s, electronics will account for a quarter of car manufacturing costs.[20]

The key priority for the industry, then, need not in the first place be to re-establish scale for final output, but rather to develop the productive capacity in all the various processes of developing and manufacturing cars, particularly in components, which range from motors down to such items as windscreen wipers. Although 1,000 suppliers supply 8,000 separate parts to a typical UK car firm, some 30 per cent of the value of the bought-in content is accounted for by 20 major suppliers including firms such as Lucas, GKN, Turner & Newall, Pilkington and BBA. The practice of buying in components worth a high proportion of the value of final output has enabled relatively small UK assemblers to reach unit cost levels competitive with those reached by much larger integrated producers.[21]

This suggests a possible model for the regeneration of the industry. While it may not be feasible to change Rover into a genuine volume producer in the immediate future, and while there would be serious problems associated with using the facilities of multinationals such as Ford even once they were taken into public ownership, the components sector is not subject to the same difficulties. It accounts for most of the employment and added-value in the industry, and is the part of the sector where most of the action will be over the coming decade.[22] In the long run, the likelihood of the car companies themselves becoming little more than final assembly operations, as the value-added shifts into components, is growing. A 1988 report by the industry and services union MSF points out that components companies 'have generally been slow to introduce the changes necessary to survive – for instance new investment – and as a result the rationalization has been severe and the industry's competitive position in Europe has been eroded'.[23] A policy of nationalizing a significant proportion of the major component suppliers, and developing within them the scale of research and development needed to enable them to provide an efficient basis for the rest of the industry, represents a way out of the dilemmas posed by the currently insufficient scale of the final producers in Britain. Such a strategy could create the conditions whereby the renationalization of the British Aerospace and Rover Group would allow an eventual return to successful volume car production. Rover itself could develop a role as a component manufacturer as well as a final producer – already in 1989 it agreed to produce 20,000 panels a week for Renault, for example.[24] Britain is well placed to knit together the different industrial processes on the basis of the most advanced technology. The main international standard for electronic data interchange in the sector, Odette, was developed in the UK with the support of the Society of Motor Manufacturers and Traders.[25]

Such a policy would chime with the current trend towards increased concentration in the components industry. During the 1980s Ford cut the number of its component suppliers in Britain from over 2,500 to 900 while Austin Rover cut its suppliers from 1,200 to 700. The onus is now on suppliers to invest in research and development, high product quality and just-in-time stock supply since producers see these as important factors in making their contracting decisions.[26]

The aim behind a policy of nationalizing components suppliers would be twofold. First, it would allow economies of scale to be realized at the level of components manufacturers – when they cannot immediately be realized at the level of final producers – by having highly specialized components producers supply a range of final manufacturers. Second, it could also reorientate the development of vehicle technology towards its overall economic and environmental effect, rather than simply towards maximizing the sales of the model in question.

This reorientation is already a trend in the world market. But it is emerging only slowly since it runs counter to the basic logic of private production and consumption. Two areas are central: pollution control and electronic-guidance, collision-avoidance systems. By taking a lead in these two areas, the sector could make a contribution to environmental standards as well as overall economic efficiency in Britain, at the same time as preparing itself for key export markets that can be clearly foreseen for the 1990s. Japanese cars (initially the Toyota Corolla) were in 1988 the only ones already complying with future EEC controls, because the Japanese government decided to go for strict US-type standards from an early date. Instead of being dragged kicking and screaming into the acceptance of emission standards, as is currently the case, the British government should, from an ecological and even from a competitive point of view, be taking a lead in setting strict standards.

A powerful components industry with the scale needed to finance the necessary high levels of research and development, combined with a strong public commitment to develop the infrastructure for advanced traffic management systems, will be needed if Britain is to benefit from these new technological developments. Under present policies, however, they are more likely to sound the final death-knell for the British industry than to herald its resurgence. If this advanced infrastructure is built up first in competing countries, they will be in a better position to supply the technology to run the networks as well as the vehicles to operate on them.

The car and the lorry have traditionally been symbolic of the private way of doing things, as against the bus and the train, which have been symbols of collective solutions. This has never been fully valid, since the car has always relied on massive public investment in roads. But the car is beginning to change. The convergence of information technology and telecommunications is permitting the development of sophisticated traffic guidance systems. The main feature of these is that the driver specifies his or her destination, and an onboard computer, linked in through a telecommunications network to a central system, proposes a route, taking into account traffic jams and accidents on the way. Large-scale research and development programmes are currently under way to develop these systems – in Europe notably the Prometheus and DRIVE programmes. In Britain, a pilot scheme, 'Autoguide', was in operation between Heathrow airport and Westminster from 1988. The accelerated development of such technologies in Britain is essential if the industry is to participate effectively in the vehicle markets of the 1990s. Studies show that these developments will permit very significant savings in fuel, time and stress. By integrating the movement of each car into a collective system, and putting the driver partly into the role of a passenger, they also begin to erode the distinction between private and public transport.

Public Transport

Government underfunding and lack of investment, combined with regionally imbalanced economic growth, has created a crisis in public transport – on road, rail and in the air. In London alone, congestion is costing industry £15 billion a year.[27] The 1987 Kings Cross Underground fire and the rail disasters at Clapham Junction in 1988 and at Purley and Glasgow in 1989 were only the most obvious signs of a system at breaking point. Overcrowding is reaching epidemic proportions on rush-hour bus, rail and underground services. Peak underground traffic grew by 35 per cent between 1980 and 1989, while off-peak traffic grew by 80 per cent.[28] The M25 motorway, instead of relieving congestion, has generated so much extra traffic that it is already unable to cope, while central London is even more congested than before. Aircraft movements in the London terminal manoeuvring area (covering Heathrow, Gatwick, Luton and Stansted) are now a major safety worry, with air traffic control working at full capacity with ageing equipment, but still unable to avoid long delays during the summer.[29]

Meanwhile, regional airports of international standard remain underused; British Rail (BR)'s provincial sector is planning to close up to 1,000 miles of rural railway lines;[30] no new electrification programmes are scheduled outside the South-east; and the signs are that any major new links to the Channel Tunnel will terminate in London. The Transport Department's answer to motorway congestion is to build extra lanes, while railways have been told to plan on the assumption that resources of rolling stock will be so tightly stretched that traffic will be turned away in peak periods, with a high fares policy to drive passengers off the system rather than providing railways with the necessary extra resources.

Any new national plan for public transport should aim to overcome these imbalances on the basis of the following principles:

- public ownership, regulation and democratic control;
- national planning with local accountability;
- investment in new projects with subsidies for day-to-day running costs.

Piecemeal versions of such strategies have been tried before. But the trend in transport policy now in vogue is running in the opposite direction. Wide-ranging policies of deregulation and privatization have been applied through the 1980s in an attempt to revitalize an industry seen as being in decline. But, far from breathing new life into the transport industry, 'Conservative government policies have left a fragmented, disjointed and exhausted transport system, barely recognizable as the public service they inherited in 1979.'[31]

An inherent conservatism towards fares policies and network planning, alongside a general scepticism about the possibilities for public transport, have been long-standing problems of transport planning in Britain. South Yorkshire's famous cheap fares policy was introduced in the late 1970s in the face of resistance from council planners.[32] In the event the policy generated an increase of 20 million passenger journeys per year. Under Department of Transport guidelines, road schemes – generating no revenue income – are assessed on the basis of social costs and benefits in terms of lessened traffic congestion and environmental effects, while rail programmes are obliged to make a profit over costs.

Rail–road trans-shipment facilities need to be encouraged as a positive step towards integrating the two forms of transport; yet grants towards them are not currently allowed unless it can be first proved that traffic would be attracted away from trunk roads. Similarly, Transport Supplementary Grant can now only be given to local authorities for road and parking projects, not for public transport schemes. Thus 'no rational prioritization of national expenditure takes place, nor any adequate assessment of needs or value for money for transport expenditure'.[33]

Even under governments with a more positive approach to public transport expenditure, roads have generally been the priority, with the question of public transport relegated to managing the existing system, as the example of the nationalized railway shows.

Why a nationalized railway?

The opportunities offered by post-war nationalization have largely been missed. The system BR inherited was never redesigned as an integrated network and post-war planning tended to separate homes from workplaces, often building new towns in areas poorly served by the existing network. BR also has a very different relationship with central government from its European counterparts. BR is distant from the decisions of Britain's transport planners, while road planners are part of the Department of Transport. In France, by contrast, Societé Nationale des Chemins de Fer Français (SNCF) and Ministry of Transport staff are regularly exchanged, and in Italy, Ferrovie dello Stato (FS) and the Italian Ministry are effectively one and the same.[34] While metropolitan Passenger Transport Executives adopt three-year policy plans for the provision of local services, BR is constrained by the necessity of producing annual plans, which rule out some prohibitively capital intensive investment items vital to the planned development of the network. Rail projects costing over £5 million have to be submitted for approval to the Department of Transport, but major trunk road projects are initiated within the Department itself.

The rail system will only be able to fulfil its potential if it is designed, planned and operated publicly and centrally. Only then could it operate efficiently, providing a vital link between sectors of the economy and giving people the greatest possible freedom to travel. When Lord Beeching began his programme of lopping off vast tracts of the railway network in the early 1960s, he justified it on grounds of financial efficiency. If a line made a loss, it had to be cut out of the system, and if enough loss-making lines were shut down, the system would steam into profitability. But Beeching's theory was fundamentally flawed. Lines do not exist on their own: they are the constituent elements in an integral system, the rail network as a whole. Large-scale closures mean inconvenience and hardship for current users, the loss of feeder traffic to the rest of the system and a still heavier burden on the roads, with all the social and environmental damage involved. And an ever-contracting network will never be able to satisfy the increasing demands of passengers or freight traffic in a potentially expanding economy. However, Beeching's theory still has its adherents on the British Railways Board today.

After the King's Cross Underground fire and Clapham Junction, Purley and Glasgow rail disasters, few would maintain that market forces can achieve a cheap, accessible, democratic, modern and safe transport system. Those in doubt need only refer to Desmond Fennell's report of the King's Cross inquiry: 'It is clear on the evidence of [London Regional Transport chairman] Sir Keith [Bright] that his Board did have proper regard to efficiency and economy: it is equally clear they did not impose the same criteria when it came to safety of operation.'[35]

The inability of market forces to measure up to the needs of a nationally-integrated rail network is clear. Government subsidy to the railways, in the form of the Public Service Obligation (PSO) grant, was cut from £950 million in 1982 to £700 million in 1986–7. In 1990–91, it will be just £539 million.[36] And yet, despite these cuts, and staffing levels only 70 per cent of what they were 10 years ago, the service BR provides is supposed to be generally comparable to that of 1974. Government attempts to drive down the PSO grants and artificially force up BR's profitability are killing off its ability to provide a reliable, safe and clean service.

The objective is privatization. Already, in an echo of the Beeching mentality, the Government has lopped off BR's hotel, catering, engineering, holiday and Sealink subsidiaries. Right-wing think-tanks like the Adam Smith Institute and the Centre for Policy Studies have been busily issuing pamphlets informing the minister how they think he should sell off the remaining network. With the objective of preparing the network for privatization by cutting government subsidy, the results in terms of quality of service have been catastrophic. Since 1983, the number of seats on BR trains has fallen by 10 per cent, while the total number of passenger journeys has risen by 5 per cent.[37] The increase in employment in the South-east led to a 15 per cent increase between 1985 and 1988 in the number of people travelling daily into central London by rail. But overcrowding is no longer something confined to the South-east. According to the 1988 Central Transport Users Consultative Committee Report, 'pockets of overcrowding are developing elsewhere on the network, not least on InterCity. Overcrowding is an epidemic and must be cured.'[38]

Overcrowding is not the only headache for travellers. Passenger complaints concerning Network SouthEast have risen by 64 per cent since 1979, prompting the Monopolies and Mergers Commission to comment that 'there is a considerable and continuing discrepancy between the British Railways Board (BRB)'s published figures [for punctuality, reliability and avoidance of overcrowding] and the daily experience of many commuters. Commuters come to regard BRB's figures with scepticism or even mistrust.'[39] It is little wonder that against the background of an expanding transport market BR has failed to maintain its share. Since 1975, BR's share of the passenger market has fallen from 9 per cent to around 7 per cent in 1986. Freight has dropped even more dramatically: in 1975, BR had 15 per cent of the freight market – by the end of the 1980s, it has around 9 per cent, most of that coal.

Local transport services

Deregulation of local bus services has fragmented urban transport networks, leading to competition between bus operators and between different forms of transport – most notably in Tyne and Wear, where bus routes no longer feed local metro interchanges, but run in parallel to the city centre.[40] While government studies show an increased bus mileage, the common pattern is over-bussing at peak periods, competing services timetabled to within minutes of each other with long gaps in between, and increased use of smaller vehicles with capacity and accessibility disadvantages.[41] The increase in bus mileage conceals the fact that bus usage has fallen by 7 per cent nationally and 12 per cent in big cities, mostly the result of huge fare increases that followed withdrawals of subsidy, as well as slower service due to the increased private traffic in big cities.

The only remaining regulatory mechanism is the government-appointed Traffic Commissioners, responsible for operator licensing and overseeing maintenance standards, but with little or no power over service registrations. This has led to a situation where local network planning is entirely the responsibility of commercial operators, and may not be directly linked with local authority decisions on planning and economic development. Even the structure of metropolitan transport authorities – joint boards of district council nominees – militates against co-ordination with highway management and educational transport needs in individual districts. While many authorities have plans for light rapid transit schemes ('supertrams') or trolleybuses, present policy dictates that they must involve the private sector in financing, constructing and operating such systems. This has obvious consequences for public policy. The record during the 1980s shows that responsibility for the control of local services needs to be returned to the public sector, and strategic regional authorities created, or re-created, with responsibility for a range of local services, including transport.

An alternative national policy

Transport is not normally a high profit industry. Rail and light rail projects involve large initial capital expenditure but offer relatively low returns. Bus operation is relatively labour-intensive and has traditionally tended to produce a well-organized, semi-skilled workforce able to bargain for above-average wages and conditions.[42] Before nationalization, both private bus and rail companies relied on local monopoly status and price-fixing to keep fares (and therefore revenue) high – but at the expense of discouraging usage. Industry commentators generally believe that the 1986–7 privatization of the National Bus Company will lead to a return to that situation. A concerted attack on the wages and conditions of bus workers and the undermining of traditional trade union structures has provided profits for some companies, as has the use of younger minibus drivers allowed for by existing driver licensing legislation. But with increasing car ownership, the potential profitability of private transport enterprises remains low.

National policy should have two objectives. First, it should aim to achieve an integrated transport system, with strict regulation over operators to eliminate wasteful competition; promotion and provision of interchange facilities; ensuring the availability of information; and, as far as possible, compatibility between fares structures. Second, an effective strategy would recognize the interdependence between transport and other sectors of economic policy – such as land-use planning, environmental controls, and economic development. New town planning and urban regeneration projects should be backed up with public transport links, not just roads. Finance should be made available for new urban transport systems, based on national guidelines for regional and local development priorities, instead of the present first-come-first-served bidding system. And while the environmental and energy advantages of a shift from road to rail are well recognized, without an overall employment policy covering transport operation and manufacturing, including private cars, the potential for division and disruption of the motor industry is enormous.

A Labour government in the 1990s should be committed to the re-municipalization of privatized local public transport, with full consultation for users and the local communities affected. Current Labour Party proposals that local authorities would have to finance this process themselves cannot be right, when it is realized that the proceeds of the sale of the seventy-odd subsidiaries of the National Bus Company went to the national exchequer.[43] Only a renewed commitment to public ownership of the transport infrastructure and its operation can ensure an expanding network providing the safe and reliable standards of service that both passengers and overall economic needs demand.

Energy

Britain is an energy-rich country. Apart from the Soviet Union, it is alone among major industrialized nations in being a net exporter of energy. Until the 1980s the industry had made substantial progress. The fragmented pre-war sector, which suffered from low wages, inefficiency and lack of co-ordination, had been transformed through nationalization, with each part becoming a successful, modern corporation. As for the inefficiencies and harsh working conditions of the inter-war period, it is enough to contrast the progress in health and safety and working conditions in publicly-owned mining as compared with the private construction industry. Before nationalization a miner's risk of fatality was 1 in 1,000; it is now 1 in 10,000.

The exception is oil which was and remains dominated by large-scale multinational corporations. By the late 1980s foreign companies had control over most UK oil reserves, as concentration in the industry leapt through a frenetic series of asset deals. Five companies now own 58 per cent of reserves and 59 per cent of current output. British ownership of reserves has fallen to 47 per cent, even counting Shell as British. A 1989 study by County Natwest Woodmac argued that the monopolization of the sector might lead to an atrophy of new ideas and approaches to the industry.[44]

But there have been problems on the publicly-owned side of the sector. Whilst public ownership has allowed relatively efficient reorganization through internal management, there has been an acute failure to co-ordinate across sectors. Different fuels wastefully compete with each other in the market place and publicly-owned corporations even battle it out in the courts. Most recently, there was the absurd instance of a court case between Scottish Electricity and British Coal over pricing policy and the commitment to purchase rather than import.

Over the years external government control has been increasingly a combination of two elements which have intensified under Thatcher, especially as a result of privatization plans. First, commercial criteria have been used more and more, to the point where British Coal treats redundancies as a matter for the welfare state. This contrasts with the original claimed objectives for the nationalized coal industry of serving the needs of workers and consumers alike while breaking even on average over the years. Second, instead of the industries being used to command the economy, the opposite has been the case with wage restraint, investment programmes and price controls being used to meet economic objectives, at the expense of the industries' long-term development. During the 1980s this took the extreme form of privatization policies to beat down the miners, allow coal imports, and favour nuclear power. The number of miners has been almost halved since the coal strike of 1984–5 as a result of scores of pit closures. The economist Andrew Glyn has shown beyond doubt that the 'uneconomic' pits are no such thing, when full account is taken of the costs of redundancy, continuing dole payments, the loss of direct and indirect taxes, the extra burden on local rates and the fuller spread of overheads.[45] The threatened import of 35 million tonnes of coal per annum, much potentially from South Africa, would more than halve the coal industry's workforce, with serious implications for power and transport workers and for the regional location of industry.

Privatization

Privatization of the electricity supply industry will result in more expensive electricity. Costs of production and distribution will be increased. Cast-iron guarantees are made for the nuclear industry despite its excessive cost and potential safety risks, especially under private control. The electricity supply industry has had an institutionalized bias towards nuclear power which has never been economic even if the overwhelming weight of expenditure on research and development is set aside. One has only to compare government research and development expenditure of £209 million for 1988–9 on nuclear energy with the insignificant £1.4 million on coal – 5p per tonne of coal burnt compared to 31p in the US, 34p in West Germany and 105p in Japan.

Competition will be difficult to ensure, even if it were to bring benefits, since the privatized industry will be dominated by a few large – and growing – corporations. The solution being offered is to give powers to a regulator, for energy as for other sectors. There are serious problems in this. Either powers will be too weak in order to guarantee profitability, or the regulator will be expected to do what has not yet been done by any post-war government – to develop and introduce a co-ordinated energy policy, taking account of its many implications. This would be to expect a regulator to do undemocratically what is the responsibility of government policy to determine. These likely deficiencies of the privatized electricity supply industry highlight what needs to be done – and what could be done under public ownership.

Britain has the worst record in Western Europe for energy conservation because the objectives of the industry are those of large-scale suppliers. The same deficiency applies in relation to alternative energy sources and combined heat and power. Vertical integration with the rest of industry needs to be planned, not left to the market. Anderson-Strathclyde, a leading mining machinery manufacturer, is already controlled by Minorco, while there are plans to construct private ports. Transnational corporations threaten to bring about major economic and political changes in the make-up of the industry. The real need, in contrast, is for a strategic plan for each energy sector as well as strategic planning across the sectors to deal with conservation, regional development and new technology. Vertically integrated public control is needed in pursuit of progressive objectives.

This implies the need for a co-ordinated plan for coal and electricity. It is absurd to have one playing off against the other when 80 per cent of coal is burnt to provide electricity and 80 per cent of electricity is coal-fired.

The past twenty years have shown that energy markets are subject to powerful economic and political forces and interests which have brought about enormous instability in the industry. Public ownership and coherent planning are essential to minimize the negative effects of this and to enable the pursuit of long-term, stable power supplies as well as job security for those in the industry. Energy should be provided increasingly as a basic right rather than as a source of profit.

Construction

Construction's safety record in Britain is appalling. Despite an inspection blitz by the Health and Safety Executive during 1987 and 1988, when 2,046 out of 8,272 building sites visited were closed down as dangerous to workers and the public, there were a record 157 construction industry deaths in the year to March 1988. According to government figures, as many workers are fatally injured in the construction industry as in the whole of the manufacturing sector.[46] Construction workers have reason to complain also about economic policies. They have been among the worst victims of the overgrowth of the City in the British economy. The speculative cycles in the value of property make the construction industry swing between hyperactivity and long periods of depression and unemployment. At the same time, Keynesian demand management by the government – so-called fine tuning of the economy – has only intensified the industry's instability. As a result,

> during the recession from 1973 ... the decline in economic activity, coupled with cuts in public expenditure, led to a fall of one-half in the flow of new contracts between 1972 and 1980. ... The severity of booms and slumps in construction activity are likely to have a particularly adverse effect on the industry in view of its labour-intensive, craft-based nature and the value to a firm of retaining men who are used to working as a team; moreover experience seems to show that recessions often lead to trained men being lost from the industry altogether. The particularly high degree of uncertainty which faces construction firms must preclude forward planning of any worthwhile kind and thus retard investment in plant and labour training.[47]

According to the chairman of Redland, a leading British building materials company, a rise of one percentage point in mortgage rates has generally resulted in a 6 to 7 per cent decline in private housing output.[48] The vulnerability of the construction industry to the insane fluctuations of interest rates which the free market has given us over recent years can therefore easily be appreciated. Construction is usually seen as requiring few imports; yet by 1988 the annual trade deficit on building materials had risen from £400 million in 1981 to £2.6 billion, accounting for over 10 per cent of the £20.5 billion deficit in visible trade.

Recent years have seen a surge in homelessness – local authorities accepted responsibility for 118,000 officially homeless households in 1987 in England and Wales alone, compared with 74,000 in 1981.[49] The single homeless are not of course accepted as homeless at all – and unofficial estimates of the number of homeless are far higher. A new wave of homelessness followed sharply higher repossessions in 1988 as a result of mortgage defaults. Yet between 1973 and 1986, construction output fell by 13.1 per cent, as against growth of 20.4 per cent for the economy as a whole.[50] The need for more housing is clearly desperate. But hundreds of thousands of the workers to build these houses are still unemployed because the free market, yet again, has failed to put needs and productive power together. In the two years to 1989, construction output again rose by a sixth, but this growth was concentrated in private sector office building and industrial construction.[51] Of the two to two-and-a-half million house purchases a year, about one tenth are accounted for by new homes. By 1989, rises in interest rates were leading to drop-outs by buyers of new homes, and starts on new homes were forecast to fall 15 per cent.

Movement towards a long-term stable growth path for the industry must be the aim. This would involve separate considerations for the residential (houses) and the business (factories and offices) sides of the industry. For houses, it is possible in principle – though complex in practice – to identify a set of needs, in terms of shortages of housing by region, and to plan a policy of public provision to meet these needs. Such a policy would provide a firm backbone of steady growth for the residential side of the sector, and would have the further advantage of calming the fluctuations of private residential construction, since the existence of a known policy of growing public provision would remove the uncertainty which underlies speculation in house prices. For industrial construction, the key is its role in investment. Construction accounts for around half – 46 per cent in 1987 – of gross investment, and output of investment goods always varies much more than the rest of the economy. The orientation suggested in this book for other sectors of the economy, based on an intensification of research efforts and investment in long-term modernization of capacity, promises a stabilization of investment demand for the construction of factories and offices, and could form the basis of a building programme designed to take account of regional and environmental policies.

Construction is a technically backward industry throughout the world. Despite the impression created by cranes and heavy earth moving equipment on large building sites, many of today's labour techniques were developed in the ancient Middle East, and have changed little since. Attempts have been made to apply factory principles of production, notably during the war and in the 1960s; but these have on the whole proved disappointing, mainly because they have really amounted to a mechanical transposition of techniques developed in manufacturing, rather than involving a serious and independent research effort. At first sight, it appears strange that no firms have invested seriously in the research and development needed to modernize construction technologies, since the existing form of labour is so arduous and dangerous – while productivity has grown much slower than in the rest of the economy:

> Over the period since 1948 the prices of capital goods in general and also of goods and services in general have increased by around 11–12 times compared with 14 times for construction. This difference is mainly explained by the fact that productivity in construction has not increased at the same rate as elsewhere.[52]

Small firms in a large industry

The main explanation of the shortage of fundamental research in construction is that no firms are large enough to take a strategic view. Between 1979 and 1987 the number of firms in the industry grew from 80,000 to 175,000, with all the increase registered among firms employing fewer than seven workers. The result has been a flourishing of the 'lump' – 'self-employed' employees without insurance or protection – who now make up more than half of the labour force.[53] Only 18 construction firms made it to the 1988 *Financial Times 500*, of which Tarmac alone is in the top 100 with a market value of £1.7 billion and 28,000 employees. The next largest, George Wimpey, has a market value of less than £700 million. For an industry which accounts for 9 per cent of male employment in Britain, these are strikingly low figures. As one analyst has put it:

> The construction industry remains, as it has long been, an industry comprised of a large number of predominantly small firms. ... There has been no growth in the average size of firms in the industry (indeed the reverse is true). ... Out of nearly 168,000 registered firms, about 90 per cent employ fewer than 8 persons.[54]

Firms of this size are not capable of mounting the scale of research effort capable of transforming and modernizing an industry. As a result construction is caught in a vicious circle underpinned by the market and the private approach to the organization of the industry. Needed research and development is simply not carried out. The contradiction is that the research and development performed is determined not by the industrial structure *after*, but by that *before* the technical scale changes as a result of the change in production technology.

This is made worse by the fact that we are talking about long-term research and development. Private firms, especially in Britain, are extremely reluctant to commit themselves to this kind of research, as they fear that others will be the ones to gain from their research. In construction this syndrome is still more pronounced, since firms have had to develop a short-term outlook to cope with Britain's highly volatile property market. The result is massive mistakes at huge social cost, because not enough resources are put into examining the appropriateness of the technical and architectural approaches adopted. Again because of the smallness of scale, there is scarcely any real market research – merely subjective and anecdotal impressions as to whether particular types of building are successes or not – and it seems to take a generation for any lessons to be learnt.

The industry is not only broken down into small firms; there is a further division between design (architecture and civil engineering) and production (construction proper):

> This division between the design and production stages ... precludes any interaction between design and production considerations except in so far as production aspects may be taken into account by the designer. Designers, however, can only do this in fairly general terms, for traditionally they have received little training in such matters and

> their practical experience is limited. ... Thus the separation of the design and production functions in construction precludes the close co-operation between designers and producers, which is important from a productivity point of view, and also limits the possibility of the feedback of production experience into subsequent design. This contrasts sharply with the close integration between design and production achieved in much of manufacturing industry.[55]

The urgency of an expansion of research efforts and a revolutionization of the sector's technology is increased by the growing relationship between construction and other industries – especially as the quantity of electronic equipment, increasingly networked, continues to rise sharply in offices, factories, and even homes. The best prospects for improvements in the underlying technology of the industry lie in the integration of production and design. And in the real world this will only happen through large-scale public intervention. The organizational basis for this development, aimed at the improvement of research in the sector, already exists. An expanded Building Research Establishment could serve as the vehicle of this approach. But on its own it would have no production arm, and would be unable to test and implement the results of its research. It would need to work in close conjunction with a nationalized public construction firm, which would probably need to be constituted from the merger of at least two currently private firms, given the lack of concentration in the sector.[56]

Pharmaceuticals

Pharmaceuticals account for only around 2 per cent of UK industry, but the sector is growing more than twice as fast as the economy as a whole. Half of its sales go to the NHS and one-third are exported. Research expenditure came to £490 million in 1984; and 15 per cent of the sector's 81,400 employees are engaged in research and development activities. Its trade surplus rose 3 per cent in 1988 to £835 million.[57] The pharmaceutical industry is already subject to extensive public control, notably through the Pharmaceutical Price Regulation Scheme (PPRS), which assigns a target rate of profit to NHS suppliers. They are permitted to retain profits above this rate if they are due to 'the launch of a new product, improved efficiency or other factors clearly arising from the company's own efforts'.

The fact that the government is in this way given a responsibility to determine the causes of profitability in the industry, produces a deep and operational involvement of the state in the sector's affairs – an involvement quite at odds with the free-market ideology that civil service bureaucrats cannot be trusted to understand and determine the day-to-day affairs of individual firms, which should be left to the cut and thrust of the market. There is no suggestion, even from the present government, of changing the situation. And with good reason: pharmaceuticals belong to a growing category of industries for which the free market is totally inappropriate. The cost of a successful drug is to a great extent determined by the cost of the research needed to develop it, rather than the later cost of producing the actual tablets. Free competition with no legal restrictions would therefore lead to an abandonment of research, since the company paying for the development of a particular drug would not benefit from the investment any more than other companies which would be equally free to produce the same drug without having paid for its development. The solution adopted is that of patents: legally enforceable, and saleable, exclusive rights to market what one has developed. 'Knowledge can only acquire a price when it is protected by some form of monopoly', with the attendant profit-maximizing incentives to increase prices even if this means lower output.[58]

Patent medicine

Such patents are therefore only valid for a limited period, currently twenty years. This is a compromise between the free market and the patent monopoly approaches, and therefore combines the advantages and disadvantages of both, without tackling the underlying problem, which cannot be solved on a market basis. Pharmaceuticals are an example of the typical industry of the future, in which direct production costs are less significant than research and development, thereby undermining the operation of the market and demanding social intervention. These vast programmes of research and development will play a growing role in the economy. And the state will increasingly be called on to take responsibility for them, since their results are intrinsically social, with the benefits spread over the whole of society, rather than being limited to the firms carrying them out.

There are two ways for this socializing process to be organized. Society can take responsibility for the widening research and development effort, but allow private firms to rake in the benefits; or it can directly receive the benefits for which it pays. The latter is clearly the more just and logical approach. Special pleading and the force of vested interests could, however, delay the generalization of this solution indefinitely, and hold back the development of advanced technology on a social scale. But it is already clear that the emerging forms of product development demand a new organization of property relations in the sphere of research and development. The clear practical implication is that the leading firms of the sector should be brought into public ownership.

Since the pharmaceutical sector is less concentrated than many, this would call for the nationalization of a significant number of firms – the top 15 account for around 55 per cent of output. Of these most are foreign-owned, but this would raise no particular difficulties from the point of view of the organization of production. On the research side, laboratories are relatively autonomous in most respects, with the implication that detachment from foreign networks and possible integration with other British units could proceed fairly smoothly. On the production side, similarly, this is an industry in which economies of scale have not yet come into play greatly, with the result that there has not been the decomposition and globalization of production to be found, for example, in the car industry. Because of this, manufacturing processes brought into public ownership would be relatively self-contained, even where they are part of the operations of a multinational firm.

Medical care: commercialization or socialization?

Thus far the case for a publicly owned pharmaceuticals industry has been made in terms of the nature of its production processes – and specifically, the importance of research and development. Looking at the demand side – at the needs of the customer – provides an independent but equally powerful rationale for taking the sector into public ownership.

In all the major capitalist countries, the increased marketization of medical care threatens the basic health standards that have been established over the past half century. The over-the-counter (OTC) section of the market, for medicines not requiring a prescription, has been growing in importance, while the OTC section is increasingly dominated by firms whose expertise lies in retailing and marketing rather than research and development. In the US, Johnson & Johnson and Procter & Gamble are now the second and third biggest advertisers of OTC medication, ahead of more research-based firms such as Merck, Ciba-Geigy, Sandoz, Upjohn and Hoechst; while in the UK Beecham's marketing dominance has dissuaded Glaxo from concentrating its efforts in the OTC sector. The importance of these developments is underlined by the fact that the OTC market is forecast to overtake the prescription market by 1990.

Profit margins for OTC are higher than in the rest of the grocery sector. This is largely because brand-name versions of drugs cost up to five times as much as their identical equivalents in different packaging, known as generic alternatives: Aspro as against aspirin, Panadol as against paracetamol. Nowhere is this trend more marked than in Britain, where the undermining of the NHS by the government is having a strong effect on the medicine business. This move towards a health world where packaging counts more than value, and image more than genuine medical benefit, offers rich pickings for the global drugs industry, but threatens to undermine the development and provision of genuinely beneficial drugs and treatments. Traditionally Britain has ensured this through an implicit understanding between the industry and government. The British state, through its licensing procedures and procurement procedures for the NHS, has insisted on high standards in terms of research and testing, and been willing to finance such standards by paying above the world market price for medicines so long as the companies have local research and testing facilities. But this kind of unwritten deal will come under increasing pressure in coming years, both from the increased dominance of the OTC section if development is left to the market, and from pressure from the EEC and the General Agreement on Tariffs and Trade (GATT), challenging support for domestic industry.

To leave these questions to the market would be to place in jeopardy the health of all, and allow the manipulations of advertisers to undermine national policy for good health. Private firms have an interest in selling as many OTC medicines as possible. This poses two kinds of health danger. First, many medicines, including OTC products, have minor side-effects, with the implication that the presumption should be against using them except where really necessary.

Second, the belief is assiduously fostered by advertising that medicines offer complete solutions when in fact they are usually only effective as part of an overall treatment involving lifestyle factors such as diet and exercise. Exclusive reliance on medicines may actually worsen the medical problem in question. Since neither the market nor the traditional deal between drugs firms and the government can offer an assurance of appropriate provision of medicines in the future, there is an urgent need for a new policy. The aim should be to ensure adequate research and development, and sufficient production, of drugs and medical supplies in Britain, as part of a plan to continue the success of the pharmaceutical industry in a revitalized health sector. A new structure for the industry should also permit exports to develop, as a counterpart of the need to import drugs, or licences for drugs, where more effective remedies have been developed overseas.

There is a clear need to bring major firms into public ownership, in order to reorientate research and development towards genuine health needs, and arrest the takeover of the sector by salespeople and packagers. But at the same time the existing network of research laboratories should not be disrupted by merging or splitting firms overhastily. The first step in restructuring the industry would need to be a study of the breakdown of research, which is currently divided between industry, higher education institutions and the health service. There are strong grounds for suspecting that access to public facilities and results is very important to private industry, but that the taxpayer is currently not receiving adequate recompense for this access – mirroring the situation in the health service proper, where private medicine is parasitical on the NHS. One possible structure would involve full and automatic access to public facilities for the nationalized section of the industry and conditional access for the remaining private parts, depending on the fulfilment of conditions for provision of research results, licensing and production.

But the most important gains from nationalizing the major pharmaceutical firms would be to permit a coherent strategy for the whole health sector, in the knowledge that the means for its implementation would be to hand. Too often plans to revitalize public health provision have lacked credibility because they have relied on the goodwill of the pharmaceutical industry, while not proposing the necessary powers to ensure this co-operation. Great advantages could be derived from joint planning of a strategy for health and a strategy for pharmaceuticals. For example, it has long been recognized that the emphasis of general health care needs to shift from cure to prevention. That implies a structural shift in the relative demand for different medicines and, more fundamentally, a reorientation of the research priorities of the whole of the medical–pharmaceutical complex, currently excessively determined by market forces which have nothing to do with health.

It is possible to imagine trying to develop a policy to achieve these goals within the existing structure of the industry, in co-operation with private firms. But the drugs firms would privately measure every proposal against their hidden agenda of profit maximization, and it would be impossible for them to contribute honestly to a strategy with quite different goals. A more realistic approach would be to hammer out a shift in the thrust of research and investment with a group of publicly-owned and democratically-run enterprises; and as a second stage to extend this agreed strategy to the remaining private firms through negotiation and the direction of public finance where possible, but if necessary by statutory powers.

Notes

1. Interview with *Marxism Today*, June 1983.
2. *Financial Times*, 25 January 1989.
3. Organization for Economic Co-operation and Development (OECD), *Country Report : Britain*, Paris 1988.
4. Wynne Godley, 'Manufacturing and the Future of the British Economy', in Terry Barker and Paul Dunne, eds, *The British Economy after Oil: Manufacturing or Services?*, London 1988, p. 10.
5. Stephen Cohen and John Zysman, *Manufacturing Matters*, New York 1987.
6. Manufacturing, Science, Finance (MSF), *Aerospace – Britain's Future; A Strategy for Britain's Aerospace Industry*, London 1988, p. 1.
7. *Financial Times*, 13 March 1989.
8. *Financial Weekly*, 23 February 1989.
9. Chris Darke, MSF National Officer, quoted in the *Financial Times*, 17 February 1989.
10. *The 146 Campaign*, TASS, 1985, quoted in MSF, *Aerospace – Britain's Future; A Strategy for Britain's Aerospace Industry*, London 1988, p. 3.
11. Sir Austin Pearce, cited in Robert Heller, *The State of Industry*, London 1987, p. 120.
12. See the argument by Chris Darke, *MSF Journal*, December 1988.
13. *Irish Times*, 18 January 1989.

14. MSF, *Aerospace – Britain's Future; A Strategy for Britain's Aerospace Industry*, London 1988, p. 9.

15. *Financial Times*, 2 September 1988.

16. Institute of Manpower Studies, *The UK Motor Industry*, 1989. Figures include electrical equipment and tyres, sectors excluded from official UK Government motor industry employment statistics.

17. *Financial Times*, 24 January 1989.

18. Garel Rhys, 'Motor Vehicles' in Peter Johnson, ed., *The Structure of British Industry*, London 1988, p. 168.

19. *Investors Chronicle*, 31 March 1989.

20. Ian Robertson, 'Clever Cars', in M. Goldring, ed., *The World in 1989*, London 1988, p. 115.

21. Garel Rhys, 'Motor Vehicles' in Peter Johnson, ed., *The Structure of British Industry*, London 1988, p. 175.

22. See *Financial Times*, 8 June 1989, suggesting that by one definition, the value of bought-in components is likely to rise beyond 60 per cent of total sale value.

23. CAITS/MSF, *The Motor Industry Today and Tomorrow – A Report for Motor Industry Representatives*, London 1988, p. 23.

24. *Financial Times*, 6 February 1989.

25. *Financial Times*, 30 March 1989.

26. CAITS/MSF, *The Motor Industry Today and Tomorrow – A Report for Motor Industry Representatives*, London 1988, pp. 24–5.

27. *Financial Times*, 30 March 1989.

28. Department of Transport, *Central London Rail Study*, London 1989.

29. Air Traffic Users Committee, *Annual Report 1987–88*, London 1988.

30. Public Transport Information Unit, *Public Transport Information*, December 1988/January 1989.

31. South-East Region TUC, *Transport Policy in the South-East*, London 1988, p. 2.

32. As argued by Alex Waugh, South Yorkshire County Council Transport Committee Chair, cited in Gavin Smith, *Getting Around*, London 1984, p. 37.

33. Association of Metropolitan Authorities, *Oiling the Wheels*, London 1988, p. 4.

34. Transport 2000, *BR: A European Railway*, London 1984, p. 1.

35. Desmond Fennell OBE QC, *Investigation into the King's Cross Underground Fire*, HMSO Cmd 499, London 1988, p. 123.

36. National Economic Research Associates, *Policies to Achieve a Busier Railway*, London 1988, p. 3.

37. British Railways Board, *National Accounts*, London 1988.

38. Central Transport Consultative Committee, *Annual Report 1987–88*, p. 5.

39. Monopolies and Mergers Commission, *British Railways Board: Network South-East*, HMSO Cmd 204, London 1987, para 2.89.

40. Norman James, 'The Tyne and Wear Metro Study', Paper to Centre for Local Economic Strategies seminar, December 1988.

41. See Transport Road Research Laboratory, 'The First Year of Bus Deregulation', *Research Report 161*, London 1988; and William Tyson, *Bus Deregulation in Great Britain*, London 1988.

42. Ken Fuller, *Radical Aristocrats: London Busworkers from the 1880s to the 1980s*, London 1985.

43. Labour Party, *Fresh Directions*, London 1987. Labour's 1989 policy review avoids the issue altogether.

44. *Financial Times*, 27 February 1989.

45. Andrew Glyn, 'The Economic Case Against Pit Closures' in David Cooper and Trevor Hopper, eds., *Debating Coal Closures*, CUP, Cambridge 1988.

46. Central Statistical Office, *Annual Abstract of Statistics*, London 1989, table 3.36.

47. Michael Fleming, 'Construction', in Peter Johnson, ed., *The Structure of British Industry*, London 1988, p. 230.

48. *Financial Times*, 2 February 1989.

49. Central Statistical Office, *Social Trends*, London 1989, table 8.4.

50. Central Statistical Office, *Economic Trends Annual Supplement*, London 1988, pp. 4, 92.

51. *Financial Times*, 1 March 1989.

52. Michael Fleming, 'Construction', in Peter Johnson, ed., *The Structure of British Industry*, London 1988, pp. 224–5.

53. Figures quoted by George Brumwell, Chair of the construction union UCATT, in his 1989 Sir Arthur Whitelegge Memorial Lecture, *Morning Star*, 18 May 1989.

54. Michael Fleming, 'Construction', in Peter Johnson, ed., *The Structure of British Industry*, London 1988, pp. 214–5, 221.

55. Michael Fleming, 'Construction', in Peter Johnson, ed., *The Structure of British Industry*, London 1988, p. 225.

56. See Michael Ball, *Rebuilding Construction*, London 1988, for a different analysis of the sector.

57. Association of the British Pharmaceutical Industry, cited in *Financial Times*, 1 March 1989.

58. Tessa Morris-Suzuki, 'Capitalism in the Computer Age', *New Left Review* no. 160, November/December 1986, p. 86.

9

Regional and Ecological Balance

Desperate diseases require desperate remedies.

Guy Fawkes, 1605

The global ecological crisis has put a question-mark over the whole meaning of economic development. The threat to the planet from uncontrolled, unsustainable economic growth is now obvious to everyone. As the interdependence of all economic activity has become dramatically clearer, so has the need for co-operative international intervention. All countries and social systems are under threat. Whatever benefits have been claimed for capitalism over the years, environmentally and regionally balanced economic development has never been among them; while in many socialist countries, a narrow and imitative view of economic growth has led to serious ecological damage.

Economic growth has clearly caused enormous ecological destruction. It can bring short-term economic benefits at the expense of long-term injury to the environment. But in the future, increases in output will nevertheless be an indispensable tool for overcoming the problems created by past growth. The key is ecologically sustainable, balanced growth: not just ensuring that new technology is used in the service of people rather than having people service the technology – but also bringing technological change itself under conscious social control. Environmental compatibility will have to be built into the design stage of new technologies. Sustainable growth needs to be long-term rather than short-term; people-centred rather than profit-centred; and balanced across different regions as well as between rural and urban areas.

Ecological Balance

Economic planning must be directed towards human needs. A central aim of future growth must be to enhance the quality of the environment. We need clean air and a planet to live on as much as we need food, kidney machines, video-recorders or cars. It would be wrong to imagine that concern for the environment means tempering economic growth with a few ecological safeguards. The smoke belching out of a factory chimney is just as important a product of that plant as the goods driven out of the factory gate. Our concept of the economy has to be broadened, to embrace and integrate ecological factors in economic analysis, measurement and policy.

Factory waste or pollution is not bought or sold on the market, but it is paid for in physical damage, illness and death by the whole of society. If private firms can continue to make society pay their costs, they will do so. If the main aim of production is to make profits rather than meet human needs, then ecological considerations will only be taken into account either where the firm would risk prosecution by harming the environment or where they impinge on the balance sheet. Companies will mount advertising and lobbying campaigns to secure as liberal regulations as possible. This is why the natural framework for integrating the ecological dimension into economic life is public ownership, which potentially allows environmental protection to be set out as a basic aim of production, rather than as an afterthought imposed on firms from outside.

The Green politician Jonathon Porritt puts it like this:

> The *costs* of pollution control are easily quantifiable; there they stand in the books as a debit. The *benefits* are not as easily quantifiable, and society's ledger doesn't have a special column to show the advantages of a cleaner environment. Since the direct expenses fall on particular industries, they have a very strong political interest in opposing pollution control; since the benefits are spread much more widely throughout society, there is often no single group that can take up the cudgels with the same single-minded enthusiasm as industry does.[1]

But like many who have taken up the ecological challenge most strongly, Porritt believes that all economic growth – by its nature – is unsustainable. He is not only wrong, but actually harming the cause of ecology when he insists that 'an increase in Gross National Product (GNP) inevitably means an increase in Gross National Pollution'.[2] On the contrary, positive intervention and planning to enhance the environment – and reduce Gross National Pollution – will often itself increase GNP as a by-product. For example, if cars are changed over to incorporate anti-pollution catalytic convertors, their production becomes more expensive and measured GNP rises accordingly – but pollution is reduced. More generally, the whole approach of economic planning is based on the need to find ways for firms to take the wider effects of their actions into account, and not merely the immediate effects on their own balance-sheets. Under socialism, that can potentially be ensured by full-scale social ownership and democratic control. But even in a capitalist society, wider public ownership and planning offer the possibility of a shift in that direction.

Ecology and planning for use

How could a programme based on planning in the 1990s contribute to increasing the quality of life, broadly defined, rather than simply increasing the standard of living measured in monetary terms? Take the case of harmful industrial emissions again. While fines or regulations require the government to define and implement rules which need an accurate understanding of the production process, a government which is not directly involved in industrial production will always be two steps behind. It can only pass laws on the emission of particular chemicals, or on the use of particular processes, once it knows that they are happening, and what their effects are. There are two alternatives. Either government will have a general supervisory duty, but no responsibility to authorize new industrial processes or the expansion of old ones; or there must be some licensing scheme for new processes. In the case of a general supervisory duty, it will in practice take a public outcry before the government acts, as it will not be in the interests of firms to publicize the introduction of processes that might be harmful. In the case of a licensing scheme, firms will inevitably perceive the government departments enforcing the regulations antagonistically, in the same way as firms currently regard –

and outwit – the Inland Revenue; and they will be able to adopt a variety of stratagems to evade the intent of the regulations. Such schemes have to involve very strong powers of inspection and high levels of staffing if they are to be even partially effective. Characteristically for Britain, pollution of water courses by British farmers reached record levels in 1988 while prosecutions actually fell – due in large part to shortages of staff in the water authorities.[3]

A simpler and more effective solution would be to build ecological concerns into the basic aims of the undertakings. This is not best done on the basis of private enterprise, accountable to profit-maximizing shareholders, since by their nature ecological issues concern the effects of processes at the global and social level, not at the level of the enterprise. The effect of chlorinated fluorocarbons (CFCs) on the ozone layer is a case in point. CFCs in aerosols and fridges are now being phased out at great expense: in the US alone, US$135 billion-worth of equipment depends on CFCs. But one can imagine the reaction from the management of a big fridge plant twenty years ago to a bright chemist pointing out the danger of CFCs. They would have responded according to the negative implications for their bottom line, rather than the positive effect on society's bottom line. And we can be sure that similar, selfishly private, technological decisions are being taken today in other areas. Public outcry seems to be the only effective policy pressure for ecological concern in a world of private profit.

Collective and public solutions can not only be made more socially accountable than private capitalist solutions. They can also allow the same job to be done while consuming less resources. This is clear from the example of public transport. The railway network has a better safety record than the road system, is cleaner, less congested and, with lower air and noise pollution, environmentally more sound. Land use per person or per ton carried is less than for cars and lorries, energy use is lower, and rolling stock has a longer life span than cars or trucks.[4] A revitalized public transport network would send less fumes into the atmosphere than the private cars that are currently being crammed into the rush-hour streets – often without passengers. In the energy sector, the same approach could be taken with publicly-financed combined heat-and-power schemes, and with proper funding of renewable energy sources.

Of course, planning for ecological balance is not cost-free. For example, before the 1987 general election, the then Labour Party environment spokesperson David Clark proposed a plan to invest £10 billion over ten years in environmental protection and pollution control, creating 200,000 jobs – though almost all of the scheme was excluded from Labour's election manifesto. If the Labour leadership had stuck to the official Labour policy of reducing military spending, the necessary funds would have been easier to allocate for these plans. If we recognize the importance of investment in the physical infrastructure, to secure the basis for secure and balanced growth, we should recognize that a clean and healthy environment is the most important infrastructure of all. The Labour movement has adopted radical policies to tackle the environmental crisis. Labour's 1989 policy review proposed far-reaching controls on atmospheric, land and sea pollution – as well as the establishment of a Ministry of Environmental Protection and a new quango to enforce pollution standards. But as with so many other of the Labour leadership's plans, it is hard to see how all this could be delivered without a major extension of direct, democratic social control and ownership of industry.

Balanced Regional Development

The present structure of regional aid is so complex that few non-specialists can have a clear picture of it. But while the list of names of the many different grants and bodies involved is confusing, the main policy trends over recent years have been towards:

- a reduction of regional aid;
- a move to bypass local government by establishing undemocratic urban development bodies on the model of the London Docklands Development Corporation; and
- a reliance on the private capitalist sector rather than local or national public enterprise.

The net effect of these policy shifts under the Thatcher governments has shown up in widening gaps across as well as within regions. In the absence of central government support for local authority involvement in local economies, even progressive Labour-controlled authorities have been forced to enter into partnership developments with private industry on terms overwhelmingly beneficial to the private sector rather than the local community.[5] Indeed, a 1988 TUC publication on the inner cities does not even attempt to work out possibilities for a properly planned and co-ordinated strategy for economic regeneration through the public sector; the emphasis is all on private capitalist investment.[6] The employment White Paper of 1944 proclaimed:

> It will be the object of Government policy to secure a balanced industrial development in areas which in the past have been unduly dependent on industries specially vulnerable to unemployment.

Almost half a century later, the government is spending £885 per head in the overheated South-east compared to £702 in Yorkshire and Humberside, helping to worsen the already serious problem of regional inequalities.[7] At the same time, the ten most environmentally and socially depressed local authority areas in England, according to the Department of Environment's misery league, are in London.

The Thatcher government argues that the solutions to problems of regional inequality should be market-driven. But it is the market – or at least private production for the market – which created the problem of regional imbalance in the first place. So it makes little sense to entrust its solution to this selfsame market. Inequality has grown, not fallen, in the recent past. Employment growth since 1983 has been concentrated heavily in the South: taking the whole period from 1979 to 1987, employment fell by 157,000 in the South, but by 1.2 million in the North.[8] A 1988 report by the North of England Regional Consortium (NOERC) argued that the elimination of regional differences in social and economic opportunities 'represents the most important challenge facing the nation', going on to comment that:

> Even a cursory inspection of regional disparities and the present response shows that a plethora of inadequately thought-out programmes is no substitute for clear co-ordination and positive policy.[9]

Regional programmes are not only inadequately thought-out; their financing is not on the same scale as the problems they address. There is a curious gap between discussions of regional policy and general discussions of the economy and private investment. The former are talked about in tens and hundreds of millions of pounds, spread over five-year periods, while the latter are discussed in billions and tens of billions per year. The government spends less than £500 million annually on regional aid, and has switched about £250 million from national programmes supposedly to the inner cities, but in practice overwhelmingly to Urban Development Corporations. Meanwhile, since 1979 over £20 billion has been cut from local authorities' rate support grant. Public money is handed out to private firms, but little or no attempt is made to extract any serious degree of control over these firms' strategies in return. Next to no resources are devoted by the regional development agencies to taking stakes in firms: the Welsh Development Agency invested £9–10 million out of its £86.5 million spending in 1987–8, while the equivalent figures for the Scottish Development Agency were £8 million out of a total budget of £140 million in 1986–7. The rest is essentially handed over to private firms as a gift. Nowhere has that been more obvious than in the Tory government's highly expensive enterprise zones, where companies are given tax holidays and allowed to ignore planning controls, but which have been useless at creating new jobs.

National and regional economic policy

Without an effective regional policy, a coherent national economic policy is impossible. Regional policy is a matter of concern for the whole country, not just the poorer parts. For example, interest rates were increased ten times – from 7.5 per cent to 14 per cent – between May 1988 and May 1989 in an attempt to head off rising inflation and balance-of-payments deficits. But while the depressing effects of this on the economy of the South-east may be welcomed by government, spending and investment is equally discouraged in the North. Government macroeconomic policies apply equally to the whole country. As long as there are major variations in the level of wealth and activity between different parts of the country, locally differentiated economic measures – which are after all what is meant by regional policy – will be needed to deal with the very diverse problems of the different areas. And the only way to create a truly single economy in the long run is by means of strategic regional policy aimed at reducing and ultimately removing the sources of disadvantage of the economically less developed regions.

The late 1980s saw some trickle-down of high southern growth into the rest of the country. But this mechanism, halting, delayed and insufficient as it was, will be still further reduced by the introduction of the Channel Tunnel in 1993, after which benefits of growth in southern Britain will be as likely to trickle down into northern France as northern Britain, and the need for a positive British regional policy will be correspondingly greater. Professor Doreen Massey of the Open University has highlighted the inconsistency of a government economic strategy that allowed imports to grow to satisfy the demands of consumer spending in the South-east, while the government was having to pay out increasing amounts on subsidizing new infrastructure to cope with congestion, on mounting mortgage tax relief, and on ever-increasing rentals on government offices.[10] As this shows, the government's real regional policy, like its real policy in other fields, has been to hand over the large sums to the richer areas which least need it, while returning a relative pittance in regional aid. The Labour MP Tony Blair summed up the contradictions as follows:

> There is congestion, overheating, rocketing house prices, skill shortages in one part of Britain and depopulation, unemployment and substantial slack in demand in the other. It is not efficient and it is not socially just. The government with its attachment to the free market, is incapable of resolving this division. It is the distinctive contribution of socialism, with its emphasis on notions of society and community, that it can.[11]

Moving headquarters to the regions

The impact of new information technology on regional location can cut either way. On the one hand advanced telecommunications reduces, and in some cases abolishes, the importance of physical distance between and within companies. Given that distance from the major markets is one of the regions' biggest handicaps, this can be expected to stimulate regional development. But on the other hand, the very same technologies create the option of locating all the strategic functions of companies and other organizations far from the production centres in the regions, and close to the main sources of producer services – consultancy, computer support, and finance.[12] Because of this ambiguity of new technology, any serious attempt to move organizations' headquarters to the regions would need to be either based on public sector decisions, or else on inducing private firms to change their behaviour. The private market solution would be an uphill struggle – in a 1988 survey of 110 chief executives and finance directors, 93 per cent said they would risk dismissal rather than move north of Watford, while 99 per cent felt that the Channel Tunnel made a move north impracticable.[13] In the late 1980s, the escalating costs and problems of working in London began to push both businesses and government to look again at moving important offices out of the capital and the South-east. But it hardly amounts to a stampede, and the likelihood must be that as the speculative growth runs out of steam, the trend will disappear.

There is an increasingly old-fashioned notion of the headquarters of any large organization as a single physical location – typically a large building – where information is centrally processed and all important decisions are made. It is usually located in London, and the idea of moving it lock stock and barrel to another part of the country raises obstacles which generally prove insuperable. However, more and more of the functions of this type of organization are nowadays contracted out – computer services, telecommunications management, strategic analysis and market research, for example. This is sometimes done for unjustifiable motives, such as the desire to use external unorganized labour where it is cheaper and more pliable. But it is often for perfectly good reasons, especially to take advantage of economies of scale in the production of expertise in these very specialized areas. This trend shows up in the growth of business services in the economy.

The technical reasons for company headquarters to be in London are disappearing, but the technical and residential infrastructure for these business support services is currently overwhelmingly concentrated in the South-east. There is therefore a chicken-and-egg problem of distributing economic functions in a way more in line with modern communications technologies. The individual units, whether with their business or residential hats on, are quite rational to resist relocation. But the result is a collective irrationality: the concentration of far too many national resources in the area with the highest house prices and greatest traffic congestion.

The only way to break this logjam and release the savings to be had in terms of reduced costs and improved quality of life, is through planned government intervention to promote a more even distribution of economy activity. Overall planning should not only provide incentives for relocation, but also create the conditions – physical, technical and cultural – to support such relocation. This would not simply, or even mainly, mean the resiting of facilities currently in the South-east. It would be focussed rather on the development of the necessary infrastructures, especially in the areas of physical transport and transport of information, to be able to run organizations at a distance, and allow the close interworking of different units located hundreds of miles apart. Foremost among these would be the installation of a national fibre-optic grid, as described in chapter 7.

International incentives

The thrust of regional policy is and has long been aimed at attracting foreign investment. At the level of Britain, this might be in the interests of the regions; but looked at on a global basis, it makes no sense for governments to be competing with each other for a limited volume of transnational investment. In a way, international capital mobility has been enforcing an international macroeconomic policy, in which investment incentives are set in each country to match those elsewhere, taking into account variations in the attractiveness of different regions and countries, in terms of wage and skill levels and proximity to markets. But this is government policy determined by the market, and operating in an unconscious and chaotic way. On the global level, it constitutes a transfer from taxpayers to private companies; and generally from taxpayers in the poorer countries – those which need to attract investment – to private firms in the more prosperous countries.

A typical example is the Nissan investment in the North-east of England. Compared to the alternative – not paying the ransom demanded by Nissan and seeing the investment go elsewhere – the subsidies given to this development might seem to make sense from a local point of view, whatever the effects on the British motor industry.[14] But measured against an alternative system, in which competition between governments for investments was reduced or abolished, the same subsidies are shown up as wasteful and irrational. A progressive government in Britain could take an international initiative to co-operate with other countries to weaken this futile cycle of competitive incentives. The problem is a little like the arms race: it is difficult for one player to withdraw from the game, and there is a competitive escalation of the incentives given, to the benefit of multinationals and at the cost of the taxpayer. The question of how to end this merry-go-round of bribes to big business also echoes the disarmament debate: there is a strong case for a unilateral cut in incentives, challenging others to respond in kind; and there are also powerful arguments for multilateral reductions on the basis of negotiations. The exact form which reductions should take is not clear; but the need for them is overwhelming, as is the possibility of mobilizing public opinion in their favour in other countries as well as here – once it is shown that cuts would be balanced, and thus not affect any country disproportionately. The removal of this blanket transfer to multinationals would furthermore release public funds for strategic intervention.

Matching local resources and needs

Local and regional authorities have a key role to play in developing locally sensitive and appropriate employment and training strategies. However successful alternative national, regional and local planning strategies might prove to be for the economy, sector by sector, such industrial strategies would not by themselves direct the right numbers and types of jobs and training to where they are most needed. So a geographical dimension of employment and training planning would be an essential complement to industrial policies, based upon direct public sector intervention, particularly at local and regional levels. A nationally planned programme of industrial investment would not, in the short term, generate enough jobs and training opportunities to eliminate unemployment, particularly given the fact that investment in new technology industries tends to be capital rather than labour intensive. The task is not just to get rid of registered unemployment, but to tackle underemployment and unregistered unemployment – which covers for example those women who are not even counted because they are not entitled to social security benefits in their own right. Even within the better-off regions, there has been increasing polarization under the Thatcher governments. A third of Britain's unemployed live in the South-east, and of those with jobs, one in three earn poverty wages below the Council of Europe 'decency threshold'. Meanwhile, rising house prices linked to the growth of better paid service sector jobs in the region have contributed to the rise in homelessness.

Sheffield's 'Employment Plan' started from the need for a vigorous city and regional dimension to national planning, proposing major investments in nationalized industries, such as the electrification of the Midland Main Line Railway, which would improve the infrastructure and at the same time create jobs, through the 'multiplier effect' in key local engineering industries.[15] Taken together with a planned expansion of local service sector jobs – in transport, health, education and social services, for instance – the Sheffield plan would have ensured that national investment plans also brought locally needed employment to the city.

The experience of local and regional authorities, over the past decade or so, has shown that they can provide the necessary local expertise to develop complementary employment and training strategies, which also meet local social needs and typically have the additional advantage, in terms of employment creation, of being labour intensive. Housing schemes, for example, meet social needs through direct labour organizations which also provide training opportunities for young local people, black and white, women as well as men. During the 1980s, local authorities developed plans for linking the need for homes and the need for jobs, starting from the dire state of Britain's housing at a time when unemployment amongst building workers stood at half a million. In parallel with their housing plans, local authorities such as Sheffield also worked on local strategies to tackle heating problems and fuel poverty, through investment programmes in energy-efficient schemes such as combined heat-and-power.[16]

Local authority programmes also provided examples of the creation of socially useful jobs in caring services, for instance as nursery workers and as care assistants for the elderly. Manchester's employment plan drew out the link between investment in the infrastructure – such as housing – with the associated jobs in children's centres and old people's resource centres. It included training objectives, backed up by equal opportunities policies to ensure that jobs and training opportunities were accessible to both men and women, to black and minority ethnic people, and to people with disabilities. The Sheffield plan had provisions for community support workers for the elderly, for welfare assistants, for health visitors, district nurses and nursery nurses. Over the five years before the plan was drafted, Sheffield created 650 jobs within the Family and Community Services Department alone. The plan proposed a further 1,261 jobs, with a particular focus on enabling the elderly to choose to stay in their own homes, by providing the necessary back-up services.

These local economic plans were also linked into other proposals to improve job opportunities and pay in welfare, catering and cleaning. Improving pay for workers such as cleaners in local authorities like Hackney has helped to stabilize the workforce and reduce recruitment costs, thereby opening up more possibilities for developing training and improving social aspects of the jobs performed by home helps and catering staff in social services.

These attempts to improve the quality of jobs and services have important implications for future strategies for the public sector more generally. The public sector has been under attack from enforced privatization and compulsory competitive tendering. In the face of these attacks, the response has often been defensive or apologetic about the present shortcomings of public provision, rather than forceful in presenting a clear strategy for developing the strengths of public provision, in terms of the ability to provide quality services which meet social needs.

The public sector loses its purpose if local authorities attempt to win contracts for public services by undercutting their private competitors in terms of pay and conditions of employment. The most coherent alternative is to concentrate upon providing quality jobs and services. Whilst such a strategy clearly cannot guarantee success in the current climate – given the nature of the private sector competition which local authorities are up against – it does offer some possibilities for short-term gains while providing the basis for a longer-term strategy for the future development of public sector jobs and services. The Haringey school meals project provides an illustration of such a strategy in practice, based on working with the trade unions and the local community to improve the quality of both the jobs and the service, and to boost the uptake of school meals in response to the combined threats of cuts and privatization.

Local Economic Strategies

The London Industrial Strategy developed by the Greater London Council[17] in the early 1980s illustrates the interdependence between the international, national, regional and local dimensions of planning. Its analysis of the car and motor components industries provided case studies of industries which are crucially affected by the global strategies of multinational capital. As spelt out earlier, Ford

UK, which was London's largest manufacturing employer, has been restructuring its operations worldwide with no particular commitment to manufacturing in London, or even in Britain. Production has been reorganized in terms of overall profitability. Ford has placed increased emphasis on international sourcing and flexibility, and this process has been associated with the breakdown of previously integrated production operations such as that at Dagenham. As a result, Dagenham risks becoming a screwdriver plant, assembling mainly imported components into kit cars. Such an outcome might increase Ford's flexibility and profitability, but it would erode the bargaining power of labour and the manufacturing base of the south of England.

In the face of the restructuring strategies of a powerful multinational like Ford, national policies are needed, as discussed in chapter 8. Short of nationalization, local content regulations can ensure that a certain percentage of British sales are produced within the UK, as can specific import controls. Such policies would need to be reinforced by controls on the company's ability to move production around, on transfer pricing, and on the disclosure of information to allow effective monitoring to take place. In addition to such direct interventions, further leverage could be obtained by co-ordinated public sector purchasing policies, including vehicle fleet purchases. Within the context of the West Midlands region, for example, there have been attempts at complementary strategies through local Enterprise Board investments in smaller and medium sized motor components companies. Local economic strategies have a role both in supporting trade unions and in combining to contribute to the development of national strategies for the car industry, and for key multinationals like Ford within the sector. Rather than representing an alternative to national policies, local strategies need to be integrated into effective national policies, as a way of reinforcing them, and of stimulating the development of effective international trade union co-operation.

Textile and clothing industries

Textiles and clothing are both strongly tied into the international economy, but in the case of clothing, this relationship takes a very special form, reflecting the division of production into a wide variety of sizes of unit. There still exist relatively large and medium sized firms, with relatively long production runs, in areas such as West Yorkshire, and to some extent in Lancashire. By contrast, in London and the West Midlands for example, production is typically carried out by very small firms, although they are themselves dominated by a small number of large retailers, who in effect determine their strategies.

An increasing challenge is being posed to the British textile and clothing industry by the import of upmarket designer goods from the EEC. Unless British firms can compete more effectively, they will fail to meet the requirements of the high street retailers. The development and implementation of a sectoral strategy for this fragmented industry would require local and regional as well as national intervention.[18] Local intervention, in collaboration with the trade unions, is crucial too, to ensure that the industry does not survive through its traditional strategy of increasing the exploitation of the most vulnerable sections of the workforce – especially women and black and minority ethnic people such as the Bengali community working in the clothing industry in East London. Local plans for the textile and clothing industries have been presented by the Centre for Local Economic Strategies as:

> the building blocks from which a national policy might be built under a future government. It is argued that such an approach to national policy would be able to build on a wealth of local knowledge, experience of intervention and sense of innovation, in marked contrast to the relatively recent historical experience of attempts to introduce interventionist industrial policy through the mechanism of Whitehall.[19]

This report, based on a review of local authority experiences of intervention in the clothing sector, does not of course argue against national policy intervention. On the contrary, it argues that restructuring is unlikely to succeed without state intervention, and that Britain is at a serious disadvantage in this respect compared with the industry elsewhere in Europe where there have tended to be more effective national sector strategies for both textiles and clothing. The point is rather that in such a diverse industry, any national strategy must draw upon local and regional expertise in production as well as in labour organization – dealing with issues such as training, health and safety, equal opportunities, and pay and conditions.

Local authorities concerned with the textiles and clothing industry have formed a joint organization, Local Action for Textiles and Clothing, and have focussed on the need for a coherent national strategy to complement their local strategies. The envisaged national framework is seen as hinging on the creation of an effective Sector Development Agency, including trade union representation, to plan national investment, linked to effective and carefully monitored agreements on working conditions and equal opportunities. Effective regulation of trade would also need to be developed, especially with developed countries in the EEC, if the industry is to survive beyond the Multi Fibre Agreement, which was renewed in 1986 to provide some weakened form of protection from imports. For the future, Labour policy should include an expansion of planned trade with developing countries, on terms that would allow an improvement in the conditions of workers in those countries as well as in Britain.

Finally, a national strategy would need to tackle training weaknesses by establishing revitalized training boards, with local authority representation, to provide the national framework for local training schemes. It is this type of national, and indeed international strategy, which could provide the policy framework within which local and regional authorities would be able to build up their own local plans.

From these different experiences, developing local and regional strategies for vehicle manufacture and for textiles and clothing, a number of local authorities have reached similar conclusions about the type of complementary national framework which they need. National sector strategies would have to be backed up by powerful controls over the operations of multinationals, including over the export of capital, together with policies for planned trade with both developed and developing countries. No radical labour movement programme for government in the 1990s based on public ownership and planning could be implemented without the widest participation in the planning effort by trade unions, workforces, local authorities and community organizations. The challenge posed by such a programme to the most powerful interests in society could only be met if large numbers of people felt that it was their programme and their government: in other words, if they were given the chance in a practical way to take greater control over their own lives.

Notes

1. Jonathon Porritt, *Seeing Green*, Oxford 1984, p. 35.
2. Jonathon Porritt, *Seeing Green*, Oxford 1984, p. 36.
3. Water Authorities Association, *Water Pollution from Farm Waste 1988*, London 1989.
4. Transport 2000, *BR: A European Railway*, London 1984, p. 1.
5. A good example is Strathclyde Regional Council, *Strathclyde – Generating Change*, Glasgow 1988.
6. TUC, *Trade Unions in the City*, London 1988.
7. Figures from Richard Caborn MP, quoted in the *Daily Telegraph*, 23 September 1988.
8. Dr John MacInnes, *Discussion Paper 32* and *Discussion Paper 34*, Centre for Urban and Regional Research, University of Glasgow 1988. These studies define the 'South' as the South-east, South-west, East Anglia and the Midlands; and the 'North' as North and North-west England, Yorkshire and Humberside, Wales and Scotland.
9. NOERC, *State of the Regions Survey*, 1988.
10. Institute of British Geographers, Annual Conference 1988.
11. *Guardian*, 11 April 1988.
12. Jeremy Howells, *Economic, Technological and Locational Trends in European Services*, Aldershot 1988.
13. Manchester Business School, *Executive Survey*, Manchester 1988.
14. See John Foster and Charles Woolfson, 'Corporate Reconstruction and Business Unionism: the Lessons of Caterpillar and Ford', where it is strongly argued that attracting multinational branch plants with no research and development attached 'hinders the full utilization of a region's human resources *comparatively* to their potential'. *New Left Review*, no. 174, March/April 1989, pp. 51–66.
15. Sheffield City Council, *Working it Out*, Sheffield 1987.
16. Sheffield City Council, *Homes and Jobs*, Conference Report 1986.
17. Greater London Council, *London Industrial Strategy*, London 1985.
18. Centre for Local Economic Strategies, *Prospects for Local Authority Intervention in the Textiles and Clothing Industry*, Manchester 1986; and Greater London Council (GLC), *Textiles and Clothing: Sunset Industries?*, London 1986.
19. Centre for Local Economic Strategies, *Prospects for Intervention in the Merseyside Clothing Industry*, Manchester 1986.

10

Planning for Positive Action

I've always had an English nanny, otherwise I'd never have left the children happily.

Margaret Thatcher, 1968[1]

The casino economy of capitalism divides the workforce, both directly in factories and offices and indirectly through the working of the market. The result is a reserve army of labour, unemployed or in insecure and unorganized jobs, but available to be drawn into the mainstream of the labour force in booms, and made redundant or part time in slumps. In Britain it is largely black, female or both. Women and black workers are the targets of discrimination in a wide variety of ways in all job categories, including skilled and professional grades. Both female and black workers have a special position in the labour market: in the latter case, through the effects of imperialism; in the case of women, because of the historic sexual division of labour. Of course women have many separate needs, and many problems are specific to black workers. Positive action for black workers would require, for example, the Race Relations Act to have teeth. Women have a particular interest in child-care facilities, given the dominant division of child-rearing tasks between the sexes. But both have much in common: not only from their subordinate position in the divisive operations of the casino economy, but also from the parallel aims and methods in planning for positive action against discrimination. A progressive shift to planned, sustainable growth in the 1990s could provide the means for genuinely social advance for all exploited groups, and allow the scale of intervention necessary for positive action against systematic disadvantage.

Women's Work and the Women's Movement

Over the past twenty years, the women's movement has challenged many of the different areas of private and social life in which women are oppressed. Over the same period, there has been a marked and long-term growth of women's participation in the labour market. More and more women have been going out to waged work. While the proportion of men in the labour force fell from 80 per cent to 74 per cent between 1971 and 1987, female participation rose from 44 per cent to 50 per cent over the same period.[2]

These two developments are undoubtedly connected. But there is no mechanical link between the strengthening and broadening of the women's movement and the increasing use of female wage labour. Many of the central issues for the movement, such as the right to abortion on demand, have not been campaigned for on purely economic grounds, though they have strong economic implications for women. Others more obviously straddle the boundaries of the economic and the non-economic, such as sharing of domestic work to allow women to leave the home and enter the paid workforce on more equal terms with men; and some issues are immediately concerned with the labour market, such as the demand for equal pay for work of equal value.

The growth of women's participation in the labour market has been a common development across all the advanced capitalist countries, even if the timing and extent of the change have varied. There are also common characteristics in the nature of women's terms of employment. Men and women have traditionally worked in different sectors of the economy and in different types of jobs. Such occupational segregation has given rise to the idea that certain jobs are suitable only for women and others only for men, even though historically women have often done jobs which are usually thought to be a masculine preserve. In conjunction with job segregation, women have also been confined to the lower levels of the labour market hierarchy, with men occupying the more senior positions.

Partly as a result of this and partly because 'women's work' is seen as unskilled and less valuable, there continues to be a substantial differential between men's and women's pay. Although these trends can be found throughout the developed capitalist world, there are marked differences from country to country. In Sweden, for example, the level of women's wages is bordering on that of men's, while occupational segregation is one of the most extreme.

The major reason for the increase in women's employment has been that more married women are going out to work who previously would not have returned to the labour market after having had children. So the new sources of female labour have been those women who have continued to hold major responsibility for housework and particularly for child care. Not surprisingly, many of the new army of wage labour have only been able or willing to serve on a part-time basis in order to be able to continue domestic work. This has been lightened, not so much by labour-saving gadgets and machines, as by a considerable decline in family size. Women have been having fewer children, at shorter intervals and, by living longer as well, have had more time available for the labour market.

Women in the labour force

In the de-industrialization of the past decade, manufacturing employment has fallen absolutely in Britain, while the service sector has been the main source of new employment.[3] From the mid 1960s to the end of the 1970s, growth in employment can be explained almost entirely by the entry of married women into the part-time workforce, accounting for over one and a half million jobs. Over the same period, more than a third of mainly male jobs in manufacturing were lost. Women's participation in the labour force is higher in Britain than in the other main European Community countries, slightly lower than in North America, and a good deal lower than in Scandinavia. In 1986 the ratio stood at 61 per cent in Britain. The corresponding figure for Spain was 35 per cent; Italy 42 per cent; Federal Republic of Germany 51 per cent; France 55 per cent; Japan 57 per cent; the US 65 per cent; and Sweden 78 per cent.[4] For Britain this translates into a share of the labour market of 42 per cent for women. However, 45 per cent of all women employees work part time, and women now make up

89 per cent of all part-timers – still an unusually high figure by international standards.[5]

Women's relative pay registered a one-off improvement of around 18 per cent during the 1970s. This was partly due to the shift of women workers into industries with lower sex differentials, and partly because of trade union pressure – including the enforcement of the 1970 Equal Pay Act, which was implemented over the five years to 1975, through collective bargaining. The 1980s, on the other hand, were far less positive. Throughout the decade, women's relative pay stuck at about 74 per cent of men's hourly rates. On a weekly basis, taking account of overtime by men and part-time work by women, this figure drops to 66 per cent.

The centrality of child care

The women least likely to play a full part in the formal economy in practice are those with a child under five. Older children seem to be a smaller disincentive to women looking for work. The significance of the constraints imposed by the lack of proper child care is demonstrated by the number of women with children who work a short distance from their homes and take evening jobs or work a five-day week with reduced hours – rather than working full time for fewer days a week – so as to fit in with school timetables. The general pressure of child care and 'husband care' on women's time is shown by the overwhelming majority (78 per cent) of married part-time women workers who say they are working part time because they do not want a full-time job. This compares with the much lower figure of 38 per cent for non-married part-time women workers, and only 29 per cent for part-time men.[6]

Women are especially concentrated in a few service sector jobs. In 1988 14 per cent of women in employment worked in health, education and welfare, 30 per cent in clerical jobs, 10 per cent in selling and 22 per cent in catering and cleaning. Female part-time service employment has been increasing while full-time male employment has been falling in manufacturing. The decline of manufacturing has provided a source of cheap female labour for services: a typical employment profile for a woman in recent years has been to move from full-time manual work through childbirth and back into part-time service employment.

In both manufacturing and services, women have been used to compensate for low productivity because of their low wage costs:

> When women have been working in manufacturing industries at cheaper wage rates, they have been supporting, in Britain, an ailing manufacturing sector, allowing it to limp along and be slightly more on a par with the cheap labour production of developing countries in textiles and clothing. Given that productivity gains have been restricted in service industries, then women are also the obvious choice of workers to try and keep down costs in these industries.[7]

In addition, the use of women in service jobs takes advantage of the skills which women have largely had to acquire at their own expense in the home – cooking, cleaning and caring for children and other relatives. So training costs are minimized to the employers. This failure to pay for the skills which women usually have acquired because of the sexist division of domestic labour is an extra reason why the service sector jobs are often filled by women rather than by the men made redundant from the manufacturing sector.

International comparisons

The special significance of women's work for the British economy can be seen from international comparisons. The US has been more successful than Britain in drawing women into the labour market, and especially in allowing the continuation of work around childbearing and facilitating an early return afterwards. Arrangements for child care in the two countries are quite different. In the US, paid child care is widely used, partly because tax relief extends to help from relatives. In Britain very limited help is available to the mother, whether from the hopelessly inadequate public provision or from the partner. As a result many women take part-time jobs either during the school day or in the evenings when their husbands come home from a standard working day. Another factor favouring women's participation in the US is the greater access to second car ownership, which widens the travel-to-work area as compared with the UK where deteriorating local public transport has to be relied on.[8] Some of these differences are explained by the higher level of income per head in the US, but the most startling difference between the US and Britain shows up in employment histories after the birth of children. When moving in and out of work around childbirth, American women generally find a better job afterwards than the one they left before childbirth. In the UK, by contrast, the tendency is for women to be forced to accept a worse job after having children.

The comparison between the two countries supports the idea that the exploitative form of women's paid labour in Britain plays a crucial role in supporting the general low level of wages. Women are so poorly supported by public child-care provision in their attempts to work, and wages are so low in Britain, that the kind of private provision of child care with tax relief which has proved successful in the US has failed to take off. Women generally cannot afford the cost. The low-wage economy in the UK has made use of women as a cheap labour force – as reflected in downward mobility over childbirth – even at the expense of wasting their skills and experience.

A comparison of Britain and West Germany shows that more reliance is placed on part-time employment in the UK (19 per cent of employment in 1983 as opposed to 14 per cent in West Germany) with women providing the bulk of part-time workers in both countries. In Britain, a greater proportion of part-time workers are drawn from the very young and the very old, suggesting that weaker sections of the workforce in general support the market for part-time labour. The dependence of the UK economy on part-time labour is illustrated by the fact that as many as 9 per cent of all part-time workers hold two or more jobs. This does not reflect any greater preference by British professionals for varied work, since both West Germany and Britain have a similar proportion of part-timers in high status jobs, while the majority are concentrated in the service sectors and low status work. And while Britain has a higher share of service industries, and hence an implied bias towards a higher overall share of part-time workers, it also has a larger share of part-timers in each separate industry. Britain's dependence on a low-wage female workforce is supported by its employment tax policy. The national insurance threshold – earnings above which attract contributions – is higher in the UK, excluding 30 per cent of part-timers as compared with 11 per cent in West Germany. So, as with the lack of tax relief for child care compared with the US, British women are discouraged from working other than part time.

The case of Sweden shows how the impact of legislation on women's labour market position involves much more than taxation alone. Through policies geared towards the unemployed – even when they are relatively few in number – in training, public works, equal opportunities, low wages and parental leave from work, Swedish women workers have advanced their position in the labour force. In Britain, on the other hand, women suffer disproportionately because of the lack of coherent, co-ordinated employment policies. This laissez-faire attitude to the labour market – except, especially under the Thatcher governments, where intervention has been geared towards lowering wages and bargaining power – has been supported by social policies which take the traditional role of women as wives and mothers as their point of departure. Even when the government is pushed by fears about skill shortages to take measures to encourage women back into the labour force its announcements are prefaced with little homilies about the importance of family life. A 1989 circular from the Home Office minister John Patten began:

> The family is central to national life, but we must make sure the best possible help is available for women who choose to work.[9]

While part-time work and occupational segregation are comparable in the two countries, female workers in Sweden earn 10 per cent less than men, compared with 30 per cent less in Britain. There is a close link between the lack of coherent industrial and social policies in the UK and the deeper dependence on women as a cheap labour force. That connection has been particularly marked in the public sector itself, since it employs so many women and has been a major source of the boost to female employment in health, education and welfare. The state as employer has had a profound effect on the conditions in which women work.

Racism and Employment

The special position of black people and other minority ethnic groups in the workforce is closely linked with the evolution of British imperialism. After the war, several European capitalist countries were able to draw on reserves of surplus agricultural workers to feed the booming new industries with cheap labour. In Britain, where the agricultural workforce was already tiny, low-paid workers were recruited both by the state and private enterprise from British colonies or ex-colonies, mainly in the Caribbean and the Asian sub-continent. In a sense, exploiting immigrant workers at home provided British capital with an alternative to investment in the Third World during the post-war boom.

Black employment in Britain has from the start been concentrated in certain sectors: notably the public transport and health services, and manufacturing sectors like textiles and steel. All those areas of employment are now the special object of shake-outs, rationalization and privatization. Since 1968, 'primary' immigration has effectively been blocked. But the new service industries that flourished in the 1980s, such as catering and tourism, have drawn heavily on a new pool of migrant workers and refugees – 'the flotsam and jetsam of latter-day imperialism' – for low-paid, casual employment.[10]

Despite three Acts of Parliament since the mid 1960s, Britain's black and minority ethnic workforce continues to suffer from systematic discrimination in employment. As one recent report commented:

> The position of the black citizens of Britain largely remains, geographically and economically, that allocated to them as immigrant workers in the 1950s and 1960s.[11]

Black people are concentrated in semi-skilled and unskilled jobs and earn less than white people at the same job levels, despite being more highly unionized and doing more shift-work. They also tend to work in industries notorious for bad conditions and low pay. Unemployment is far higher among blacks than among whites. In the late 1980s, the unemployment rate for workers of West Indian origin was twice that of whites; and Pakistanis and Bangladeshis were almost three times more likely to be unemployed than whites. And whereas better qualifications significantly reduce the chances of being unemployed if you are white, they have much less impact if you are Asian or Afro-Caribbean.[12]

Attempts have been made to explain the higher level of unemployment among blacks in various ways which focus on factors other than discrimination. For example, the black population is younger than the average, and unemployment has been worst among young people; black workers are concentrated in some areas which have been most badly hit by industrial decline. But the evidence is overwhelming that these have had only a marginal effect on the differences in unemployment rates between blacks and whites. The most serious reason for the subordinate and peripheral position of blacks *in* work, and for their persistent exclusion *from* work, is racism, both at an individual and institutional level. And any government programme aiming to tackle black economic disadvantage has to focus on that central fact.[13]

Policy Levers

Women's position in the labour market is affected by both economic and social factors, and economic policy can influence the economic position of women even where it does not have an explicit gender content. So it is crucial that all of the agencies formulating and implementing economic policy should have a strong commitment to equal opportunities. This applies, for example, to transport, education and taxation, all of which have an impact on women as workers and as consumers. Black and minority ethnic workers also find themselves in disadvantaged positions in the workforce because of a range of pressures, the most important of which is institutional racism. Better organization and representation of unskilled and semi-skilled workers would certainly benefit black and minority ethnic workers, as would proper access to training facilities. But again, a broader awareness of and commitment to equal opportunities is essential, both on the part of employers – local and national government, nationalized industries, and, as far as they can be cajoled or compelled, privately owned industries – and on the part of trade unions themselves, if all areas of discrimination and inequality are to be effectively tackled. Trade unions have a particular responsibility to ensure the fullest recruitment, participation, and representation of women and black workers.

The Labour Party is committed to setting up a Ministry for Women. Such a new department could play a central role in initiating and responding to policies that affect women, in enforcing sex equality legislation and in pressing for gender awareness in economic policy-making. While falling family size has allowed women to participate more fully in the labour market, this merely highlights how the burden of housework, and of child care in particular, continues to disadvantage women at work as well as more generally. Britain's welfare policies are moving increasingly towards a US-style 'workfare' system which makes welfare benefits conditional on compulsory working. While such policies have no place in any progressive economic programme, the American slogan 'no workfare without child care' has a certain relevance in Britain. Universal and freely available public provision of child care must be a top priority. Since the mid 1980s there has actually been a tax on workplace nurseries; Labour is committed to its abolition. Some of the more immediate and major priorities for a Labour government in the 1990s would need to include the establishment of a national child-care system, covering creches both at workplaces and in the community, as well as nursery schools; a substantial increase in child benefit and its index-linking to average earnings; and the combining of the Sex Discrimination and Equal Pay Acts so that indirect discrimination in wages – for example through paying different rates to part-timers – could be tackled.[14]

Many other policy measures would automatically tend to benefit women because the sexist division of roles means that women currently perform a vastly disproportionate share of the unpaid 'caring' tasks in society. The policy of 'community care', whereby geriatric and mental institutions have forced patients back into private homes, has resulted in working women, far more often than men, cutting back on their paid work so as to carry out support tasks previously undertaken by those institutions. Changing the policy would therefore primarily benefit women. Three and a half million women are significantly involved in caring for elderly relatives. The need for more public provision, including home-based services, can only grow as the population of the very elderly increases. Legislation for positive action would need to apply to all sectors of the economy, private as well as public, to ensure for example that child-care leave would not detract from subsequent promotion evaluations by being subtracted from years of service. Legislative measures such as these could be strongly supplemented by contract compliance operated by public industries as well as central and local government.

Contract compliance

Contract compliance has been used by local councils in Britain – often drawing on US experience – to make sure that private firms carrying out contracts for them meet acceptable standards of quality, fair wages, union organization and equal opportunities. The local authority simply refuses to give any contracts to firms who fail to live up to these standards. The Tories' 1988 Local Government Act limited the powers of local authorities to require contractors to maintain minimum employment standards and was specifically geared to outlawing equal opportunity practices. A Labour government would need not only to remove this limitation, but to go further by making such compliance compulsory across society through the use of its own huge purchasing and contract leverage. However, because of the difficulty in checking up on the activities of companies in the private sector, most rapid progress could be expected from publicly owned firms. As argued in earlier chapters, one of the fundamental reasons for needing a broadly expanded public sector in the 1990s is because privately owned and controlled firms cannot realistically be expected to pursue the interests of the wider community, no matter how seriously attempts are made to regulate such enterprises. When it comes to control, there is no substitute for ownership. The second best option is to control the purse strings via the order books. But the greater the degree of direct public ownership, the greater too can be the degree of such indirect contract-compliance control.

Extending public ownership into a new area of product or service provision could, through contract compliance, be used to take positive action in favour of women's and black rights over a far wider area than just that workplace or company. Not only could the newly nationalized company be redirected to follow equal opportunities practices, it could also implement contract compliance on the whole array of its supplier firms – whether in the area of materials and components, or in services such as transport, cleaning or maintenance.

In the public sector, equality targets could be phased in for central government departments, local authorities and nationalized industries, as suggested by the Labour Party's Black Sections. They should set a percentage target for the number of black employees, proportionate to the percentage of black people in the catchment area of the particular factories and offices. Equality targets would need to be set for all occupations and grades of the workforce to avoid the crowding of black people at the bottom of the pile. Recruitment, training and promotion procedures would then have to be regularly reviewed so that the targets were actually met. Equality targets could also be extended to the private sector, backed up by contract compliance. Special training programmes should be geared to redressing the race and gender balance in the longer run. This could be linked to an overall planning effort for the 1990s, particularly in the newly nationalized industries and the industrial sectors where national policy is planning for expansion.

Conclusion: Equal Opportunities for Change

It is ironic that equal opportunities vocabulary and issues – as well as arguments for flexibility between work and home – have been used by management in the civil service, local government and the health service to cut women's full-time work down to part-time jobs; split shifts and introduce unsocial hours; and contract out jobs. The demand for flexibility in the 1970s meant something very different from the type of flexibility that was imposed in the 1980s.[15] The role which flexibility of employment and production will play in the next decade will depend on the political and economic route taken in Britain. It is not predetermined by technology. Industrial advance will demand both increased size and flexibility of operations. A publicly-owned, expanding core of the economy around which supplier and other related sectors could grow – along with the broader local government, educational and community sectors – would provide the scale on which flexibility could offer increased scope both of products and employment opportunities. Without such a political shift in the 1990s, the resulting failure of British industry to develop the modern scale achieved in competitor countries will result in greater use of flexible production to squeeze increased scope out of inadequate productive scale.

Progressive policies to regenerate the British economy and break with its role as a low-wage and low-productivity economy, depend on the full use and development of the talents of women and black workers and positive action to enhance pay, working conditions and job prospects, so that they can enter the labour market on equivalent terms to those of white men. Quite apart from the need for social justice in principle, failure to pursue such positive action would allow low-wage employers to undermine progressive economic policies and work conditions thoughout the economy.

Comprehensive equal opportunities policies must be adopted across the whole range of conditions. Contract compliance for equal opportunities should become standard in all public sector tendering. Women and black workers must have greater access to training opportunities. For women, training structures must be redesigned to fit in with having children. A more positive legal framework and an active review body for equal pay for work of equal value must be created to ensure the effective implementation of equal pay. This approach is needed because the simple requirement of equal pay for a given job is not enough to ensure real equality. Men and women systematically do different jobs, while minority ethnic workers are concentrated in particular industries and occupations. Conditions for part-time workers must be levelled up to those of full-time workers, with equal hourly wages. In all of these issues, a lead can be taken in the public sector.

Breaking down the divisions within the workforce – which are so profitable to capital – itself assists in the building of a united movement for social change. Some of the policies to help such a process would include a statutory national minimum wage, which would be of particular importance to women and black workers who form the vast majority of the low paid; the right to go part time and to go back to full-time work; the right of all workers to a 'career break', with a guaranteed job back on at least the previous level of pay and no break in service qualifications for rights or benefits; and the right to paid time off when children or other dependants are ill. Such comprehensive positive action would need to be based on making equal opportunities policies universal in both the public and private sectors, contract compliance, and a major extension of the public sector.

Capitalist production leads to fluctuating output and employment levels. It creates the demand for a reserve army of labour to be brought in and thrown out of work as orders rise and fall, and the trend to resort to enforced part-time working or contracting out when future markets are uncertain. These pressures are an incentive to divide the workforce, which is then affected differentially as the economy fluctuates. Most politically dangerous is the way in which the groups who form the poorly-paid insecure reserve pool of workers not only lose their jobs in times of recession – and thus directly bear the brunt of the hardship being passed onto the workforce – but are then portrayed by racist ideologies as the cause of the unemployment which they are suffering. So they have an even greater material interest than other sections of the workforce in seeing Britain move beyond the casino economy. But direct interest does not necessarily translate into political action. That is one reason why any move towards social and economic progress in Britain depends on the political mobilization that only the labour movement can provide, to bring together all those who stand to gain from an economy planned for positive action, not just plundered for private advantage.

Notes

1. *Newcastle Journal*, 3 December 1968, quoted in Melanie McFadyean and Margaret Renn, *Thatcher's Reign*, London 1984.
2. Central Statistical Office, *Social Trends*, London 1989, p. 70.
3. Martin, J. and Roberts, C., *Women and Employment: a Lifetime Perspective*, London 1984.
4. OECD, *Employment Outlook*, 1987.
5. Lloyds Bank *Economic Bulletin* no. 115, July 1988.
6. *Department of Employment Gazette*, London April 1989, p. 186.
7. S. Dex, *Women's Occupational Mobility: a Lifetime Perspective*, London 1987, p. 127.
8. S. Dex and L. Shaw, *British and American Women at Work: Do Equal Opportunities Policies Matter?*, London 1986.
9. Home Office, *News Release*, 11 April 1989: our thanks to Tess Woodcraft for drawing this to our attention.
10. A. Sivanandan, 'New Circuits of Imperialism', *Race & Class*, vol. 30, no. 4, April–June 1989, p. 15.
11. Colin Brown, *Black and White*, Policy Studies Institute, 1984.
12. Central Statistical Office, *Social Trends*, London 1989, table 4.26.
13. See Ashok Bhat, Roy Carr-Hill and Sushel Ohri, eds, *Britain's Black Population: A New Perspective*, Aldershot 1988, pp. 75–81; and C. Brown and P. Gay, *Racial Discrimination: 17 Years after the Act*, Policy Studies Institute, London 1985.
14. As advocated in the Labour Party's 1988 Policy Review report on democracy for the individual and the community.
15. Ruth Elliot, 'Women, Restructuring and Union Strategies', paper presented to the *Women and Economy* Conference, May 1988.

PART IV

Towards a New Programme

The previous two parts have focused on the causes of the underlying weaknesses in the British economy and the kind of supply-side interventionist policies that could start to overcome its chronic problems and injustices, both in specific industries and through the structure of employment. The point has now been reached where these ideas can be drawn together in the context of a policy package that could realistically be implemented by a Labour government in the course of one five-year parliamentary term.

Chapter 11 fleshes out the social and economic objectives that such a programme would aim to meet and the basic policy tools that would be needed, building on current policy debates and controversies. A general structure for a programme of planning and public ownership is sketched out, and it is argued that the problem of nationalization compensation is less of an obstacle than is often supposed.

Chapter 12 puts the programme in the context of a broader political strategy for the socialist transformation of society. Only large-scale and mass participation in a real political movement could turn any of these proposals into a practical political reality.

11

The Framework for Change

The trouble with the profit system has always been that it is highly unprofitable to most people.

Elwyn Brooks White, 1944[1]

The absence of an economic programme both credible and radical enough to inspire and help weld together a coalition of electoral support was at the heart of Labour's problems during the 1980s. The response of the Labour establishment has been to try and scale down expectations, embrace the market as the main motor of economic development, and abandon any policy commitments – such as public ownership, planning agreements and exchange controls – which are thought to be potential electoral liabilities. The net result has been to deprive the labour movement of the tools it would need in government to meet the growing demand for change and a better quality of life.[2]

Goals

From the point of view of the labour movement and its supporters, re-industrialization and economic modernization cannot be aims in themselves. They are simply the indispensable prerequisites of its more immediate goals and demands, and its longer-term perspective of a fundamental and irreversible shift in the balance of power and wealth towards working people. It is a common enough assumption outside government circles that better living standards and comprehensive social provision for the majority in Britain can only be secured with the modernization and re-equipment of the country's industrial base. But the underlying argument of this book goes one step further. In current British conditions, such a thoroughgoing restructuring of the economy would only be possible if important centres of economic power were wrested from the large private interests which currently monopolize them and brought under democratic ownership and control. Weakening the grip of the giants of capitalist enterprise in the economy should also be a welcome development in itself because it would help to erode the oligarchic, anti-democratic class domination of our society and open the way for progressive political changes. But the essential point to grasp from an economic point of view is that – even taking account of redistributive measures – no Labour government would be able to deliver higher working-class living standards, better services, housing and education and decent child-care facilities without mounting a practical challenge to the right of the banks and the largest companies to follow their own investment and production priorities as they please. Britain's international economic relations would also have to be radically restructured.

The basic material goals of the labour movement are straightforward and well-established, despite a tendency in recent years to adopt more modest aims as part of the Labour leadership's move to the right. They can be drawn from the policy decisions of the Labour Party and TUC. The key short- to medium-term economic objectives include:

- Minimum standards of provision in public services, including health, education, transport and housing;
- A qualitative boost to environmental protection;
- A national child-care system;
- Full employment;
- A statutory national minimum wage;
- Regionally balanced economic development;
- A genuine training and retraining programme;
- Rising and sustainable living standards for the whole working class.

Of course such a list is by no means exhaustive, nor does it take in other political priorities – such as the fight against racism, the expansion of organized working-class influence through an unfettered trade union movement, the widening of civil and human rights, the abolition of the House of Lords, or a non-aligned foreign policy. The fact that these are mostly beyond the economic scope of this book in no way implies that such reforms are secondary.

One of the most striking features of the 1980s has been the divisions within the working class that have been opened up and nurtured by the Thatcher governments: divisions between the employed and unemployed, between skilled and unskilled workers, women and men, those living in the South and North, between black and white, those in the public and private sectors, in core and peripheral employment, trade unionists and the unorganized, home owners and council tenants, younger and older workers. These divisions have been at the heart of the Thatcherite strategy for maintaining the Tory parliamentary majority and for heading off an effective extra-parliamentary challenge to its continued rule and the implementation of its programme. Labour lost the 1979 general election principally because large numbers of skilled and better-paid workers, whose take-home pay had been cut by a combination of incomes policies and inflation-fuelled tax increases, voted Tory for the first time. In 1987 Labour started to win back some of the unskilled workers who deserted it in 1983, though the party still failed to mobilize millions of the unemployed, pensioners in poverty and most heavily exploited workers who are its natural supporters. And many better-paid skilled workers, particularly in the new industries, decided not to return to Labour.[3] Working class unity must be a key objective. Labour can only form a government successfully if it mobilizes support around a programme that unites all significant sections of the working class and also has the appeal to attract voters from potential social allies – teachers, small business owners and the like. That cannot be done by mixing and matching a hotch-potch of policies tailored to different interest groups. But it does mean that concentrating all efforts, as the Labour leadership appears to be doing, on those workers who have done relatively well financially out of the Thatcher years, could be counter-productive.

In parallel with governments in other advanced capitalist countries, Thatcherite dominance in the 1980s was built on what is sometimes called the 'two-thirds society': in other words, on a systematic attempt to marginalize the poorest sections of the working class and isolate them from their natural social allies. Any movement for radical change depends on overcoming such divisions and turning the two-thirds society on its head. A potential Labour government has to be able realistically to offer rising living standards – in the form of both better wages and public services – to the majority of the population, as well as a drastic cut in unemployment. Consistently rising incomes for the whole working class can never be guaranteed, but the only way to make them a credible policy objective in the 1990s would be through large-scale economic and industrial restructuring. Nor can any government guard against unforeseen external shocks. But it would be grossly irresponsible not to prepare for the kind of predictable shocks experienced by every single Labour government – balance of payments crises, runs on the pound and inflationary pressures – which have consistently blown them off course in the past.

Living standards

Labour's record on delivering better living standards in office is distinctly patchy. The pattern has been strikingly similar under all three post-war Labour governments: a surge in public spending in the first year or so, followed by tight incomes policies and a squeeze on services. During the last Labour government, the Social Contract forced down the real value of take-home pay two years in succession without even the compensation of higher social spending, cut as part of the IMF austerity package of 1976.[4]

Under the Tories the picture has been more complicated. For most working-class people, real wages stagnated or fell in the early 1980s, while soaring unemployment and the squeeze on benefits and other social spending meant big cuts in living standards for a large minority.[5] In the mid 1980s, the growth spurt in the British economy boosted real wages for some sections of the working class, while at the bottom end of the labour market the combination of unemployment, toothless or abolished wages councils, regional depression and downward pressure on wages from government training schemes cut or held back living standards. Inadequate spending on health, education and housing hit most of the population, and the squeeze on benefits and pensions exacerbated poverty. Tory tax changes during the 1980s increased the tax burden for many of those on average or below-average earnings.[6] Inequality ballooned with enormous increases in high incomes and asset values for the wealthy. In the ten years after 1979, gross earnings for the bottom tenth of the population rose by 11 per cent in real terms, while the equivalent figure for the top tenth was 69 per cent. Between 1979 and 1985, the real income of the poorest fifth fell by 2 per cent in absolute terms.[7] Nevertheless, steadily rising real wages for the majority of those in work after 1982 gave the Thatcher government the 40-odd per cent of the vote at the 1983 and 1987 general elections it needed to stay in office.

A Labour government could not hope to maintain the breadth of social support it would need in office if it repeats the squeeze on working-class living standards experienced under previous Labour governments. That rules out from the start the option of savage deflations to deal with balance of payments crises, currency problems and inflationary pressures. More controversially in the labour movement, it also rules out wage controls – whether imposed by statute or by agreement with union leaders. Experience of different kinds of incomes policies over forty years or more has shown, not only that they always lead to reductions in real wages, but that they also cut the ground from under the feet of organized workers at exactly the time when a high degree of industrial and political mobilization is essential. The case against wage controls has been strengthened by recent economic and statistical research which casts doubt on the conventional view that it is necessary to hold down wages if expansionary government policies aimed at cutting unemployment are to work.[8]

Rising wages in the private sector depend on an expanding economy and strong trade unionism. A planned expansion of output in all sectors of the economy would also produce the buoyant tax revenues that are needed to finance better wages and salaries in the public services. But rising living standards for the majority should involve far more than higher pay. They would mean a boost to the basic pension which was amongst the lowest in the European Community by the end of the 1980s, a major increase in child benefit, decent social security benefits, a sharp cut in unemployment itself and a sustainable rise in living standards. The only basis for regular increases in public spending is a growing economy. But there is also plenty of room for deepening the tax base: reversing the tax cuts for the rich, introducing a wealth tax, turning corporation tax into a genuine levy. A better political climate for transferring spending from the military to social needs should give a Labour government in the 1990s more room for fiscal manoeuvre. Britain's £20 billion annual arms budget is by far the highest as a proportion of national income of all advanced capitalist countries except the US. If NATO–Warsaw Pact tension continues to be reduced, the demand for cuts in Britain's military budget could be made overwhelming.

A minimum wage

After many years of controversy, the labour movement is now united on the need for a statutory, index-linked national minimum wage to fight the poverty and exploitation of the lowest paid.[9] Traditional opposition within the movement focussed on the concern that a minimum wage could undermine collective bargaining and be used to justify and enforce wage controls on other workers. Phasing in a legal minimum would require renegotiation of differentials for those workers whose pay rates were close to the minimum. An obvious example is the health service, where wages are low and there is a complex grading structure. But there is no logical connection between the adoption of a statutory minimum wage and incomes policies as normally understood. The process of adjustment of differentials can and should be left to the unions and employers concerned. Indeed, such a legal minimum could only be a back-up for effective collective bargaining and trade union organization among the pool of part-time, temporary, casual, and subcontracted labour that has been deliberately enlarged by the Tory governments during the 1980s. But in the labour market conditions of the 1990s, it is seen as essential.

Rejection of a statutory minimum by employers' organizations and the Tories has always been based on claims that it would be inflationary and would lead to job losses. A general increase in the earnings of the low paid could well push up what was seen as the 'going rate' for other workers. Whether such a trend would be inflationary would depend entirely on how fast the economy – and productivity in particular – was growing. In sweatshop industries, higher wages might lead to some layoffs by small businesses, but these jobs are effectively being paid for at present by social security subsidies, and marginal employment losses would be far outstripped by the job-creating effects of other parts of the programme and the extra demand from higher wages for low-paid workers.[10]

A national child-care system

The single greatest practical contribution that any Labour government could make to giving women more control over their own lives would be the creation of a comprehensive, free child-care system.[11] In the conditions of the 1990s, where the number of school leavers coming into the labour market will continue to fall until 1995,[12] it is also an economic necessity. A handful of large employers, like the Midland Bank, established some basic child-care provision in the late 1980s in response to the need to attract women employees. But typically the private sector is hopelessly ill-informed and ill-prepared for the demographic pressure on labour supply.[13] Without economic planning and public provision, it will be at sea in the 1990s. The Tory government's contribution was actually to tax workplace nurseries from the mid 1980s.

Britain lags far behind most capitalist countries – let alone the most advanced socialist countries – in child-care provision at all age levels. The British child-care record is the worst in the European Community: 3.4 per cent of pre-school children are in full-time education, compared with 19.1 per cent in France, for example.[14] The country has only half as many publicly-funded day-care places as at the end of the war. Less than one in a hundred under-fives has a place in a local authority day nursery in Britain. Taking private as well as council day nurseries, child minders, nannies and au-pairs all together, they only provide care for about 7 per cent of Britain's three and a half million under-fives.[15] By contrast, in East Germany, 81 per cent of under-threes had places in free creches by 1986, and 89 per cent of children between the ages of three and six – when compulsory schooling starts – were attending kindergartens.[16]

In the late 1980s, the child-care issue was at last taken up by the Labour leadership as a political priority. A Labour government in the 1990s would need to put the establishment of a comprehensive, flexible, free and democratically-controlled child-care system at the top of its agenda. Not only would it make possible the rapid creation of a large number of public sector jobs and help meet skill shortages at a time of rapid economic restructuring, it would also help win essential political support from women for a broader radical programme.

Full employment

The scale of mass unemployment which persisted throughout the 1980s in Britain and in most of the rest of the advanced capitalist world – at a time when its leaders were so pleased with themselves about the booming market economies they were presiding over – remains a remarkable indictment of the waste and human degradation that is built into the modern capitalist order. Apologists for 1980s-style capitalism – taking their cue from monetarist economists, who believe that there is a natural rate of unemployment – claim that in an era of new technology full employment is no longer possible; they argue that since the introduction of the latest wave of labour-saving technology based on the micro-chip has destroyed jobs, unemployment has therefore become an unavoidable, permanent feature of society. Even some on the left think the answer is to share out what employment there is more fairly. In fact, there is every reason to believe that with today's new technologies – as with earlier bursts of innovation – full employment is fully possible. It is undeniable that under capitalist production relations, full or near-full employment cannot be guaranteed or maintained. But that has nothing to do with labour-saving technology as such. Even many capitalist economies – such as Japan, Austria and Sweden – maintained relatively low unemployment during the crisis years of the 1970s and 1980s.

Full employment should be brought back to the centre of the labour movement's agenda. At the 1987 general election, the Labour Party promised to cut unemployment by a million within two years. At that point, the official total stood at around three and a half million. By the spring of 1989, official unemployment was below two million. That was partly the result of removing unemployed workers from the dole figures through changes of rules or bogus training schemes. But it was mainly because high growth rates from the mid 1980s boosted employment. Clearly Labour's target – far from being the dangerous, spendthrift plan it was portrayed to be during the 1987 general election – was in fact a rather modest goal. The growth rates of the late 1980s are most unlikely to continue into the early 1990s, when the threat of renewed slump conditions will hang over all plans for economic change. But they show what is possible. The aim of full employment within one full five-year parliament looks more plausible than when the Campaign Group of Labour MPs published its 1985 proposals for the creation of a million jobs a year.[17]

The retreat from the post-war commitment to full employment in Britain did not begin with Mrs Thatcher, but with the decision by the Wilson government of 1964–70 to sacrifice it on the altar of the City of London and its interest in an over-valued pound. A return to full employment therefore requires a decisive break with such political traditions. The experience of the advanced capitalist world since the post-1973 crisis also shows that sustainable growth is only one necessary condition for maintaining low unemployment.[18] Specific forms of intervention are required: direct public investment needs to be prioritized over consumption; active labour-market measures, public works, vocational re-training, and public service employment need to be massively expanded; tax structures need to be changed. The labour movement's conception of full employment also has to take full account of the role of domestic labour, the growth of women's participation in the labour market, and the need to have flexible employment as a right for all.

Methods

To achieve better social and public services, a fully-funded national child-care programme, ecologically and regionally balanced development, greater social justice, rising living standards for the majority of the population and full employment in the conditions of the 1990s, old-style Labour policies are plainly not enough – still less in their Policy Review form. It should by now be obvious that the instruments used by the Wilson and Callaghan governments to greater or lesser effect – and dished up again in a modified form by the Labour leadership at the 1987 general election – now have little credibility, particularly if we are talking about the need for a radical shift in the balance of wealth and power. The methods needed to achieve the labour movement's essential policy goals cannot be read off a shopping list of radical-sounding slogans and demands. They have to be derived from the specific requirements of the re-industrialization and modernization drive which would be the only long-term basis for meeting people's demands and aspirations. Drawing on the arguments of earlier chapters, the basic building blocks for a programme of modernization and progressive change need to include:

- a planned public ownership and investment programme in a core of strategic and advanced industries as the foundation of a new British industrial base;
- the nationalization of banks and financial institutions to funnel cash into industrial and regional priorities;
- enforceable planning agreements with all major private monopolies operating in the country as a major tool of democratic national planning.

As argued in chapter 5, the heart of a successful programme of economic change in the 1990s would depend on the phased development of a group of core industries which are essential to Britain's future as a modern industrial economy, particularly with the declining importance of oil to both the exchequer and the trade balance. Without that secure economic foundation, any attempt to expand the economy for jobs, services and better living standards would be bound to fail.

But the giant capitalist companies which control those industries or markets in Britain have their own quite different priorities. The underlying criterion of all their economic decision-making is private profit; social or national priorities are only taken into account insofar as they affect that basic yardstick. Such companies also mostly operate as transnationals, making their investment, production and marketing decisions on a global scale. By contrast, the proposal systematically to build up modern domestic industry and services in the emerging international economic conditions of the 1990s is based on a completely different set of criteria which are bound to cut across the plans of the private monopolies that dominate the economy.

Public ownership

The most rational, long-term solution to the problem – and this would be one of the necessary conditions for the development of a socialist society – would be to turn those few hundred companies into democratically-owned and accountable public bodies. The basic priorities of those enterprises could then be set in line with those of the elected government in negotiation with their workforces. But in the foreseeable circumstances of the next few years, the socialization of all large-scale private enterprise seems highly unlikely to be a viable political option for a Labour government. Such a fundamental change in the structure of ownership and power in the country could only come about as part of the revolutionary transformation of society and class relations. That does not mean it is a utopian solution that should be forever banished from the political agenda. But it does limit what can plausibly be proposed as part of a feasible programme for a Labour government in the coming years – even one elected in an atmosphere of radical expectations.

Without an extension of public ownership into all major sectors of the British economy, however, large-scale industrial restructuring and expansion would be impossible. In view of the political, financial and organizational constraints on the sort of massive extension of public ownership necessary to create the conditions for stable democratic national planning, the strategy of nationalizing at least one major company in each of the couple of dozen principal economic sectors remains a creative one. This approach owes its origins to a Labour Party National Executive Committee working group in the early 1970s which included Lord Balogh, Tony Banks, Judith Hart, Stuart Holland and Ian Mikardo. Its proposals were championed by Tony Benn on the NEC itself. At that time they favoured taking at least 25 of the top 100 private industrial companies into public ownership. The proposal was aimed at securing a planning foothold in every sector.

The thinking behind the proposal was as follows. Outright ownership of a company in each industrial sector would not only provide a focus for industrial expansion and investment in all the key sectors of the economy: it would also give the planning institutions the knowledge of the way the industries functioned, as well as their cost and demand structures, allowing them to draw up meaningful planning agreements with the majority of industrial giants still in the private sector. In addition, the government would have a measure of direct control over the industry.

Lord Balogh, one of Harold Wilson's economic advisers during the 1964–70 Labour government and vice-chair of the British National Oil Corporation in the late 1970s, explained why he believed ownership of at least one company was essential if a Labour government was going to have the means to plan the development of an industrial sector effectively:

> We want immediate access to facts about costs and prices, and access to facts cannot be had if you are not a partner. That is, it cannot be had unless you wish the Inland Revenue to crawl over their books all the time, which they would not like, and I do not think it would be well done by the Inland Revenue because it is a very complicated business.[19]

Although the principle of nationalizing at least one firm in each major sector is still a sound one, in some sectors it would make more sense to take over a group of related businesses – as advocated for the construction industry and for pharmaceuticals in chapter 8.

The real failure of the nationalized industries established by successive Labour governments is not simply that they were undemocratic, bureaucratic and inefficient, but that they were never used as a lever to change the way the economy was run. All nationalizations in Britain have been based on the 'public corporation' model, established by the Tory and National governments in the 1920s and 1930s for the Central Electricity Board, the BBC and the British Overseas Aircraft Corporation. The formula was borrowed by the right-wing Labour politician, Herbert Morrison, in the 1940s. National Boards were appointed to run each concern at arm's-length from the government, effectively in the same way as any large capitalist business. From the beginning the nationalized industries were loaded with debt and leant on to keep their prices down and provide cheap coal, gas and electricity to the private sector. Not surprisingly, they quickly developed a reputation as inefficient loss-makers, and their remote and bureaucratic management methods brought little benefit to those who worked in them. The benefit mostly went to private capitalists. Both Labour and Tory governments over the years used nationalizations to save important 'lame-duck' industries that were in danger of going under. British Leyland (now the Rover Group) was put together by Labour, Rolls-Royce was taken over by the Tories. The 1974–9 Labour government bailed out Ferranti and Fairey Holdings. All this helped to give public ownership an image of failure.

No Labour government ever used the nationalized industries as a strategic springboard for planned investment and growth. All administrations, both Labour and Tory, in practice set the publicly-owned businesses a basic target – whether it was to cover their costs or reach a particular rate of profit – and then left them to get on with 'the job'. The exception would be at election time when the government would twist the boards' arms to postpone price increases or bring forward investments. The public sector was hampered by its inability to borrow freely, since loans to nationalized industries are counted as part of the public sector borrowing requirement. The publicly-owned companies were and are subject to nit-picking government interference, without ministers being able to impose clear, democratically agreed priorities because of the restrictive legislation under which they were nationalized. In the case of majority government shareholdings – which used to be the arrangement covering British Petroleum (BP) and is the basis of the current Labour leadership's proposals for British Telecom (BT) – ministers have even less power, since under the terms of the Companies Act they are obliged not to discriminate against the interests of the minority private shareholders (see chapter 7).

A public ownership programme in the 1990s would have to change the way nationalized industries and companies are run in a root-and-branch way. Public enterprise has to be liberated from the legal and bureaucratic straitjacket it has been tied into. Publicly-owned companies would need to be at the heart of the planning process, with the full participation of their unions and workforces. The internal organization of the nationalized businesses would have to be opened up to consumer and local representation, and the bargaining role of the trade unions expanded. As well as providing their vital strategic role in a programme of economic change, publicly-owned companies should become model employers, leading the way in positive action against racist and sexist employment policies.

Public ownership is, of course, only one form of social ownership, and a Labour government would want to encourage the development of the co-operative sector and municipal ownership, particularly in the small business and service sectors. In some industries, it might want to encourage the development of Swedish-style wage-earner funds, whereby a tax on profits could be used to build up collectively-owned and controlled stakes in large companies as another method of influencing the largest monopolies that remained in private hands and of redistributing income and wealth. But neither co-ops nor local authority enterprises – still less the American-inspired fad for employee share ownership plans (ESOPs) – can serve as an alternative to nationalization, as some in the labour movement have tried to imply.[20] In an economy where decisive economic power is concentrated in fewer and fewer hands, only full-scale public ownership can be the basis for the radical change that is needed.

Planning

The extension of the public sector on such a scale would create an important bridge-head to carry out a planned expansion of the core industries of the future. But it would still leave the decisive centres of economic power in Britain in private hands. The experience of past Labour governments in trying to convince large private companies to carry out their part of an indicative plan has been a dismal one. The only plausible way of ensuring that big business sticks to democratically agreed priorities – short of nationalization – is through the use of legal sanctions. That means some form of enforceable planning agreement. This was the strategy advocated by Labour in opposition in the early 1970s. Once in office, however, Harold Wilson used his authority to remove all threat of statutory enforcement for such agreements from the 1975 Industry Act; in the event only one voluntary agreement was signed with a private firm. This involved handing over large quantities of government money to the UK branch of the American company Chrysler. Having taken the cash, Chrysler tore up the agreement and sold out to the French-owned Peugeot.

It is the existence of real conflicts between the interests of private shareholders and ordinary people that requires powers of compulsion over capital. The approach of Labour's 1989 policy review does not recognize these real conflicts, and therefore believes it is sufficient to encourage and cajole capital:

> The irony is that the apparent divergence between the short-term private interest and the long-term national interest is in fact a delusion. No firm can operate successfully for very long in an under-educated, under-trained, under-invested economy, with a crumbling infrastructure and outdated equipment. Eliminating the apparent gap between the national interest and private interests is a fundamental task of economic policy.[21]

This would be correct if the conflicts were only apparent. But the conflicts of interest are real. One hundred and fifty billion pounds' worth of British capital has drawn a slightly different conclusion from the same analysis of British decline, and left for greener pastures abroad, in the US or South Korea. Working people have nowhere else to go, and therefore have an unshakeable interest in the regeneration of Britain's economy. This is one major reason why a Labour government will need to force capital to reinvest and re-equip.

So how could statutory planning agreements work? The authors of a semi-official Labour Party publication on economic strategy published in the run-up to the 1987 general election argued that while 'voluntary planning agreements offered nothing to make it worthwhile for firms to negotiate', compulsory planning agreements were 'a contradiction in terms' which assume that 'companies can be forced to agree to certain commitments.' Their alternative, which they claimed went beyond planning agreements, was based on a combination of using commercial leverage on particular firms and developing sectoral strategies with worker participation.[22] This is a step back from the positions adopted in the early 1970s; there is no reason to believe such proposals would be any more successful than the sort of indicative planning which was attempted by the first Wilson government in the mid 1960s and led to such disillusionment in the labour movement.

Labour's *Programme 1982*, for all its glaring weaknesses in the area of economic policy, sketched out a more realistic approach to planning what would of course be – as Neil Kinnock pointed out at the 1988 Labour Party conference – a market or capitalist economy. It proposed a combination of statutory powers which could be used to ensure that private companies negotiated and carried out what it called development plans to cover purchasing policy, import penetration, investment plans, pricing strategy and training poiicy. Those powers included price controls, which could be relaxed for compliant firms; credit from a National Investment Bank; import controls for a sector where leading firms had agreed plans in line with sectoral priorities; and discretionary financial support. It also proposed other ill-defined powers of industrial intervention.

The planning agreements necessary for industrial and economic redevelopment in the 1990s would have to include some of these mechanisms. They would need to be enforced by a mixture of commercial and legal pressures, backed up by a legal enforcement procedure for recalcitrant companies – with the promise of nationalization as a final incentive. A nationalized financial sector and a democratized Bank of England could become a central part of the planning process. They would be able to amass information necessary for building up the planning process, monitor the behaviour of the large private monopolies and funnel investment funds to underpin the planned reconstruction effort. In the early stages of any new government, before the necessary legislation was on the statute-book, pressure would have to be exerted using existing legislation. But it is important to remember the political context that such a government would have been elected in: such a change would only be possible with mass popular support. In 1974, when Labour was re-elected and Tony Benn appointed Industry Minister during the miners' strike, leading industrialists beat a path to his door in their enthusiasm to co-operate with the new government's planning proposals. It was only when the Prime Minister, Harold Wilson, threw his weight behind the effort to block the more radical plans that the Confederation of British Industry (CBI) formed a common front against planning agreements.[23]

Economic planning and intervention would thus have to go much further than anything attempted by previous Labour governments. Paul Hare describes the failure of the 1964–70 attempts:

> The plan was sacrificed to the exigencies of short term macroeconomic policy, though even if it had not been it contained so little provision for implementation that it is hard to believe it could have had much impact on the economy. With its unclear objectives, and being produced at a time when planning was briefly 'in fashion', it is tempting to conclude that the National Plan was largely a political exercise, without much serious intent. ... The National Plan hardly began the task of changing the real constraints facing the economy, and its rapid failure following a period of quite unjustified optimism left planning in Britain discredited for many years.[24]

The institutional structure of planning would also take time to develop. Planning would have to be built from the bottom up on the basis of the detailed knowledge of the workforce, the trade unions and local authorities – as well as sympathetic sections of corporate management. Early on in the life of the government, a team of economists, trade unionists, ministers, civil servants and sympathetic business people would need to be brought together immediately to begin the process of drafting sectoral plans for expansion and to form the nucleus of a new planning council or commission. In the longer run, the DTI would have to be reorganized with some of the Treasury's existing powers as a Department of Planning, working closely with the new public financial sector. Regional and local planning institutions would need to be developed to mesh with the national effort. A training programme to develop planning skills would need to be established. Negotiations over enterprise plans would be held between the government and the private company management, with the government drawing on the advice and knowledge of trade union and shop floor organizations.

Industrial Democracy and Workers' Control

The focus of this book has been overwhelmingly on the failure of capitalism and private enterprise on a social level, and on how power could be wrested from big business to redirect the way the whole economy operates in the interest of the working class and its potential allies. There has been plenty of discussion about how public ownership and intervention could change the way companies do business with each other, but very little about how publicly-owned companies should be run internally, about workers' control or whether there is a role for industrial democracy in the private sector. The most important reason for this approach is that workers' struggles for control over the production process or strategic company decisions are not technical problems that can be legislated for by a sympathetic government. They can only grow out of effective trade union and political organization on the shop floor.

The disappointment with the experience of the bureaucratic and undemocratic nationalized industries in Britain led many in the labour movement to focus on the internal organization of the companies as the key to their failure. On the right of the movement that translated itself into a view that ownership was unimportant and what mattered was industrial democracy. On the left it veered off into a demand for workers' control first and foremost. That tendency needs to be corrected. The reason the nationalized industries never even began to fulfil the hopes that were invested in them was that they were never used as the centrepiece of a strategy to challenge the dominant political and economic interests in society – which would have been a struggle all workers could take part in: once they were condemned to being commercially-orientated corporations whose main role was to service the private sector, the demand for participation made little more sense than in any ordinary business.

No strategy aimed at challenging class power throughout society can seriously include industrial democracy schemes which put a token trade unionist or two on the board. Even in normal circumstances, such arrangements end up compromising the nominee, who is at best a lone voice bound by commercial obligations, and they achieve nothing for the trade union. Likewise, workers' control under capitalism – even if an enterprise has been taken into public ownership as part of a radical political programme – is effectively a contradiction in terms. At best, it would have the effect of turning a publicly-owned company into a co-operative. More likely, it would amount to little more than a glorified Japanese quality circle.

In the context of a socialist society, the development of self-management becomes a practical possibility. The current experiment with the election of enterprise managers in the Soviet Union is a step in that direction. But in the context of the kind of programme outlined in this book, the most effective government action would be to extend workers' and trade union statutory rights in both the public and private sectors. Rights to company information and consultation could be a powerful lever in the hands of an effective trade union organization. Real control could then be exercised through collective bargaining and negotiation rather than as part of some half-baked participation scheme. In a curious way, the right that the National Union of Mineworkers won during the 1984–5 coal strike to an exhaustive pit closure review process with full information rights gives a pointer to what could be achieved in different circumstances. Complete access to commercial information would not only enormously strengthen trade unions at the workplace, but could also provide a basis for grassroots democratic participation in a national planning process.

Of course the internal structures and organization of new publicly-owned companies do need transforming. In addition to their key strategic economic and political role, nationalized firms should be models of good employment practice. New publicly-owned companies could quickly pick up a reputation for efficient and open organization and first-class terms and conditions, which would strengthen political support for public ownership. They would need to be at the forefront of positive action programmes and their organization could be opened up to consumer and community representation at all levels.

The Macroeconomic Framework

Economic forecasts for the 1990s are highly uncertain. If it were clear that the economy was heading for a recession, with the prospect of under-used economic capacity, then relatively modest plans for more government spending might be up to the job of cutting the dole queues. If on the other hand firms' capacity utilization were already high – as was the case at the end of the 1980s – any intervention to reduce unemployment and improve the quality of services would need to be more far-reaching. But it could at least be limited to dealing with that specific situation by planning trade, diverting resources from unproductive to productive uses and so on. As it is, a Labour programme not only has to be flexible enough to impose both such sets of measures onto a private capitalist economy, but would also need to be ready to pursue more radical policies to offset the destabilizing effects of what are likely to be major economic fluctuations – international as well as domestic – from blowing the government off course.

At the time of writing,[25] the British economy was coming to the end of its eight-year recovery from the trough of 1981 – itself the result of the worst slump since the 1930s, between 1979 and 1981. Growth rates throughout this upswing had not been particularly high. Certainly they were no higher than the post-war average for cyclical upswings. In many respects the economy had merely recovered its 1979 position: ten years on and not much advance. However, that cyclical recovery from slump had relied on a credit-fuelled consumer boom to sustain it, and the result was a swelling balance of payments deficit and manic speculation in the financial markets. The question for the early 1990s will be whether that consumer boom can be sustained, and if not, as seems most probable, whether some other source of economic expansion could take its place. The alternative will be, at best, economic stagnation and rising unemployment.

It is unlikely that the consumer boom of the late 1980s could continue without continued credit expansion. In theory it could be financed by earnings growth, but that seems a bit of a tall order. Although much has been made of increasing average earnings, this has largely been the result of increased productivity rather than any increase in the share of output going to labour. If anything labour's share has declined, with a shift from wages to profits. Wage rises have lagged behind increasing profits. Returns on assets by Britain's 100,000 leading companies rose by 19 per cent in 1988, compared with an 8 per cent increase in wages.[26] As high interest rates lead people to borrow less, it is implausible that the resulting gap in final demand could be made up by higher investments from profits. In fact the greater probability is that investment in consumer goods industries and their supply industries would be scaled down accordingly, exacerbating the shortfall in demand.

Nevertheless, if the consumer boom carried on, a radical Labour government would need to move quickly to take control of the economy out of the hands of the international financial markets and thus allow the possibility of economic policies not tailored first and foremost to maximizing profits and pleasing the markets. The scope for independent government intervention could then be used to divert resources into investment projects, particularly in potential export and import-substitution sectors. The immediate priorities would be to reduce inflation, the balance of payments deficit and interest rates. The key for all these targets would be to divert resources from unproductive to productive uses. A counter-inflation strategy would be based on direct action to ensure that increased credit and demand was matched by increased output rather than higher prices. As for the post-North Sea oil balance of payments deficit threat, the priority would be to avoid the need for crisis reductions in imports – whether through import controls or via the free market operating through domestic recession. Stable interest rates would mean the abandonment of the Tories' vain attempts to use a single instrument – the interest rate – to control three targets simultaneously: investment, domestic consumer credit, and the exchange rate. Instead, direct quantitative controls would need to be used.

If the economy faces a downswing in the early 1990s, measures would be necessary to expand demand. But productive capacity would still have been scrapped and would certainly be far below the level required to achieve full employment and an increased standard of living. So there would still be a need to expand capacity, using the lever of public ownership and investment. The focus would have to be on linking the demand and supply sides of the economy, through intervention in and expansion of the public sector. Public ownership itself increases possibilities for bringing stability to the economy and its markets, since decisions about the scale of major investments, output and employment are taken in the democratic arena and do not depend on the secret whims of massive private transnational companies. The way in which a publicly owned core of the economy could be developed as a mutually reinforcing process of expansion and modernization has already been discussed in detail in chapters 7 and 8. The point to stress here is that the recessionary threat to the

British economy in the 1990s would need to be met by an expansion of productive capacity as well as a matching expansion in demand.

Where Would the Money Come From?

The question of how the sort of interventionist economic policies outlined in this book could be financed is a vital one, both from a political and an economic point of view. In particular it is often asked how widespread public ownership of industry could be paid for. The starting point is to realize that the financial issues involved depend fundamentally on real economic forces. The Conservative government succeeded in raising money from privatizing publicly-owned assets because the paper shares being sold represented claims on real productive resources owned by those firms – capable of producing goods and services, and thus revenue and profits. The wealth of society is measured in statistical terms by monetary accounting, but the actual wealth lies not in the money itself, but on what real resources that money can lay claim to.

The proposals in this book are aimed at laying the ground for a more productive economy, which would increase these real resources in Britain, through investment, research and development, by redirecting efforts away from the unproductive waste of military production and the shuffling of stocks and shares in the City. So why is there any question of where the money comes from to pay for it? Since wealth would be increasing, there should be a surplus to be distributed, rather than a bill to be paid. Part of the answer to this riddle lies in the costs of compensating the previous owners of the industries taken into public ownership. If no compensation were paid, there would have been a transfer of wealth, in the form of paper claims on real assets, from the previous shareholders to the taxpayers. And to the extent that public ownership would allow expansion of these industries, the increase in the wealth of the taxpayer would be greater than the loss of wealth of the previous shareholders: net wealth would have been created. So in theory the taxpayer could compensate the previous shareholders in full – leaving them just as well off as before the nationalization of the firm in which they held shares. The taxpayers would still be better off by the amount of extra wealth generated by the increased level of economic activity.

When a firm is taken into public ownership, compensation takes the form of issuing government bonds. These are equivalent to the shares for which they are exchanged, in the sense that they represent both a stock of wealth – which can be realized by selling the bonds just as the shares could have been sold – and an income stream in the form of interest payments rather than the share's dividend payments. The value of the shares corresponded to the real productive assets of the company and the dividends derived from the profits arising from the use of those assets. In the same way, the bonds given in exchange for shares would correspond to the real productive assets now in common ownership, and the wealth generated by those assets for the community would be the real basis of the interest payments on any such government bonds.

This argument is sometimes put more simply: the profits or financial surplus from the public sector would provide the income stream from which the interest payments would be paid. That would certainly be one option – to market the goods and services produced by the newly nationalized business so as to ensure enough profits to service the debt. But once the assets are in public hands there is no need for their use to be restricted in this way. Running publicly-owned firms to meet a much broader range of social and economic criteria than simply maximizing profit – as would be essential for the central programme of building a modern industrial base in this country – would be likely to conflict with the narrow requirement to pay the interest on the bonds entirely out of the nationalized business's profits. If British Telecom were installing a national fibre-optic grid and distributing free Minitel-like terminals, as proposed in chapter 7, it would not be making the £2.4 billion as it did in 1988/89. So a modest net cost of compensation would probably have to be accepted. But there is no reason why it should reduce a Labour government's social spending programmes, since it would be more than outweighed by the positive effects of publicly-planned investment throughout the economy, which would show up in expanded activity and tax revenues.

Historically, governments in capitalist countries have tended to be unnecessarily generous to the private shareholders of firms they have nationalized, even taking account of the political pressures of the time. Seen from the perspective of the recent wave of privatizations, their policy has been the unusual one of buying dear and selling cheap. In Britain, nationalized industries like the Coal Board were overburdened with the cost of their own compensation bills, and then denied the freedom to borrow for capital investment because any money they raised was, and is, counted quite unnecessarily as part of the restricted 'public sector borrowing requirement'. A Labour government in the 1990s would need to develop a new system of public accounting that would encourage investment rather than stifle it.

Public Spending, Taxes and Inflation

Whatever kind of Labour government might be elected in the 1990s would be faced with enormous pressures for higher public spending of all kinds and would certainly be committed to a range of priorities. Quite apart from the complexities of compensating the shareholders of twenty or thirty transnational giants, the short to medium term goals that a radical Labour government in the coming period would need to put first – a national child-care system, minimum standards in public services, a quality training and retraining programme, not to mention higher wages for public sector workers – would all drive up departmental budgets. As the investment and expansion programme started to take off, new tax revenues would be generated to help finance such colossal undertakings. But even a phased programme of increased public spending would demand new sources of finance in the short term. Income tax would have to be raised among those income groups beyond the social base of the new government. A wealth tax would be an urgent measure, and military spending could and should be drastically reduced.

But whether government securities are issued in compensation for taking privately owned industries into public ownership or in order to raise money for public expenditure, the economic effect depends on the willingness of financial institutions to hold large quantities of them. If privately-owned financial institutions proved unwilling to hold new bonds issued by a progressive Labour government, this would lead to a fall in the price of those securities and a rise in interest rates, making any further bond issues that much more difficult. This apparently technical problem needs to be placed in the more general context of the City's potential reaction to a radical government. If politically-motivated destabilization was provoked by policies such as cuts in military spending or withdrawal from NATO, the bond market could be disrupted regardless of whether or not new bond issues were planned by government. As argued in chapter 6, the surest way of overcoming such problems would be to take the City itself into public ownership. Short of that, even the TUC is on record as arguing that if a Labour government faced problems because of an unwillingness of financial institutions to hold government securities, then the government should take strongly interventionist measures:

> Whether this was allowed to disrupt the Government's funding of its spending programmes on health, education and so on would depend on what measures the Government were prepared to take to ensure that securities were held – on the degree of control which the Government was prepared to exercise over the financial institutions. One option would be for Government to *oblige* the financial institutions to hold a certain portion of their assets in the form of government securities.[27]

Such requirements could then be set at whatever level proved necessary to prevent the price of such securities falling.

Incomes Policies and Employment

The last Labour government presided over high inflation. In a period of recession in the international capitalist economy, it persisted in allowing demand to be expanded without having the political will to follow its own manifesto and intervene to expand output to meet that demand. Given the level of demand, the key determinant of inflation is the level of domestic production of goods and services. Incomes policies are thus at best a diversion. At worst they can undermine the key counter-inflation need for investment in high productivity domestic production facilities. On the one hand, by transferring company finances from wages to profits incomes policies allow firms to make profits without making those new investments. And on the other hand, by keeping wages low incomes policies can keep outdated capacity profitable, adding a further motivation to employees to perpetuate Britain's low investment, low productivity, low wage economy.

A quite separate argument in favour of incomes policies is that they allow the expansion of employment. A large body of academic literature appeared throughout the 1970s and 1980s establishing an inverse relation between wage and employment levels, implying that reducing wages would increase employment – a policy conclusion most explicitly stated in a 1985 contribution from the Treasury. However, there is actually no such correlation between cyclical employment growth and wage reductions. Wages in the business cycle show no significant pattern. Wage reductions are just as likely to be associated with a fall in employment as with an increase. Indeed, an incomes policy may itself tend to reduce employment – either by reducing expectations of future demand for consumer goods or by allowing out-of-date equipment to remain profitable thereby inhibiting its replacement with newer technology.[28]

The International Dimension

The last few pages have looked at the domestic macroeconomic challenges for a Labour government in the 1990s in implementing a programme aimed at fundamental change in the economy and society. But in reality the British macroeconomy can no more be considered in isolation from the rest of the international capitalist economy than British industry can be separated from the division of labour favoured by the transnationals. In chapter 2 and chapter 6, the need for trade planning, exchange controls and a strongly interventionist programme of international economic co-operation was examined. To recap briefly, a growing trade deficit would threaten the kind of balance of payments crises that dogged the Labour governments of the 1960s and 1970s – and was the immediate cause of the U-turn by the Mitterrand government in 1983. Particularly in conditions of a downswing in the international economy, expansion of the British economy would tend to suck in imports at an unsustainable rate. A Labour government in the 1990s would therefore need to adopt a policy of trade planning, allowing a sustainable growth in both exports and imports, as well as allowing Britain's participation in the creation of a new international economic order.

Policies designed to allow a balanced increase in imports alongside expanded exports could be most effectively pursued under a form of socialization of foreign trade – in the sense that there would need to be public control over the size of the overall increase in imports each year. Such a scheme for a planned growth of trade would need to ensure that trade developed in a way compatible with the overall national planning framework, while at the same time permitting private firms to continue their normal import and export operations.

One option would be to proceed from a target rate of nominal growth for imports as a whole, to the definition of nominal growth rates for thirty or forty major categories of imports, such as machine tools or luxury products. Within each category, a process of bidding for import licences could then determine which particular commodities or services were imported. By this method of deciding how much of what categories of goods and services to import, the government could take account of market demand as well as industrial, social and regional needs.

The technical details of another scheme were spelled out by Professor Wynne Godley in the 1970s as part of his proposal for import controls, under which all the foreign currency allocated for imports would be auctioned off. His particular approach could be criticized for over-reliance on the market and favouring the wealthy, while not providing for rational co-ordination of trade. Another option might be the direct allocation of import licences for the bulk of trade, supplemented by a market for some unallocated portion of import allowances – presumably luxury consumer goods. In this case central government could obtain a financial surplus from the auction of these quotas, which would in effect be an additional tax on luxury imports. Whatever the exact form of the scheme, the important point would be to give the government strategic control over the growth of trade and its integration with the rest of the economy, while at the same time allowing firms to use their detailed knowledge of international product markets efficiently.

All such policies would be unworkable in the absence of comprehensive exchange controls. Under the Common Market's Treaty of Rome, exchange controls are permitted in an emergency, but this exemption would not cover their permanent re-introduction as part of a long-term strategy to remove power over the British economy from the hands of international finance capital. A realistic scheme for the repatriation of overseas investment has been set out involving the issue of government bonds in return for such assets.[29] In the discussion of nationalization compensation the possibility was raised that institutions issued with such bonds might wish to sell them. Some degree of non-transferability of such bonds would then need to be considered. The same considerations would also apply to this capital repatriation scheme, but with this addition such a scheme would be perfectly feasible.

Many in the labour movement recognize the threat posed by international financial disruption and instability in the exchange markets, but regard the exchange rate mechanism of the European Monetary System (EMS) as a far safer and preferable alternative. The exchange rate mechanism of the EMS ties the currencies of most EEC members into a tightly-defined range; but membership of the exchange rate mechanism would place an extra obstacle in the way of a Labour government intent on following independent economic policies. Under the terms of the EMS, financial support for the pound would be conditional upon Britain taking 'adjustment measures'; in the early 1980s both France and Belgium had to slash social security spending in the name of these adjustment measures.[30] In effect it is West Germany which determines economic policy through the exchange rate mechanism, as it is the largest and the lowest-inflation member. For this reason the EMS is generally regarded as a Deutsche Mark zone. Being a full member of the EMS would be as great a barrier to radical economic policies as the IMF proved to be in the 1970s.

The fundamental reason for the Labour Party to adopt the type of economic programme outlined in this chapter would be political rather than purely economic. It would be one aspect of a programme to challenge the power and control which monopoly capital currently has over the economy, society and our lives. But by itself a Labour government would be virtually helpless in attempting to confront that wealth and power, whatever the coherence or otherwise of its legislative proposals. Attempts to introduce an element of democratic control and planning into the economy and to redirect resources away from military waste towards social use could only succeed with mass popular support and mobilization.

Notes

1. Elwyn Brooks White, *One Man's Meat*, New York 1944.
2. This was the thrust of Labour's two-year policy review. The final documents, published in May 1989, probably went even further than the Labour leadership had itself originally intended.
3. See Professor Ivor Crewe's analysis of a BBC/Gallup 1987 general election exit poll in the *Guardian*, 15 June 1987. Labour's vote among unskilled and semi-skilled workers increased from 44 per cent in 1983 to 50 per cent in 1987 – though that was

still 5 per cent fewer than in 1979. But its vote among skilled workers actually fell by 1 per cent in 1987 to just over one third.

4. Deflating the index for weekly wage-rates from *National Institute Economic Review* February 1986, by the Retail Price Index from *Economic Trends (Annual Supplement)* 1986, shows that real wages fell by 8 per cent in 1977 and – unlike earnings – had not recovered their 1976 level by 1983. The tax and price real wages index used by *Labour Research* shows that take-home pay dropped in both 1977 and 1978.

5. The real wage index derived from the *National Institute Economic Review* and *Economic Trends (Annual Supplement)* used above shows that real wage rates fell in 1981 and 1982.

6. See Malcolm Wicks's analysis of tax changes in *New Statesman and Society*, 10 March 1989, which shows that a married couple with two children and the husband in work on average earnings paid 35.1 per cent of their income in tax in 1978/79 and 37.3 per cent in 1988/89. Families on half average income saw their tax burden rise from 2.5 per cent to 7.1 per cent over the same period.

7. See John Hills, *Changing Tax: How the System Works and How to Change It*, Child Poverty Action Group, London 1989.

8. See the evidence on the lack of correlation between wage restraint and employment in Göran Therborn, *Why Some Peoples Are More Unemployed Than Others*, London 1986, pp. 59–64; see also Jonathan Michie, *Wages in the Business Cycle – An Empirical and Methodological Analysis*, London 1987, pp. 133–4, which argues that there is no counter-cyclical pattern to real wages and that the view that counter-cyclical reflation must be accompanied by wage cuts is therefore invalid.

9. Both the Trade Union Congress and the Labour Party Conference in 1988 confirmed support for a statutory national minimum wage. The Labour Party resolution called for a legal minimum of £135 a week, with pro rata payments for part-time workers.

10. See 'Fair Wages Strategy: National Minimum Wage', *TUC Consultative Document*, TUC Publications, London 1986, for a discussion of possible employment effects.

11. For a fuller discussion of child care, see chapter 10.

12. Eurostat, *Basic Statistics of the Community*, Brussels 1988. In 1995, the proportion of 15–19 year olds in Britain will be around 74 per cent of the 1985 figure.

13. A 1988 NEDO survey found that six out of seven private firms were either ignorant of, or had seriously underestimated, the coming shortfall of young recruits.

14. *Eurostat*, Brussels 1988, pp. 114–15.

15. Bronwen Cohen, *Caring for Children, Services and Policies for Child Care and Equal Opportunities in the UK*, Brussels 1985.

16. Staatliche Zentralverwaltung für Statistik, Berlin 1988. In 1970, the comparable proportions were 29 per cent and 65 per cent respectively.

17. Andrew Glyn, *A Million Jobs a Year*, London 1985.

18. See the analysis by Göran Therborn, in *Why Some Peoples Are More Unemployed Than Others*, London 1986.

19. Thomas Balogh, 'Britain's Planning Problems', in Stuart Holland ed., *Beyond Capitalist Planning*, Oxford 1978, p. 136.

20. A recent example is Oonagh McDonald, *Own Your Own: Social Ownership Examined*, Fabian Society, London 1989, pp. 36–42, 79.

21. Labour Party, *Final Report of Labour's Policy Review for the 1990s*, London 1989, p. 10.

22. Diana Gilhespy et al., *Socialist Enterprise*, London 1986.

23. Tony Benn, interview with Seumas Milne, 26 January 1989.

24. Paul Hare, *Planning the British Economy*, London 1985, pp. 39–40.

25. June 1989.

26. Dun and Bradstreet, *Key Business Ratios*, London 1989, cited in *Financial Times*, 2 May 1989; *Department of Employment Gazette*, May 1989.

27. TUC, *Industries for People*, 1986, Appendix 1: How Governments Acquire Assets, p. 36 [emphasis added].

28. See Jonathan Michie, *Wages in the Business Cycle – An Empirical and Methodological Analysis*, London 1987. In a critical review in the *Economic Journal*, vol. 99 no. 394, March 1989, J.S.V. Symons continues to claim that regardless of the actual correlation between wages and employment, lower union militancy 'will lead to lower wages and a higher level of expected employment'. But his discussion remains at the level of 'other things being equal'. And in his own model, lower wages could equally lead to lower employment through a shock to the employment-determining equation from the wage reduction. That could be the result of reduced capitalist expectations of future consumer goods demand or loss of world market share as productivity growth is lowered because investment plans are postponed as productive capacity at the margin becomes profitable at the reduced wage levels.

29. See Karel Williams, John Williams, Tony Cutler and Colin Haslam, 'The Economic Consequences of Mrs Thatcher – Labour's Economic Policy Options for 1991', unpublished paper, 1988.

30. Jacques van Ypersele, *Le système monétaire européen*, Luxembourg 1984, pp. 90–93.

12

Beyond the Casino Economy

Matters cannot go on well in England until all things shall be in common.

John Ball, 1381

This book set out to show that the technical obstacles to a programme of radical economic change can be overcome and that, contrary to the fashionable view, many current economic developments in fact favour policies of public ownership and democratic planning rather than a market-based approach. They also point the way to what the French Socialist Party used to call the need for a 'break' with capitalism and the potential of socialism as a more rational and efficient – as well as a more just – type of society.

It has been necessary to go into such detail because so many in the labour movement have become convinced that facts and events are moving against them: that trends of new technology, industrial reorganization and globalization mean that socialist economic strategies are no longer viable. We have tried to demonstrate that this is very far from being the case, and that the technical instruments needed to put progressive policies into practice can be made to work. But at the same time it is important not to get too bogged down in technocratic minutiae about what a Labour government should do with this or that industry, or about a run on the pound – or even the Common Market. Progressive change does need to be practical. But the economic and institutional arguments can only make sense in a political context.

A Framework for Political Action

Radical economic and industrial reforms could not conceivably be implemented without a far higher level of mass political action and participation than has been achieved in Britain in recent years. Even for such a programme to be adopted by the Labour Party and translated into unequivocal manifesto commitments would require constant political pressure from both inside and outside the labour movement and the confidence to take industrial and political action to achieve clear goals: pressure from party activists and trade unions, women's organizations, black groups, the peace and environmental movements, community groups, the unemployed, tenants and consumer organizations – in other words, the whole range of social and political bodies in which people organize themselves to defend and advance their interests.

The lack of any mass popular agitation for social change was at the root of the failure of the French Socialist–Communist government elected in 1981 to live up to the promise of the 1972 Common Programme on which its policies were loosely based. There were many special factors and failures which explain the particular circumstances in which President Mitterrand's government decided to carry out a political U-turn and retreat from the policies of the left. But in the absence of mass pressure from below, it was inevitable that the uncertain commitment to progressive change at the top would evaporate. The ebbing of the mass political and trade union struggles of the early 1970s ironically helped the Socialist government to be elected in the early 1980s because the parallel electoral decline of the French Communist Party convinced wavering middle-class voters that it was at last safe to return a restructured left to office. But that was not the kind of political foundation which could have kept a progressive government on course, and from the start the radical economic measures – in particular the public ownership and planning policies – were implemented in a formalistic way without a clear commitment to the political thinking behind them.[1]

In Britain, mass political action has only broken through its normal barriers twice since the 1945–51 Labour governments: in the early

1970s, during the trade union-led struggles against the Heath government's industrial relations legislation and the two miners' strikes; plus, at least arguably, in the last year of the Callaghan government and the early 1980s, when different groups of workers revolted against wage restraint, public spending cuts and closures, and hundreds of thousands of people were drawn into demonstrations and public campaigning against the revival of the Cold War. One by-product of both periods was a revulsion at the record of previous Labour governments, a sharp shift to the left inside the Labour Party and its adoption of more radical economic policies. In the early 1970s, for example, Labour's new programme proposed the nationalization of twenty-five of Britain's largest private manufacturing companies[2] and at its 1982 annual conference, the Labour Party re-adopted the policy as part of a radical employment strategy.

When Labour was returned to office in February 1974 after the defeat of the Heath government on its 'Who Runs the Country?' platform, the ruling class in Britain was temporarily knocked off balance. Labour had a golden opportunity at that time to start to bring about the 'irreversible shift in the balance of wealth and power' that party leaders had talked so much about. Tony Benn, the then Labour Industry Secretary, recalls:

> Capital was utterly demoralized at that time. Their reading of the miners' strike was that it had been a sort of re-run of the General Strike and that they had lost. There was a New Realism on the side of capital. I remember a man from Smiths Industries coming to see me and saying: 'Don't worry, we've got no problems with planning agreements, we've worked with MITI in Japan, you know.' If the Labour government had pushed, it would have fallen into our hands. But Wilson pulled the rug on us and remoralized a demoralized capitalist class. By 1976, we'd turned a Labour victory into a Tory victory.[3]

What was missing was both the mass external pressure which could have forced the Labour cabinet to stick by its commitments and a developed political leadership within the labour movement which could have focussed different sectional and local struggles on the central political battle.

Reaction on the Wane

Even to propose radical measures in the atmosphere of today runs the risk of seeming utopian. Both in Britain and elsewhere the ideological right remains politically dominant. Socialist and social-democratic governments around the world are at best only modifying the essential demands of big capital and its drive to find a way to re-establish conditions for profitable growth. The economic and political upheavals in the socialist countries have allowed the Western media and politicians to put a question mark over the viability of any alternative social system to capitalism. For those working class parties in the advanced capitalist states trying to find a way back to office, New Realism is the order of the day.

But at exactly such an unpromising time as this, real life is creating the conditions for a renewal of socialism and a gradual realization of the necessity for a radical change of political direction in the capitalist world. The 1980s were years of political paradox in Britain. On the one hand many of those active on the left and in the labour movement lost confidence in some of their deepest values, even in the very possibility of social justice and advancing working people's interests. On the other, most of the rest of the population moved to the left as the effects of Thatcherite policies sank home.

The proportion of those who believed that the government should 'increase taxes and spend more on health, education and social benefits' rose from 32 per cent in 1983 to 50 per cent in 1987.[4] The proportion who believed that 'income and wealth should be redistributed towards ordinary working people' increased from 47 to 57 per cent over the same period.[5] The popularity of trade unionism was at a 33-year high – with 71 per cent thinking trade unions were 'a good thing'[6] – and by 1988, 49 per cent of those questioned said they wanted 'a mainly socialist society in which public interests and a more controlled economy are most important.'[7]

The Thatcher governments have been a historic setback for the left and the labour movement, which suffered many defeats during the 1980s. But the period has also seen advances, and the survival of a remarkably resilient commitment to collectivism which is often overlooked. Among the least noticed, but most dramatic, victories were the overwhelming mass votes by trade unionists in favour of the right to political trade unionism and to affiliate to the Labour Party in the political fund ballots of the mid 1980s.

Tory market-dominated policy has partially succeeded in remoulding society, while at the same time sowing the seeds of a rejection of these policies, as their inadequacy to the long-term needs of the British people become apparent. That has been reflected in a growing alienation of the majority of the population from both the direction and the detail of Thatcherite politics and a new attraction to the ideals of collectivism and solidarity. Throughout the world there is an increasing realization that capitalism is by its nature utterly unsuited to tackling the ecological crisis, that its latest phase of growth is driving half the developing world further into hunger and destitution, and that even in its most successful heartlands, poverty and marginalization are once again becoming endemic.

In Britain, capitalism's failures and the fragility of its successes are more obvious than in many other advanced capitalist countries. Capitalism in Britain is more parasitic, more monopolized, more speculative and more environmentally destructive than elsewhere. Capitalism in Britain, including under Thatcherite management, has consistently failed to modernize. More clearly than for example in West Germany or Sweden, there is a telling case in Britain for sacking the board of directors and forcing through a complete restructuring and change of direction. Yet it is in precisely these conditions that the labour movement and the left is becoming increasingly timid, more and more tailoring its demands and policies to the prevailing reactionary orthodoxy in a desperate attempt to stem the tide. The solutions being offered by the current Labour Party leadership are at best half-measures, or at worst based on an attitude of 'if you can't beat them, join them'.

As the people move left, the left moves right. As the scale of the task of necessary reconstruction grows, so the Labour Party abandons the policy tools that could equip it to do the job. There is a lag between what is happening in the real world and the politicians' perception of it: a lag which could rob the labour movement of a historic opportunity to make its ideas the common sense of the coming decades.

The Transition to Socialism

But what if the implementation of a radical economic programme simply became the means to pull capitalism out of the mess it has got Britain into and even gave it a new lease of life? After all, nothing proposed in this book would of itself break the boundaries of capitalist society. Capitalism is still capitalism, even with large-scale public ownership and planning. Whether such a programme would end up restructuring and stabilizing capitalism in the face of public discontent – as some of its potential supporters would undoubtedly want – or whether it could open the way for a fundamental transformation in the social system is not something that can be answered in the abstract. A political or economic programme is not necessarily reformist or revolutionary in itself: everything depends on the political forces that are mobilized behind it and whether they are strong enough to take it further.

A programme for radical economic and social change which grew out of the demands of the labour movement, the peace movement and community and progressive organizations of all kinds, would involve a serious challenge to the interests of big business which dominate life in this country. It would be a challenge that would eventually either lead to retreat or to a level of political and social struggle that could begin to call into question the whole social system and raise the alternative of a socialist society: a society based on common ownership where the working class and its allies hold political power.

The class character of such a programme would effectively be an anti-monopoly one. In other words, it would be aimed at trying to solve the accumulated problems of the British economy and to deliver a better life for the majority of the population at the expense of the interests of the largest few hundred transnationals which control the British economy and their political protectors. Even to begin to go down that road would call for a wide range of social forces to be drawn in around the goals and struggles of the working class.

The implementation of such a radical political and economic programme is thus one way in which the conditions for a socialist transformation of society could come about on the democratic initiative of the working class and its supporters. Instead of the classical revolutionary scenario of the ruling class being unable to continue ruling in the old way and the working class refusing to carry on as before because of some disaster brought about by the breakdown of the old system, the same conditions could come about because of a political crisis over a popular programme of political and economic change.[8]

Of course, all this is speculative and far from today's political situation. What is needed now is to win support both inside and outside the labour movement for policies which do not simply repeat the mistakes of the past or merely offer a more caring version of the

Tory policies of the 1980s. But the left would be quite wrong to abandon its strategic perspective of a complete change in the social system in the interests of a specious realism. The logic of industrial and economic change in recent years quite clearly points to the long-term viability and necessity of a modern socialism in the twenty-first century.

Notes

1. See Philippe Herzog et al., *Un Chemin Pour Sortir de la Crise*, Paris 1985; and Alain Lipietz, *L'Audace ou L'Enlisement*, Paris 1985.
2. Labour Party, *Labour's Programme for Britain*, London 1973, p. 34.
3. Tony Benn, interview with Seumas Milne, 26 January 1989.
4. Roger Jowell, Sharon Witherspoon and Lindsay Brook, *British Social Attitudes*, Aldershot 1988, p. 96.
5. 1983 figure from *British Election Studies*; 1987 figure from *Gallup*; both quoted in John Rentoul, *Me & Mine – The Triumph of the New Individualism?*, London 1989.
6. MORI, 1987.
7. MORI, June 1988. A similar question asked by MORI in the summer of 1985 found 46 per cent favouring a socialist society and 46 per cent favouring a 'mainly capitalist society in which private interests and a free market economy are most important'. By 1988, support for the capitalist option was down to 43 per cent. The argument that there has been a underlying shift to the left in public attitudes during the 1980s is set out in detail in John Rentoul, *Me & Mine – The Triumph of the New Individualism?*, London 1989.
8. As argued for example by the Danish Communist Ib Nørlund, quoted in Konstantin Zarodov, *Leninism and Contemporary Problems of the Transition from Capitalism to Socialism*, Moscow 1976, p. 133.

Bibliography

Abrams, Mark and Rose, Richard, *Must Labour Lose?*, Penguin, Harmondsworth 1960.

ACAS, *Labour Flexibility in Britain*, London 1988.

Advisory Committee on Science and Technology (ACOST), *Opto-Electronics: Building on our Investment*, London 1988.

Aglietta, Michel, *A Theory of Capitalist Regulation: The US Experience*, Verso, London 1979.

Air Traffic Users Committee, *Annual Report 1987–88*, London 1988.

Aksoy, Asu, Miles, Ian, Morgan, Kevin and Thomas, Graham, 'The Changed White Heat of Technology', *Guardian*, 8 June 1989.

Amdahl Executive Institute, *Clues to Success: Information Technology Strategies for Tomorrow*, Hartley Wintney 1989.

Appleby, Colin and Twigg, David, 'Computer Aided Design in the United Kingdom Car Industry', *National Westminster Bank Quarterly Review*, August 1988, pp. 39–52.

Association of Metropolitan Authorities, *Oiling the Wheels*, London 1988.

Atkinson, John, 'Manpower Strategies for Flexible Organizations', *Personnel Management*, August 1984.

Atkinson, John and Meagre, Nigel, *Changing Working Patterns*, National Economic Development Office, London 1986.

Ball, Michael, *Rebuilding Construction*, Routledge, London 1988.

Balogh, Thomas, 'Britain's Planning Problems' in Stuart Holland ed., *Beyond Capitalist Planning*, Basil Blackwell, Oxford 1978.

Bank of England, 'Takeover Activity in the 1980s', *Quarterly Bulletin* no. 1, 1989.

Barker, Terry and Dunne, Paul, eds, *The British Economy after Oil: Manufacturing or Services?*, London 1988.

Bernstein, Eduard, *Evolutionary Socialism*, New York 1961 (1898).

Bhat, Ashok, Carr-Hill, Roy and Ohri, Sushel, eds, *Britain's Black Population: A New Perspective*, Aldershot 1988.

Blackburn, Phil and Sharpe, Richard, eds, *Britain's Industrial Renaissance?*, Routledge, London 1988.

British Railways Board, *National Accounts*, London 1988.

Brown, Colin, *Black and White*, Policy Studies Institute, 1984.

Brown, C. and Gay, P., *Racial Discrimination: 17 Years after the Act*, Policy Studies Institute, London 1985.

Bruntland, Gro Harlem, *Our Common Future*, Oxford 1987.

Bryant, Ralph, *International Financial Intermediation*, The Brookings Institution, Washington 1987.

Buck, Trevor and Cole, John, *Modern Soviet Economic Performance*, Basil Blackwell, Oxford 1987.

Bukharin, Nikolai, *Imperialism and World Economy*, Monthly Review Press, New York, 1972 (1914).

CAITS/MSF, *The Motor Industry Today and Tomorrow: A Report for Motor Industry Representatives*, London 1988.

Campaign for Labour Party Democracy, *The Case for Public Ownership*, London 1986.

Castro, Fidel, *Nothing Can Stop the Course of History*, Pathfinder Press, New York 1986.

Cecchini Report, *Economics of 1992*, European Commission, Brussels 1988.

Central Office of Information, *United Kingdom National Accounts*, HMSO, London 1987.

Central Office of Information. *Britain 1989: An Official Handbook*, HMSO, London 1989.

Central Statistical Office, *Annual Abstract of Statistics*, HMSO, London 1988.

Central Statistical Office, *Economic Trends*, HMSO, London February 1989.

Central Statistical Office, *Economic Trends Annual Supplement*, HMSO, London 1988.

Central Statistical Office, *Social Trends*, HMSO, London 1988.

Central Statistical Office, *Social Trends*, HMSO, London 1989.

Central Statistical Office, *Financial Statistics*, HMSO, London April 1989.

Central Statistical Office, *General Household Survey*, HMSO, London 1989.

Central Transport Consultative Committee, *Annual Report 1987–88*, London 1988.

Centre for Local Economic Strategies, *Prospects for Local Authority Intervention in the Textiles and Clothing Industry,* Manchester 1986.

Centre for Local Economic Strategies, *Prospects for Intervention in the Merseyside Clothing Industry*, Manchester 1986.

Charles, David, Monk, Peter and Sciberras, Ed, *Technology and Competition in the Telecommunications Industry*, Frances Pinter, London 1989.

Child Poverty Action Group, *Changing Tax*, London 1989.

Coakley, Jerry, 'The Internationalisation of Banking Capital', *Capital and Class*, no. 23, Summer 1984.

Coakley, Jerry and Harris, Laurence, *The City of Capital*, Basil Blackwell, Oxford 1983.

Cohen, Bronwen, *Caring for Children, Services and Policies for Child Care and Equal Opportunities in the UK*, Brussels 1985.

Cohen, Stephen S. and Zysman, John, *Manufacturing Matters: The Myth of the Post-Industrial Economy*, Basic Books, New York 1987.

Computer Services Association, *Annual Report*, London 1988.

Computer Users Year Book, 'Salary Survey', London 1988.

Confederation of British Industry, *Investing for Britain's Future*, London 1987.

Coventry, Liverpool, Newcastle and North Tyneside Trades Councils, *State Intervention in Industry: A Workers' Inquiry*, Coventry 1980.

Department of Transport, *Central London Rail Study*, HMSO, London 1989.

Devine, Pat, *Democracy and Economic Planning*, Polity Press, Cambridge 1988.

Delors Committee, *Report on European Economic and Monetary Union*, European Commission, Brussels 1989.

Department of Trade and Industry, *Communications Steering Group Report: The Infrastructure for Tommorrow*, HMSO, London 1988.

Dex, Shirley, *Women's Occupational Mobility: a Lifetime Perspective*, Macmillan, London 1987.

Dex, Shirley and Shaw, L., *British and American Women at Work: Do Equal Opportunities Policies Matter?*, Macmillan, London 1986.

Donaldson, P. and Farquhar, J., *Understanding the British Economy*, Penguin, Harmondsworth 1988.

Dornbusch, Rudiger, 'Mexico: Stabilization, Debt and Growth' in *Economic Policy* no. 7, pp. 233–73, October 1988.

Elliot, Ruth, 'Women, Restructuring and Union Strategies', paper presented to the Women and Economy Conference, Women's Studies Unit, 383 Holloway Road, London N7, May 1988.

Elson, Diane, 'Market Socialism or Socialization of the Market?', *New Left Review* no. 172, November/December 1988.

Estrin, Saul and Jones, Derek, 'Can Employee-Owned Firms Survive?' LSE Centre for Labour Economics *Discussion Paper* no. 316, 1988.

Eurostat, *Basic Statistics of the Community*, Statistical Office of the European Communities, Brussels 1988.

Evans, George, 'Sectoral Imbalance and Unemployment in the United Kingdom,' LSE *Discussion Paper* no. 300, 1988.

Fabian Society, *ABC of Thatcherism*, London 1989.

Fagerberg, Jan, 'International Competitiveness.' *Economic Journal*, vol. 98 no. 391, June 1988.

Fennell, Desmond OBE QC, *Investigation into the King's Cross Underground Fire*, HMSO Cmd 499, London 1988.

Fine, Ben and Harris, Laurence, *Peculiarities of the British Economy*, Laurence & Wishart, London 1985.

Fine, Ben, 'Segmented Labour Market Theory: A Critical Assessment', Birkbeck College *Discussion Paper in Economics*, 87/12, 1987.

Fleming, Michael, 'Construction', in Peter Johnson, ed., *The Structure of British Industry*, London 1988.

Forbes, Ian, ed., *Market Socialism – Whose Choice?*, Fabian Tract no. 516, 1986.

Forecasting and Assessment in Science and Technology (FAST), *Human Work, Technology and Industrial Strategies: Options for Europe*, European Commission, Brussels 1988.

Freeman, Christopher and Soete, Luc, eds, *Technical Change and Full Employment*, Oxford 1987.

Freeman, Christopher, 'Information Technology and Change in Techno-Economic Paradigm', in Christopher Freeman and Luc Soete, eds, *Technical Change and Full Employment*, Oxford 1987.

Fuller, Ken, *Radical Aristocrats: London Busworkers from the 1880s to the 1980s*, Lawrence & Wishart, London 1985.

Ganguly, P., *UK Small Business Statistics and International Comparisons*, Harper & Row, London 1985.

George, Susan, *A Fate Worse than Debt*, Penguin Books, Harmondsworth 1988.

Gerry, Chris, 'Working Class and Small Enterprises in the UK Recession', in Redclift, N. and Mingione, E., eds, *Beyond Employment: Household, Gender and Subsistence*, Blackwell, Oxford 1985.

Gerry, Chris, 'Notes on the Informal Sector in Historical Perspective', paper presented to the Questions of Restructuring Work and Employment Conference, University of Warwick, 1988.

Gershuny, Jonathan, *Social Innovation and the Division of Labour*, OUP, Oxford 1983.

Gershuny, Jonathan, 'The Future of Service Employment', in P. Marstrand, ed., *New Technology and the Future of Work and Skills*, Frances Pinter, London 1984.

Gershuny, Jonathan, 'Addendum to the Future of Service Employment: the Recent History of Service Employment', mimeo, University of Bath 1985.

Gershuny, Jonathan and Miles, Ian, *The New Service Economy*, Frances Pinter, London 1983.

Gilhespy, Diana et al., *Socialist Enterprise*, Spokesman, London 1986.

Gillespie, Andrew and Hepworth, Mark, 'Telecommunications and Regional Development in the Information Society', Newcastle Studies of the Information Economy Working Paper no. 1, CURDS, University of Newcastle upon Tyne 1986.

Glyn, Andrew, *A Million Jobs a Year*, Verso, London 1985.

Glyn, Andrew, 'Capital Flight and Exchange Controls', *New Left Review* no. 155, January/February 1986, pp. 37–49.

Glyn, Andrew, 'A Case for Exchange Controls', University of Oxford Institute of Economics and Statistics, Applied Economics Discussion Paper, no. 36 1987.

Glyn, Andrew, 'The Economic Case Against Pit Closures', in David Cooper and Trevor Hopper, eds, *Debating Coal Closures*, CUP, Cambridge 1988.

Glyn, Andrew, Hughes, Alan, Lipietz, Alain and Singh, Ajit, 'The Rise and Fall of the Golden Age', World Institute for Development Economics Research, Working Paper, Cambridge 1988.

Godley, Wynne, 'Manufacturing and the Future of the British Economy', in Terry Barker and Paul Dunne, eds, *The British Economy After Oil: Manufacturing or Services?*, Croom Helm, Beckenham 1988.

Goldman Sachs, *UK Economics Analyst*, London 1989.

Goldring, Mary, ed., *The World in 1989*, Economist Publications, London 1988.

Goldthorpe, John, Lockwood, David, Bechhofer, Frank and Platt, Jennifer, *The Affluent Worker*, 3 vols., CUP, Cambridge 1968–9.

Goodhart, Charles, 'The Economics of "Big Bang" ', *Midland Bank Review* 1987.

Goodhart, David and Grant, Charles, *Making the City Work*, Fabian Society Tract no. 528, London 1988.

Gordon, David, 'The Global Economy: New Edifice or Crumbling Foundations', *New Left Review* no. 168, March/April 1988.

Gramsci, Antonio, 'Americanism and Fordism', in *Selections from Prison Notebooks*, Lawrence & Wishart, London 1971 (1929–35).

Grant, Wyn, *The Political Economy of Industrial Policy*, Butterworths, London 1982.

Grassman, S., 'Long-Term Trends in Openness of National Economies', *Oxford Economic Papers*, 1988.

Greater London Council, *London Industrial Strategy*, London 1985.

Greater London Council, *Textiles and Clothing: Sunset Industries?*, London 1986.

Greater Manchester Low Pay Unit, *The Bottom Line*, Manchester 1989.

Greenhalgh, Christine, 'Employment and Structural Change in Britain: Trends and Policy Options', Oxford Institute of Economics & Statistics, *Applied Economics Discussion Paper* no. 42, March 1988.

Hall, Stuart, 'Brave New World', *Marxism Today*, October 1988.

Hare, Paul, *Planning the British Economy*, Macmillan, London 1985.

Harris, Laurence, Coakley, Jerry, Croasdale, Martin and Evans, Trevor, eds, *New Perspectives on the Financial System*, Croom Helm, London 1988.

Heller, Robert, *The State of Industry*, Sphere, London 1987.

Henley Centre for Forecasting, *The United Markets of Europe*, London 1988.

Herzog, Philippe et al., *Un Chemin Pour Sortir de la Crise*, Messidor/Editions Sociales, Paris 1985.

Hilferding, Rudolph, *Finance Capital: A Study of the Latest Phase of Capitalist Development*, Routledge & Kegan Paul, London 1981 (1910).

Hills, Jill, 'The Internationalization of Domestic Telecommunications Law: US Industrial Policy on a Worldwide Basis', unpublished paper, The City University, London 1988.

Hills, John, *Changing Tax: How the System Works and How to Change It*, Child Poverty Action Group, London 1985.

Hirst, Paul and Zeitlin, Jonathan, *Reversing Industrial Decline?*, Berg, Oxford 1989.

Hobsbawm, Eric, *Industry and Empire*, Penguin, Harmondsworth 1969.

Hobsbawm, Eric, *The Age of Capital 1848–75*, Weidenfeld & Nicolson, London 1975.

Hobson, J.A., *Imperialism: A Study*, Allen & Unwin, London 1938 (1902).

Hodgson, Geoff, *The Democratic Economy*, Penguin, Harmondsworth 1984.

Holland, Stuart, ed., *Beyond Capitalist Planning*, Basil Blackwell, Oxford 1978.

Holmes, Martin, *The Labour Government 1974–79,* Macmillan, London 1985.

House of Lords, *Select Committee on Overseas Trade*, Session 1984–85 (238-I) 1985.

Howells, Jeremy, *Economic, Technical and Locational Trends in European Services*, Avebury, Aldershot 1988.

Institute of Manpower Studies, *The UK Motor Industry*, Sussex 1989.

International Telecommunications Union, *Yearbook of Common Carrier Statistics*, Geneva 1988.

James, Norman, 'The Tyne and Wear Metro Study', paper to Centre for Local Economic Strategies seminar, December 1988.

Johnson, Peter, ed., *The Structure of British Industry*, London 1988.

Joshi, Heather, 'The Cash Opportunity of Childbearing: An Approach Using British Data', Centre for Economic Policy Research *Discussion Paper* no. 208, London 1987.

Jowell, Roger, Witherspoon, Sharon and Brook, Lindsay, *British Social Attitudes*, Gower, Aldershot 1988.

Kaldor, M., Sharp, M. and Walker, W., 'Industrial Competitiveness and Britain's Defence', *Lloyd's Bank Review* no. 162, 1986.

Kay, John, ed., *1992: Myths and Realities*, London Business School, Centre for Business Studies, London 1989.

Kay, John and Vickers, John, 'Changes in the Stock Exchange', *Bank of England Quarterly Bulletin* 1985.

Kay, John and Vickers, John, 'Changes in the Stock Exchange and Regulation of the City', *Bank of England Quarterly Bulletin* 1987.

Kay, John and Vickers, John, 'Regulatory Reform in Britain', *Economic Policy* no. 7, pp. 286–343, October 1988.

Keynes, John Maynard, *The General Theory of Employment, Interest and Money*, Macmillan, London 1936.

Labour Party, *Labour's Programme for Britain*, London 1973.

Labour Party, *Labour's Programme 1982*, London 1982.

Labour Party, *Low Pay: Policies and Priorities*, statement adopted by Conference 1986.

Labour Party, *Fresh Directions*, London 1987.

Labour Party, *Social Justice and Economic Efficiency*, London 1988.

Labour Party, *Meet the Challenge, Make the Change. Final Report of the Labour Party Policy Review*, London 1989.

Labour Research Department, 'Can Contractors Comply on Equality?', *Labour Research*, vol. 77 no. 10, October 1988.

Labour Research Department, *Europe 1992*, London 1989.

Leighton, Patricia, 'Employment Restructuring and Management Strategy – Case Study Evidence on "Atypical" Employment Relationships', paper presented to the Questions of Restructuring Work and Employment Conference, University of Warwick, 1988.

Lenin, Vladimir Ilyich, *Imperialism, the Highest Stage of Capitalism*, Progress Publishers, London and Moscow 1982 (1917).

Lipietz, Alain, *L'Audace ou L'Enlisement*, Editions La Découverte, Paris 1985.

Lipietz, Alain, *The Enchanted World*, Verso, London 1985.

Logica, *European Communications Systems*, London 1986.

London Strategic Policy Unit, *The London Labour Plan: Black Workers*, London 1986.

Luxemburg, Rosa, *The Accumulation of Capital*, trans. Agnes Schwarzchild, Routledge & Kegan Paul, London 1951 (1913).

Luxemburg, Rosa, *Reform or Revolution*, Merlin Press, London 1968 (1900).

MacInnes, John, *The Question of Flexibility*, DSER, University of Glasgow, August 1987.

MacInnes, John, *Discussion Paper 32*, Centre for Urban and Regional Research, University of Glasgow 1988.

MacInnes, John, *Discussion Paper 34*, Centre for Urban and Regional Research, University of Glasgow 1988.

Machin, Howard and Wright, Vincent, eds, *Economic Policy and Policy Making Under the Mitterand Presidency 1981–84*, Frances Pinter, London 1985.

Maddison, Angus, *Phases of Capitalist Development*, OUP, Oxford 1982.

Manchester Business School, *Executive Survey*, Manchester 1988.

Martin, J. and Roberts, C., *Women and Employment: a Lifetime Perspective*, HMSO, London 1984.

Marx, Karl and Engels, Friedrich, *Manifesto of the Communist Party*, Pelican, Harmondsworth 1967 (1848).

Marx, Karl, *Capital* Volume 1, Lawrence & Wishart, London 1954 (1867).

Mason, Colin, 'Explaining Recent Trends in UK New Firm Formation Rates', *Urban Policy Research Unit*, Southampton University 1988.

Mayer, Colin, 'New Issues in Corporate Finance', Centre for Economic Policy Research, *Discussion Paper* 181, 1987.

McFadyean, Melanie and Renn, Margaret, *Thatcher's Reign*, Chatto & Windus, London 1984.

McKinsey's, *Strengthening the Competitiveness of UK Electronics*, London 1988.

Michie, Jonathan, *Wages in the Business Cycle: An Empirical and Methodological Analysis*, Frances Pinter, London and Columbia University Press 1987.

Miller, Edythe S., 'Potential Abuses in the Application of Social Contract and Incentive Regulation', privately transmitted paper, 1988.

Minns, Richard, *Take Over the City*, Pluto Press, London 1982.

Monopolies and Mergers Commission, *British Railways Board: Network SouthEast*, HMSO Cmd 204, London 1987.

Morgan, Kevin and Pitt, Douglas, 'Coping With Turbulence: Corporate Strategy, Regulatory Politics and Telematics in Post-divestiture America', in Nick Garnham, ed., *Proceedings of the Communications Policy Research Conference*, London 1989.

Morgan, Kevin and Sayer, Andrew, *Microcircuits of Capital: Sunrise Industry and Uneven Development*, Polity Press, Cambridge 1988.

Morris-Suzuki, Tessa, 'Capitalism in the Computer Age', *New Left Review* no. 160, November/December 1986.

MSF, *Aerospace: Britain's Future; A Strategy for Britain's Aerospace Industry*, London 1988.

Mulgan, Geoff, 'The Power of the Weak', *Marxism Today*, December 1988.

Murray, Fergus, 'The Decentralization of Production: The Decline of the Mass Collective Worker?', in R.E. Pahl, ed., *On Work*, Oxford 1988.

Murray, Fergus, 'Restructuring the Third Italy: The PCI and Flexible Specialization', paper presented to the Questions of Restructuring Work and Employment Conference, University of Warwick, 1988.

Murray, Robin, 'Benetton Britain: The New Economic Order', *Marxism Today*, November 1985.

National Communications Union, *Submission to the Labour Party Policy Review*, London 1988.

National Economic Development Office, *Comparative Education and Training Strategies*, London 1988.

National Economic Research Associates, *Policies to Achieve a Busier Railway*, London 1988.

Neuberger, Henry, *The Economics of 1992*, commissioned by the British Labour Group of Euro MPs, published by the Socialist Group of the European Parliament 1989.

North of England Regional Consortium (NOERC), *State of the Regions Survey*, 1988.

Nove, Alec, *The Economics of Feasible Socialism*, George Allen and Unwin, London 1983.

Organization for Economic Co-operation and Development, *National Accounts*, Paris 1969.

Organization for Economic Co-operation and Development, *National Accounts*, Paris 1982.

Organization for Economic Co-operation and Development, *Merger Policies and Recent Trends in Mergers*, Paris 1984.

Organization for Economic Co-operation and Development, *Employment Outlook*, Paris 1987.

Organization for Economic Co-operation and Development, *New Technologies in the 1990s: A Socio-Economic Strategy*, Paris 1989.

PA Consulting Group and PA Cambridge Economic Consultants, *Evolution of the United Kingdom Communications Infrastructure*, HMSO, London 1988.

Pahl, R.E., ed., *On Work*, Oxford 1988.

Palmer, John, *Trading Places*, Radius, London 1988.

Pavillet, Axel, 'Integrated Circuits for US Defence – and the Defence of US Integrated Circuits', *Military Technology*, May 1988.

Pavitt, Keith and Patel, Pari, *National Institute* Economic Review, November 1987.

Perez, Carlota, 'Structural Change and the Assimilation of New Technologies in the Economic and Social Systems', *Futures*, no. 15, 1983.

Perkins, Helen, *Graduate Salaries and Vacancies*, Price Waterhouse, London 1989.

Piore, Michael and Sabel, Charles, *The Second Industrial Divide*, New York 1984.

Plender, John and Wallace, Paul, *The Square Mile*, Hutchinson, London 1985.

Ponting, Clive, *Breach of Promise: Labour in Power, 1964–70*, Hamish Hamilton, London 1989.

Porrit, Jonathon, *Seeing Green*, Oxford 1984.

Prais, Sig, *National Institute* Economic Review, February 1989.

Public Transport Information Unit, *Public Transport Information*, December 1988/January 1989.

Rainnie, Al, 'Continuity and Change: Uneven Development and the Small Firm', paper presented to the Questions of Restructuring Work and Employment Conference, University of Warwick, 1988.

Redclift, N. and Mingione, E. eds, *Beyond Employment: Household, Gender and Subsistence*, Blackwell, Oxford 1985.

Reid, Margaret, *All-Change in the City*, Macmillan, London 1988.

Rentoul, John, *Me & Mine*, Unwin Hyman, London 1989.

Reskin, Barbara, ed., *Sex Segregation in the Workplace: Trends, Explanations, Remedies*, National Academic Press, Washington DC 1984.

Rhys, Garel, 'Motor Vehicles', in Peter Johnson, ed., *The Structure of British Industry*, Unwin Hyman, London 1988.

Robertson, Ian, 'Clever Cars', in Mary Goldring, ed., *The World in 1989*, Economist Publications, London 1988.

Robinson, Colin and Hann, Danny, 'North Sea Oil and Gas', in Peter Johnson, ed., *The Structure of British Industry*, Unwin Hyman, London 1988.

Rowthorn, Bob and Wells, John, *De-industrialization and Foreign Trade*, CUP, Cambridge 1987.

Rubery, Jill, Tarling, Roger and Wilkinson, Frank, 'Flexibility, Marketing and the Organization of Production', *Labour & Society*, January 1987.

Ruggie, M., *The State and Working Women: A Comparative Study of Britain and Sweden*, Princeton University Press, Princeton 1984.

Sabel, Charles, 'Flexible Specialization and the Re-emergence of Regional Economies', in Hirst, Paul and Zeitlin, Jonathan, *Reversing Industrial Decline?*, Berg, Oxford 1989.

Schoer, Karl, 'Part-time Employment: Britain and West Germany', *Cambridge Journal of Economics*, vol. 11 no. 1, March 1987.

Sheffield City Council, *Homes and Jobs*, Conference Report 1986.

Sheffield City Council, *Working it out*, Sheffield 1987.

Sivanandan, A., 'New Circuits of Imperialism', *Race & Class*, vol. 30 no. 4, April–June 1989.

Smith, Gavin, *Getting Around*, London 1984.

Smith, Keith, *The British Economic Crisis*, Penguin, Harmondsworth 1984.

Smith, Ron, 'Military Expenditure and Capitalism', *Cambridge Journal of Economics*, vol. 1 no. 1, 1977.

South-East Region TUC, *Transport Policy in the South-East*, London 1988.

Strange, Susan, *Casino Capitalism*, Basil Blackwell, Oxford 1986.

Strathclyde Regional Council, *Strathclyde: Generating Change*, Glasgow 1988.

Sweezy, Paul and Magdoff, Harry, 'A New Stage of Capitalism Ahead?', *Monthly Review*, New York, May 1989.

Symons, J.V.S., Review of 'Wages in the Business Cycle' by Jonathan Michie, *Economic Journal*, vol. 99 no. 394, pp. 211–4, March 1989.

TASS, *The 146 Campaign*, London 1985.

Therborn, Göran, *Why Some Peoples Are More Unemployed Than Others*, Verso, London 1986.

Tomlinson, Jim, *Can Governments Manage the Economy?*, Fabian Society Tract 524, London 1988.

Trade and Industry Committee, *Information Technology*, vol. 1, HMSO, London 1988.

Transnationals Information Centre, *Working for Big Mac*, London 1987.

Transport 2000, *BR: A European Railway*, London 1984.

Transport Road Research Laboratory, *The First Year of Bus Deregulation*, Research Report 161, London 1988.

Treasury and Industry Select Committee, *Report on Information Technology* 1988.

TUC, 'Fair Wages Strategy: National Minimum Wage', *TUC Consultative Document*, TUC Publications, London 1986.

TUC, *Low Pay: Policies and Priorities*, statement adopted by 1986 Congress, TUC Publications, London 1986.

TUC, *Industries for People*, TUC Publications, London 1986.

TUC, *Trade Unions in the City*, TUC Publications, London 1988.

Turnbull, Peter, 'Employment Restructuring and Management Strategy', paper presented to the Questions of Restructuring Work and Employment Conference, University of Warwick, 1988.

Tyson, William, *Bus Deregulation in Great Britain*, Association of Metropolitan Authorities, London 1988.

Ungerer, Herbert, *Telecommunications in Europe*, Brussels 1988.

University of Sussex, *Government IT Policies in Competing Countries: Report for the National Economic Development Office*, London 1988.

Walsh, Tim, 'Segmentation and Flexibility: Part-time and Temporary Work in the Retail and Hotel Trades', paper presented to the Questions of Restructuring Work and Employment Conference, University of Warwick, 1988.

Water Authorities Association, *Water Pollution from Farm Waste 1988*, London 1989.

Whitehead, Geoffrey, *Economics Made Simple*, WH Allen, London 1979.

Whitson, Colin, 'Some Problems of Restructuring from the Macro View', paper presented to the Questions of Restructuring Work and Employment Conference, University of Warwick, 1988.

Williams, Karel, Cutler, Tony, Williams, John and Haslam, Tony, 'The End of Mass Production', *Economy and Society*, vol. 16 no. 3, 1987.

Williams, Karel, Williams, John, Cutler, Tony and Haslam, Colin, 'The Economic Consequences of Mrs Thatcher: Labour's Economic Policy Options for 1991', Unpublished Paper, London 1988.

Williams, Karel, Williams, John, Haslam, Colin and Wardlow, Andrew, 'Facing Up to Manufacturing Failure', in Paul Hirst and Jonathan Zeitlin, eds, *Reversing Industrial Decline?*, Berg, Oxford 1989.

Wilson, Harold, *The Labour Government 1964–70*, Weidenfeld & Nicolson and Michael Joseph, London 1971.

Wilson, Harold, *Report of the Committee to Review the Functioning of Financial Institutions*, HMSO, London 1980.

World Bank, *Debt Tables* 1988.

Zarodov, Konstantin, *Leninism and Contemporary Problems of the Transition from Capitalism to Socialism*, Progress Publishers, London and Moscow 1976.

Index